PRAISE FOR *THE PUNK ROCK QUEEN OF THE JEWS*

". . . Rossi holds onto her strength, her rage, her humor, her joy, her neshama (soul) and her heart. . . . This wild ride of a memoir pays tribute to the human spirit."
  —LESLÉA NEWMAN, author *A Letter to Harvey Milk* and *Heather Has Two Mommies*

"Rossi is a very special storyteller. Take my word about the book as someone in the book: READ the book."
  —RABBI SHARON KLEINBAUM, Senior Rabbi, Congregation Beit Simchat Torah, world's largest LGBT synagogue

". . . Rossi was fearless and hungry for experience . . . The rest can be read as the funny, terrifying coming-of-age/coming out of one intrepid soul, or as a vibrant portrait of 1980s New York, or as an underbelly view of Crown Heights, because Rossi does it all in this exhilarating, satisfying read."
  —LEAH LAX, author of *Uncovered*

the PUNK ROCK Queen of the JEWS

the PUNK ROCK Queen of the JEWS

A Memoir

Rossi

SHE WRITES PRESS

Published 2024
Printed in the United States of America
Print ISBN: 978-1-64742-697-2
E-ISBN: 978-1-64742-710-8
Library of Congress Control Number: 2023914399

For information, address:
She Writes Press
1569 Solano Ave #546
Berkeley, CA 94707

Interior Design by Tabitha Lahr

She Writes Press is a division of SparkPoint Studio, LLC.

I dedicate this book to two sisters, one by blood and one by choice, both now gone.

For my sister of the soul, Suzanne Leon.

"Starlight child now you're gone, rays of moonbeam blowed you on."

I'll look for you in the sky, Suzy Starlight.

For my sister by blood, Lillian Ross.

Yaya, it's hard to comprehend that you are really gone. Your wild infectious laughter and childlike abandon seemed as though they would last forever. I hope and pray that now you are light, airy, peaceful, and free. I know we will meet again.

CHAPTER 1

THE QUEEN OF THE JEWS

I stood off to the side of the large banquet hall, waiting to make my entrance.

There had been a short, simple email in my inbox that morning. I sifted through the words in my mind as if they were flour.

It's been too long. We may see you in Naples, Danny Cohen.

I rubbed the scar on the knuckle of my right middle finger. My Fuck You finger. It always itched when rain was coming. In retrospect, trying to punch the door open had probably been ill-advised, but one doesn't think about such things when a rifle is pointed at your head.

I scanned the room. There was no sign of him. I let out my breath, now aware that I'd been holding it.

On with the show.

The room, filled to capacity, put me in mind of the Golden Globes, only instead of lobster and champagne, the audience ate bagels and lox with a *schmear* and drank decaf coffee. Ted, the director of the Naples, Florida Jewish Book Festival, walked to the podium and started his introduction.

"It gives me great pleasure to introduce, all the way from New York City . . ."

When I'd met Ted at the hotel, he'd excitedly announced, "We're sold out! Over two hundred people. We're gonna have to turn them away at the door!"

I'd come down with the flu before I left New York and had taken so many cold pills to survive the flight that I was seeing two of him.

"I'll try to be entertaining," I told them both.

Looking into the crowd, I forced down the lump that had climbed up my throat like a regurgitated meat ball—or, in this case, matzoh ball.

An hour earlier, I'd taken three non-drowsy sinus pills. The directions on the back of the box read, "Do not exceed two pills in twenty-four hours." The three pills kicked in like three lines of cocaine.

My scar itched. I shoved my hands in the pockets of my Levi's and squeezed them into tight fists. *Be funny. Don't think about the gun, the locked door, the sound of screaming. Breathe, remember to breathe.* I scanned the room again. There was no sign of Danny. Good. *Good.* It was going to be hard enough to entertain the room with a whopping case of non-drowsy-cold-pill jitters; I was grateful Danny wasn't there.

"The owner of New York City's wildest catering company, the author of the hit memoir . . ."

A year before, I'd never even been to a Jewish book festival. Now I had appeared at such things everywhere from Denver to St. Louis to Hartford, Connecticut.

"Voted best wedding caterer six years in a row, she's been called the wildest thing this side of the Mason-Dixon line by Zagat . . ."

I took a deep breath and scanned the faces in the crowd one more time. My chest buzzed. The lump fought to crawl back up my throat. I needed something to shake myself out of it. Something to make me laugh. *What a bunch of* punims*!* My mother's voice whispered in my ear, coated with the Yiddish accent she could pull on and off like a pair of slippers.

Punim literally means "face" in Yiddish, but really, for those in the know, it means *Jewish* face. Two hundred *punims* were chewing their bagels and looking at Ted. And were about to look at me. Most of them had that air of general dissatisfaction I'd come to know from decades of facing my Jewish relatives: *I'm okay, but the coffee's cold, and I have hemorrhoids.* Jews have a fear of showing too much joy, lest we jinx ourselves.

"*The New York Times* called her 'a new breed of rebel anti-caterer.' She's been touring the country, but today, she's all ours!"

I watched a woman go to the buffet and discreetly place a half-dozen oranges into her purse. I smiled and took it as a sign that my mother was watching.

"Please give a warm welcome to Chef Rossi!"

As I climbed up onto the stage, I stumbled into a large woman with a challah roll hanging out of her mouth.

"Sorry," I said to her stunned face.

She never stopped chewing.

I grabbed the microphone and went into my spiel. After my first Jewish book festival, I'd been anointed "the Henny Youngman of book tours." I liked the tag, but lately it seemed not so many people knew who Henny Youngman was.

It sucked to be old.

"Yes, I'm Rossi, better known as Chef Rossi, but perhaps you'd like to call me by the name I grew up with. It may surprise you to know that I was not born Chef Rossi. My name was Slovah Davida Shana bas Hannah Rachel Ross."

It had taken me three decades to embrace "Slovah," my Yiddish name. It was the name my mother had called me in a sweet, adoring singsong-y way when I was a kid, but it had turned into a shrieking battle cry of frustration by the time I was a teen.

Everything fell apart when I was a teen.

Hearing my Yiddish name used to make me wince. Now I proclaimed it proudly.

"Jewish names, as you know, are supposed to be 'of the father,' not the mother—but that 'bas Hannah Rachel' means 'of Hannah Rachel'—my mother's name. This was one of the few marks of feminism stamped on my childhood."

Now I had them.

"A lot of people ask me why I wrote a memoir, and I say, if you grew up lowly Orthodox and highly white trash, were kidnapped and sent to live with the Chasids at sixteen, escaped two years later, became a bartender, and then a chef, and then New York City's wildest caterer, you'd write a memoir, too!"

Their jaws always dropped (challah and all) when I got to the part about being sent to live with Chasids.

After telling some crazy-but-true stories, mainly from the New York City kitchens I'd worked in, I ended my presentation by asking for questions from the audience.

A white-haired woman dressed entirely in pink waved Ted over and grabbed the microphone.

"Would you consider a career as a stand-up comedian?"

"Only if they provide two-ply toilet paper. The sandpaper this hotel has is for the birds."

"What's the most interesting event you've catered?"

"Hmm . . . I'd have to say that was when I was asked to cater the after-party for *The Vagina Monologues*, and they wanted all the food . . . shall we say . . . *anatomically correct*."

Pinkie looked puzzled. "You mean—?"

"Yes. I fed the crowd a sea of vaginas. Oval croutons with Korean barbecue beef folded in the center, a sprinkling of black seaweed . . . use your imagination."

Some people shifted nervously in their seats. I've never understood why the word *vagina* makes so many people uncomfortable. Where would the human race be if not for the vagina?

A tall, gray-haired, baby-faced man in the back of the room stood up. I hadn't noticed him until he did, even though he was one of the few men in the audience.

"Why did you run away from home so young?" he piped up. "You were just a kid."

I recognized that high-pitched Mickey Mouse voice immediately. He was three decades older, and his red curls had turned gray, but his squinty eyes and freckled face were unmistakable.

It was Danny.

Thank God I hadn't seen him earlier. My scar began to itch like it was on fire.

Don't think about it. Try not to think about it. The scream, the gun, the scream, the gun.

I nodded, not about to let on that I recognized him.

"I wish someone had told me I was a kid back then," I replied. "I thought I was thirty-five!" I approached the edge of the stage and looked squarely at him. "I have to admit, there were times when I wished I'd stayed home a little longer. I could have used one more year to be a child."

One more year to trust, I thought to myself, as my next interrogator motioned for the microphone.

CHAPTER TWO

ESCAPE FROM
MESHUGA MOUNTAIN

For as long as I could remember, I'd carried a secret. It had followed me like a shadow, except this shadow lived on the inside. I simply didn't belong with the people who called themselves my family.

As an adult, I viewed an old black-and-white film my father had made using a 1960s eight-millimeter movie camera. For years, it had sat in mothballs in the family attic, until my younger brother Mendel converted it to VHS. Nice of him, since he wasn't in it. He wasn't born until eleven months after it was taken.

In the video, my sister Yaya was two-and-a-half years old. I was one. My mother Harriet and father Marty were both thirty-nine. They had been married ten years before having children.

A few things about the film captivated me: seeing my mother still beautiful, before the extra hundred pounds and diabetes; seeing my parents in love, laughing and rejoicing in the simple pleasure of each other and their two babies. They were yet to embark upon three decades of sleeping in separate bedrooms. But mostly, I was fascinated by watching baby me standing in my crib, holding onto the side for balance with a look on my face that could only be read as, "Get me away from these crazy people!"

Harriet wanted to raise her three 1960s children with values she'd internalized in the 1930s. She wanted her *kinderlach* to have as few *goyish* friends as possible, hoped that her daughters would marry Jewish doctors or lawyers and that her son would become the doctor or lawyer other mothers wanted their daughters to marry. Her children were expected to provide as many Jewish grandchildren as possible. Harriet might accept small deviations from her plan, but she drew the line at even the hint of intermarriage. She was convinced that the Messiah might one day sprout from one of her children and had no intention of allowing the line to be poisoned with Christian blood.

The moment we could understand English, she taught us a bedtime prayer, drumming it into us like an army sergeant. No one was permitted to go to sleep without reciting it: "I pledge allegiance to the Torah, and to the Jewish people. I promise to live a good Jewish life and marry a nice Jewish boy" (or, in Mendel's case, "girl").

One night when I was six, after I'd recited my prayer, I closed my eyes and tried imagining what the Jewish boy I was expected to marry might look like. Try as I might, I couldn't conjure his image.

After months of fruitlessly smothering my face in my pillow and searching for my imaginary spouse, the image of Wonder Woman from one of my tattered comic books appeared. I had a sense that there was something wrong with this. Still, no matter how hard I tried replacing her, every night Wonder Woman appeared in place of my future Jewish husband.

A few months after WW's initial appearance, I tried running away from home for the first time. It was while our family was summering in Florida—"cheaper then," Mom had said. I collected all the pears that had fallen from a tree outside our bungalow and filled up a pillowcase with them. While my parents were out trying to find kosher food in the Florida Panhandle, I dragged the pillowcase out of the yard, down the street, and fifteen blocks to the highway, intent on selling the pears.

A few concerned citizens pulled over. Before long, I'd sold all the pears, which, besides being half-rotten to begin with, had been dragged fifteen blocks by a six-year-old.

"What are you raising money for?" an elderly lady asked in a deep Southern accent.

"I's running away from home!" I answered, mimicking her drawl.

I walked back to my family with an empty pillowcase, five dollars richer and proud that I was a little bit closer to striking out on my own.

My second escape attempt was the raft.

I have a vague recollection of my dad as a fun-loving guy in a faded white T-shirt wrestling my sister, brother, and me on the living room floor in Bradley Beach, New Jersey. We were playing a game he'd invented called "Get 'em, Boys," and I loved it. Dad played rough; I guess the Navy had neglected to teach him the fine art of taking it easy on children. Long after my sister and brother hobbled away, I was still playing.

I would let Dad think he won, then dive in for one more wrestling move. I always lost—hey, I was six—but I'd like to think I gave him a rough go of it.

Mom's idea of a fun kid's game began with calling us over to the couch to sit on her lap. The idea was to slide down one of her short, wide legs onto the carpeted living room floor. At forty-four, she already suffered from an array of illnesses I didn't understand, but I did know there was something fragile about her. I would often forgo the sliding game out of fear of breaking her. Plus, to be perfectly honest, it was no "Get 'em Boys." I was a budding tomboy, and it was my GI Joe dad, with his hammers and saws and Ford pickup, who suited my tastes. I didn't want to play with dolls; I wanted to dig in the dirt.

By the time I turned seven, a seismic shift was occurring inside me that it would take me decades to understand. Despite my best efforts to the contrary, I began looking like a girl. Seemingly overnight, Dad pulled away, uncomfortable with any physical contact with his daughter. Why had he suddenly put a wall between us? All I knew was, for reasons beyond my understanding, I had been abandoned. That feeling grew venomous, until the very sight of him made me angry.

"Get 'em, Boys" was retired and a harsh division emerged, leaving my dad and brother on one side of the cavernous gender divide and my sister, mother, and me on the other. The problem was that my little brother, the youngest of us, wanted to remain on Mom's side, while I wanted to dig in the dirt with Dad. My sister, with her growing collection of dolls and aspirations to become the next Miss America, was the only one of us who seemed fine with the whole arrangement.

Mom loved to reminisce about her days as a teacher. She had skipped so many grades that she'd gotten her Master's degree by the time she was twenty and immediately entered the workforce. She put my father through law school on her teacher's salary and was her hometown beauty queen.

I would love to have known Harriet the beautiful career woman, but I never got to meet her. She suffered through eight miscarriages before she managed to carry a pregnancy to term. The moment she gave birth to Yaya, she abandoned teaching and proceeded to drown her boredom in food, coupon-collecting, and mothering her children like an overprotective Jewish hen on acid. The only Harriet I ever knew was a five-foot-tall, three-hundred-pound stay-at-home mom. She wasn't exactly passive, but when it came to Marty, Harriet had a mantra: "Your father is right."

Mendel was issued a catcher's mitt and baseball bat and sent off to Little League and any other sport he was willing to play.

Marty encouraged him to look under the hood of the truck and taught him to top off the oil, among other manly things.

Mendel was about as interested in these macho pursuits as I was in paper dolls.

I did manage to talk my folks into buying me a GI Joe, but only by telling them that my sister's Barbie needed a boyfriend. Maybe they figured out that sweet, fey Ken would never produce any grandchildren.

One afternoon after school, I went into the backyard to play with our mangy half sheepdog–half beagle, Scout. In theory, he was white and fluffy, but since he lived in the yard, he mostly looked like dirt. At the far end of the yard, near the garage, I discovered a large pile of newly cut lumber. *A gift from God!* I began to hatch my plan.

Every day after school I ran home and, using Dad's hammer and hundreds of nails, worked on my masterpiece. My raft. It would be just like the ones I'd seen on TV. Huckleberry Finn had built one and gone off on great adventures, so why not me? Our house was six blocks from the ocean . . . surely I could create a raft sturdy enough to sail away from my family!

Day by day, board by board, I laid the lumber out and nailed it together. I fashioned cross-pieces to hold the wood in place and made borders around the perimeter that I could hang on to if the wind picked up. Oh, it all made perfect sense to me. As soon as I was done, I would drag the massive structure (which probably weighed a hundred pounds) out of the yard, across busy Main Street, down six blocks, across another busy street, up the stairs to the beach, down the stairs onto the beach, across the sand, and into the ocean. Then I'd sail off to a distant land where nobody cared whether I was a boy or a girl.

One afternoon, about two weeks into my project, I was upstairs in my bedroom working on the next part of my plan: how to steal enough food for my voyage. *Peanut butter and fish sticks*, I was thinking, trying to be practical about it.

That's when I heard the screaming.

I don't recall what that new lumber had been meant for, but I do know what it had not been meant for: a giant tangle of planks that may have looked like a raft to me but to Dad probably looked like a bad car wreck.

I'd never heard my father make the kind of sounds that emerged as he tore apart my masterpiece, but they did seem somehow familiar. Then I realized: Godzilla movies.

"*AAAHHH!*" came the cry accompanying the sound of splintering wood.

"*AAAHHH!*" had come the screams of the Japanese people running from the fifty-foot lizard.

I hurried down to the yard to find my beautiful raft in pieces.

In 1971, parents saw nothing wrong with spanking their children, but Marty liked to up the ante by using his belt. The angry welts on my behind paled in comparison with the horror of seeing my creation destroyed.

Right there was where Dad and I froze in time: he the dictator, and I the rebel leader.

It would stay like that for decades.

CHAPTER 3

NOT-SO-NICE JEWISH GIRL

"**D**on't forget your prayers!" my mother yelled up the stairs. I buried my face in my pillow. The two large, fleshy orbs that had erupted from my chest over the past year made it uncomfortable to sleep on my stomach. I'd been unprepared for the horror of those two watermelons hanging from what had been my boy-power chest. For each bra size I went up, I added a layer of clothing. By the time I reached a *C* cup, I looked like the Michelin Man.

I walked into Forestdale Elementary School in the seventh grade a seemingly fat girl in sweaty layers of hand-me-down clothes. I grew my hair long and let it fall over my eyes. Maybe if I couldn't see them, they couldn't see me.

It worked about as well as wishing away my *C*-cup breasts.

Harriet and Marty had thought they were doing their kids a favor when they plucked us out of Bradley Beach and moved to the wealthy country-club town of Rumson. They'd figured the school would be better and safer, and maybe they were right. The problem was, they sent us off to our new über-rich preppy grammar school dressed as if we were from the boondocks of Kentucky. Rumson kids belonged to a khaki-panted, Izod-alligator-shirted army. In our Kmart flannel shirts and thrift-store jeans, we three were an easy target.

I spent seventh and eighth grade eating lunch in the restroom and navigating an obstacle course of snickerers and bullies. I might have survived until graduation if the worst bully at Forrestdale hadn't made me his pet project.

Bulldog—who more than lived up to his nickname—would seek me out wherever I hid and perform his monstrous chant: "Mooo! Mooo! It's Bigfoot. *Biiigfoot!* Where you going, Sasquatch?" When that ceased to amuse him, he'd throw a handful of pennies on the floor and yell, "Pick them up, dirty Jew!"

For the rest of my childhood, I threw any pennies that crossed my palm directly into the garbage. I doubt Bulldog figured out that the graffiti of a fat, ugly dog being anally penetrated by a chimpanzee was created by me.

It was quiet revenge.

At two o'clock, I would start staring at the classroom clock, waiting for it to turn to three and mark the end of my daily torture. When the final bell rang, I'd race the two blocks to our house, run up the stairs, and bury my head under a stack of pillows. There, under pillow mountain, I would daydream. My favorite scenarios were the one in which I saved the school from a sniper, and the one in which I was a rock star. In reality, I would have been happy just to have a friend.

In eighth grade, a new girl walked down the hall wearing a 1940s black cocktail dress and black stiletto heels. It was like a scene from an old movie starring Bette Davis.

I loved Bette Davis.

I was still wearing my Kmart clothes, but I'd saved up enough from my paper route to buy a pair of red Converse basketball sneakers.

She took one look at my sneakers and gave me the thumbs-up.

While Sonya Katz looked like a movie star, her sister Sarah, one year younger, looked as if she'd just returned from Woodstock. She wore a peace necklace, and her wild mane of hair grazed her buttocks. Sonya was a beauty queen with carefully cultivated sex appeal, while Sarah was knockout-gorgeous without a bit of makeup. They lived in a sprawling, ranch-style house in the ritzy part of Rumson. Their folks were expatriates from mystical Manhattan.

In our house, my mom occasionally stuck posters of puppy dogs on the wall with thumbtacks. In the Katz home, there were paintings with artists' signatures at the bottoms. They had a huge, L-shaped beige leather couch in the living room that Sonya said was a Calvin Klein.

I didn't know who Calvin Klein was, but I sure liked that couch.

Sonya taught me how to smoke Marlboro Lights. She taught me how to break up a clump of marijuana, remove the seeds and hide them in the houseplants, then roll the pot into a tight joint and lick the sides while keeping the ends all together. She taught me how to light the joint and suck in, holding the smoke in my lungs as I counted slowly to ten, then let it all out in one *whoosh*.

"Let me show you how to shotgun!" she announced one day. When it came time to let out her *whoosh*, she pressed her lips over mine and blew it into my mouth.

As Sonya pulled her lips away, I shifted uncomfortably on the couch, trying to make sense of what I felt. There was a buzzing feeling on my lips. *Must be the pot*, I thought.

When we'd killed the joint, Sarah put a Todd Rundgren record on the family stereo, and we danced around the house. Sonya followed that up with a bootleg import punk-rock disc she'd bought in the back of Jack's music store and carried home in a brown paper bag. It was the Sex Pistols' "God Save the Queen." She jumped up and down, and I mirrored her every move. After two years of being bullied, I was thrilled to jump and scream along with Johnny Rotten. Bouncing madly, shaking my head, I lost myself in the angry music.

My grades began suffering as I hung out endlessly with Sonya and Sarah. My mother wasn't worried, though, as the sisters met her ultimate criterion. "Thank God Slovah's finally got some Jewish friends," she announced over a dinner of iceberg lettuce salad, no dressing, and microwaved kosher fried chicken.

By the time summer ended, and I entered Rumson Fairhaven High School, the fat, smelly girl was dead and someone resembling the love child of Janis Joplin and Joan Jett had stormed in to take her place.

I reveled in my newfound power. I was the queen of badassery: pint of Hiram Walker blackberry brandy in my hip pocket, Marlboro Lights rolled up in the sleeve of my torn Ramones T-shirt held together with safety pins.

A lot of kids I'd gone to grammar school with didn't recognize me, but Bulldog did.

"Mooo!"

"Blow it out your fat fucking ass!" I shot back.

He was frozen in confusion. Kids aren't used to major transformations. I mean, is anybody?

After two years of being bullied, my suffering-in-silence days were over. "Why don't you suck your own dick, you fat tub of lard!" I added for good measure. I thought the boy would pass out from shock. Too bad he didn't.

Years later, Mom would call my seventh- and eighth-grade period the years I "wasn't there." She'd worried about her sad daughter, lost in daydreams, but had appreciated the good grades and relatively proper behavior. This new alien creature, however, she was not to Harriet's liking one bit.

She searched my bedroom looking for clues and found a marijuana pipe. "What's this for!?" she demanded.

"School project."

She picked up the downstairs phone while I was talking to Sonya, trying to listen in.

"Mom! I can hear your breathing!"

"Slovah Davida Shana! Maybe you'd rather I was dead! Then my breathing wouldn't bother you!"

One morning, Valerie Walcott, who was a year older, and who had never really interacted with me before or since, anointed me in the hallway.

"Hey Rossi! How ya doing?"

The name was a derivative of Ross. My father and his brother Sam had taken the Jew out of *Rosenthal* in the 1950s to avoid anti-Semitism. In one swoop, Valerie turned me Italian, and the name stuck. By the end of the week, I was *Rossi*.

It was the perfect name for a girl in a punk-rock getup who drank booze from a coffee cup during lunch. I felt as though I had crawled out of a cocoon, but really, I'd exploded out of it. My newfound confidence and brash behavior earned me loads of new friends, and there was no way I was crawling back in to please my mother or anybody else.

From then on, I rarely heard her voice below a bellow or a scream.

"I thought I was raising children, not snakes!"

"I raised a nice Jewish girl named Slovah, not this creature called Rossi!"

My father had given up any moderate form of communication as well.

"Button your top button!" he'd shout without even looking at me.

I had to escape.

I bought an ounce of weed from my buddy Kim's older brother for twenty bucks and rolled it into a hundred joints using pink rolling paper—my new trademark. I christened myself the Pink Lady, and soon everybody knew that if the joint was pink, it would be good. At a dollar a pop, I was racking up an easy eighty-bucks-an-ounce profit. It went straight into my runaway fund.

My parents were oblivious to my new vocation, of course. I'd found the perfect hiding spot for my merchandise, under the rug behind the never-used vacuum cleaner.

I amused myself by leaving female-empowerment land mines around my bedroom for Mom to find on her regular snoops. I stuck a "Women's Lib" pin on the chest of my teddy bear, pierced his ear with a safety pin, and placed a copy of Simone de Beauvoir's *The Second Sex*—stolen from Sarah and Sonya's mother's bookshelf—in his lap. On my nightstand, I left a 1972 copy of *Ms.* magazine with Wonder Woman on the cover—a gift from Sonya after I confessed my childhood crush.

One day, I came home from school to find my dresser drawers thrown open and all of my clothing in a heap on the floor. My Wonder Woman magazine lay open across the top of the heap like a flag on Mount Everest. Mom had gone from snooping to raging.

Women's Lib was not smiled upon in our house on Carton Street, where rules followed strict boy-girl etiquette. Mendel was allowed to stay out all night and do anything with girls he could get away with, because "the rules are different for boys." The only caveat was that if he was going to "defile" a girl, she had to be Christian; the purity of Jewish girls must be safeguarded until marriage.

Of course, no girls, Christian or Jewish, were interested in being defiled by Mendel.

Yaya and I, by contrast, were not allowed out after 10 p.m., not allowed to go to R-rated movies, not allowed to date anyone but Jewish boys—and then only with a chaperone—and not allowed to have male Christian friends.

The days of our female Christian friends were numbered. Mom would start a scorecard before proclaiming that one or another of them was verboten. When she spotted my friend Jenny Marvin wearing a cigarette lighter around her neck, that was one demerit. When she saw her hitchhiking, that was two demerits. When she found out Marvin was sleeping with her boyfriend, it was over. "Your friend Jenny Marvin is a slut! You are never allowed to associate with her ever again! Ever!"

I finally had a circle of friends, but my mother chipped away at them. Sonya and Sarah, their Judaism a shield, were forgiven most sins. But my Christian pals were on eternal probation.

I raged against my prison, dying my hair pink, getting into trouble at school, drinking, painting bad portraits of Jim Morrison, and making a point of dating just about anyone who wasn't Jewish. Bonus points if they weren't white. I got no pleasure from kissing boys, but figured there must be a fire in me somewhere, waiting to be ignited.

Marvin introduced me to a guy in his twenties named Billy who was best pals with her boyfriend Clint. Billy met all my criteria: He had long hair, dressed like a rocker in faded jeans and T-shirts, smoked, drank, had a car, and would horrify my parents. I made sure to have him pick me up from school where everyone could see, and when I was sure they were looking, I dropped a long kiss on him.

"Get a room!" one of the football jocks yelled.

"Fuck off!" I responded, thrilled.

The Jewish Community Center acted as a cover for many of my exploits. I pretended to be going to a teen Jewish singles dance there, then snuck off to Clint's basement apartment. One night, we were down there with Marvin and Clint. After we'd been drinking for a bit, Marvin grabbed Clint's hand and pulled him into the bedroom. "See ya later," she winked.

"Y'all may want to turn up that music," Clint added.

They closed the door, leaving Billy and me sitting on the couch in silence, nursing our Southern Comfort and orange juice. He started to kiss me, then slid his hand under my shirt. At first, I kind of liked the sensation of his fingers on my breasts; then he began to grab at them roughly, like he was in a hurry.

"Hey!"

"Sorry. I'll kiss it and make it better."

I laid back and closed my eyes.

Come on fire, ignite.

We kept kissing, and I felt him tugging at my pants.

I didn't protest. My pals at school talked about sex as if it were the ultimate pleasure. I wanted to understand what all the fuss was about.

Billy slid his own pants down. This was the first time I'd seen an erect penis up close. I supposed it was ample, having nothing to compare it to. It looked flushed and veiny. I felt a pang of nausea.

Marvin had told me that Clint loved to kiss her body head to toe before penetrating her. That clearly wasn't Billy's style. He simply climbed on top of me and proceeded to jam himself in.

He hit a wall inside of me, and I felt a sharp pain. My hymen clearly thought his dong was as grotesque as I did.

"Stop, stop! It hurts!"

He pulled out, dumbfounded.

"You're a fucking virgin?"

I tried to cover. Rossi the badass rocker chick simply could not be a virgin.

"A girl needs some foreplay, dumbass . . . not a jackhammer."

He wasn't buying it. "Clint said you'd been around. Fuck this shit. I ain't into no virgins."

I had him drop me off at the JCC, where I found Yaya standing by the soda machine in the lobby.

"Where ya been, Doo?" (This may sound affectionate, but it's actually short for *Doodyhead* and has always been my siblings' pet name for me.)

"Right here with you, if Mom and Dad ask."

"Okay . . . but where ya been, Doo?"

"At Marvin's getting a little too close to Billy's pecker."

"I hate those things. Why can't guys just be happy kissing and feeling you up?"

Dad picked us up in his two-seat Datsun pickup truck. Yaya wedged herself in the middle and I sat in the passenger seat, pushed up against the glass. I stared out the window, wanting to be as far away from my father as I could get.

Billy's erect penis, the hurried uncaring way he had grabbed at me . . . if that was what sex was all about, I wanted no part of it.

Dad didn't say anything, just handed us each a tangerine. He was always a man of few words, but my bad-girl transformation had literally left him speechless.

"Thanks," I muttered.

"Tangerine, like my lip gloss," Yaya chirped.

A week later, coming into the house after hanging out with Sarah, I attempted to whisk past my mother as she sat at the kitchen table, clipping the expiration dates off a pile of coupons.

"Slovah Davida Shana bas Hannah Rachel! You smell like cigarettes!"

"Mom! You know Sonya and Sarah's mom smokes!"

"Were you smoking with her? You smell like an ashtray!"

As I slid by and headed for the safety of my room, she called after me, her voice getting louder as the distance between us widened. "No nice Jewish boy is going to want you! Only sluts smell like ashtrays! The next time you come home smelling like smoke, you're grounded! *You're going to hell in a handbasket, young lady!*"

"*I don't have to die to go to hell!*" I screamed, the rage filling my nostrils. I felt like I could spit fire.

"*You think this is hell? A warm bed and plenty to eat!? Try Auschwitz!*"

CHAPTER 4

THE END OF THE PARTY

I met Jeni Webster in French class and immediately dubbed her "Webs." She was dressed in a pink sweater with khaki pants and Docksider shoes, a typical preppy Rumson look. I walked in ten minutes late, in my Sex Pistols T-shirt and torn jeans, and shoved into the seat next to her.

"Here comes trouble," she said.

We were instant friends.

I often escaped my mother's ranting by spending the weekend at Webs's. I knew it was only a matter of time before Mom built up enough demerits against her to banish her from my life. She started a campaign the moment she found out Webs was German.

"Don't stand too close to the oven," she sneered. "Your *friend*, Jeni Webster, might push you in."

Webs got me into her community theater group as a stage manager's assistant. They were putting on a production of *Cinderella* employing the music of David Bowie and the B-52s. The first time I walked into the theater, I felt as if I'd stepped into some sort of alternate reality. A woman who looked like an Amazonian giant wore a pink leather miniskirt. That was

Magnolia. Another woman with crayon-red hair practiced on her unplugged bass guitar. That was Cindy Butler. In the back, behind the sound booth, two men were kissing.

"Is this heaven?" I asked Webs.

"No, doll. It's theater."

"Jeni, darling . . . who is this gorgeous creature?" Magnolia asked with a nod in my direction.

"This is Rossi," Webs replied.

"Rossalinda! I am so happy to meet you!"

A perky woman who looked a bit like a cheerleader skipped over. Annie. "Hiya, honey!" she said, offering a smile that featured the whitest teeth I'd ever seen.

The mastermind behind the production was a tall, skinny guy named Matthew. The handsome bearded man he'd been kissing was a hairdresser named Wolf.

I couldn't take my eyes off Cindy. I'd never seen a woman in leather pants before. To me, she looked like a punk-rock Audrey Hepburn. It was pretty easy to look exotic in New Jersey, but there was something more than that about Cindy. She drew me in.

I started hanging out with Cindy after rehearsals. I'd tell my mother the show went late, and Cindy and I would go punk-rock barhopping.

I had a hard time sleeping after spending evenings with Cindy. I felt jumpy, like electricity ran through my veins. One night, after saying my prayers, I shoved my face in the pillow and finally fell asleep. I woke up with a start. Cindy had replaced Wonder Woman in my dreams.

And we were kissing.

The next night, after we'd been jumping around for an hour or so on the dance floor of a club appropriately called Toad Hall, we went into the bathroom to freshen up.

I lit my eyeliner pencil, then drew it across my lower lids. Cindy spiked up her red hair.

"Hey, Cindy . . . I had the weirdest dream . . ."

"What was it?"

"I dreamed I kissed you. I mean like a real . . . Hollywood kiss."

"Oh yeah?" she said. She grabbed me by the cheeks, pulled me in, and stuck her tongue in my mouth.

I was so stunned I froze. But then, as she fished around in my mouth, I felt like I was floating in a sea of *moist*. Parts of my body I'd barely known were there, like the back of my neck, were suddenly on fire.

We stood in that bathroom, under the harsh light, making out for what felt like hours, but probably was five minutes. When she finally pulled away, I had to lean against the sink. My head spun with confusion, but also with an excitement the depths of which I'd never felt before. I felt like someone had just turned the lights on in a dark room.

"I'm gonna go get us a couple of drinks," she said, as if the world hadn't just shifted on its axis.

As the door slammed behind her, I stared into the cracked mirror in front of me. "That's why!" I screamed to no one.

In bed later, I started into my nighttime prayer as usual. "I pledge allegiance to the flag, to the Torah, and to the Jewish people. I promise to live a good Jewish life and marry a nice Jewish—"

I froze when I got to the word *boy*. All those years of Mom trying to squash the boy out of me . . . Had this been what she was really afraid of?

◆ ··· ◆ ··· ◆ ··· ◆ ··· ◆ ··

After that night in the bathroom, Cindy and I spent a lot of time driving around in my mom's Volaré. Sometimes we skipped barhopping altogether and parked on a dark, quiet street and made out. I felt like I was melting right into her.

Once, she directed me to a dark, quiet side street in Long Branch. I parked away from the lights, pulled out my Hiram Walker, and we took turns sipping out of the bottle. Then she lifted my T-shirt and licked and kissed my breasts agonizingly slowly. Goose bumps spread all down my arms. It was as if she had nothing else to do in the world but spend an eternity worshipping my breasts. Then she slid her hand down my jeans.

This was nothing like my experience with Billy. This time, whatever it was that lived inside my "lady parts," as my mother called them, exploded outward.

My fire had been ignited.

And ignited and ignited.

Hours later, I pulled up to Cindy's house to drop her off.

"That was fun," she said, and blew me a kiss.

"I love you." The words had just tumbled out, and I immediately wished I could shove them back in. But it was too late.

"*Aw*. That's sweet. I love you, too." She walked up the stairs to her porch and disappeared inside without even turning back to wave.

The next seven times I called her house, Cindy was too busy to come to the phone.

One afternoon, Mom came home from gallivanting around looking for deals and found Magnolia sitting on top of our backyard picnic table, smoking a Moore's cigarette out of a long pink holder. Our play had ended months ago, but I'd been pretending it was still going on. I'd started hanging out with Mag to distract myself from obsessing about Cindy. One look at my flamboyant friend and my mother made up her mind. My theater days were numbered.

"There is something wrong with that creature!" she wailed later on, when I came into the house for dinner. "Is she even a woman? Just *what* are you doing with those . . . *theater people* anyway?"

Up for anything that got me away from my parents' nightly lectures, I started taking an art class at Brookdale Community College two nights a week. I loved painting, but I didn't love this kind of painting: realistic oil depictions of the same three tulips in a vase. My teacher kept scolding me for being two-dimensional.

I also spent a lot of time in Piping Rock Park. A nineteen-year-old named Doug who'd managed to graduate a few years before—"by the skin of my teeth," he liked to say—hung out there as well, smoking cigarettes with some of the burnout high school kids. There wasn't anything creepy about Doug; he just hadn't found any sort of direction and seemed to want to hang on to his teen years a little longer. Doug had a car, so naturally I recruited him as a barhopping pal.

Somehow, I was also keeping up with the "rapid promotion program" I'd enrolled in so that I could graduate from high school in three years. My parents thought I was eager to start college. In reality, I planned on running away from home the moment I got my high school diploma.

I arranged with my buddy Doug to pick me up in his Chevy the moment I gave him the signal. My bags had been packed for a month. I decided the best plan of action was to get thrown out of the house; that way my folks wouldn't come looking for me.

I smoked Marlboro Lights and blew the smoke down the stairs. I played "Hell Is for Children" by Pat Benatar so loud that the walls in the house vibrated.

"Slovah Davida Shana!!! Wait till your father comes home! There will be hell to pay!"

I got grounded, reprimanded, and screamed at.

One early evening, my father demanded I button the top button of my denim cowboy shirt. I refused and instead opened another button. He slapped me across the face.

The last time Dad had hit me, I had been eight years old. I'd refused to go to sleep, and had stayed up giggling with Yaya.

When the belt came down on my ass, I'd turned my head and laughed at him.

"Stop laughing or you get another whack!"

I laughed harder. He brought the belt down again.

The pain stung like fire, but my anger was far more searing. Each time Marty brought the belt down, I laughed even harder.

Scared, Yaya pulled the sheets over her face.

The sixth time Dad hit me, I turned and glared at him defiantly.

We'd crossed some sort of a threshold; we both knew it. I had never seen that look in my father's eyes before: terror.

He never hit me again—until now. And he'd never before hit me in the face.

All I could remember after the slap was throwing my fist. I thought I'd punched him in the nose but had no memory of connecting.

I was standing by the fridge drinking a Diet RC Cola when he got home. He brushed past me without saying a word. There were two white strips of surgical tape across the top of his nose. He told everyone he'd broken it playing racquetball.

The swearing, screaming, and smoking didn't make my mother happy, but they weren't enough to get me thrown out. That would take a phone call from Sonya and Sarah's mother.

I'd written a poem to Sarah about my deep love for her as my friend. Leona Katz felt it was something else. Looking back on it, I suppose it was.

"Your daughter is a lesbian!" Mrs. Katz screamed at my horrified mother.

That did the trick.

"We're going grocery shopping," announced my father. "When we come back, be prepared to obey the rules in this house, which are going to be ten times tougher, or don't be here!"

I put my hands on my hips. "You'll see how well I do!"

The moment they drove away, I called Doug. True to his

word, he pulled up fifteen minutes later. I filled his Chevy with TV dinners and canned tuna fish and made him drive me to a sleazy motel I'd picked out in Long Branch. At seventy bucks a week, it was the only thing I could afford. The parking lot was full of delivery trucks, and a Puerto Rican gang sold drugs behind a perpetually parked eighteen-wheeler. The room next to mine was used by a prostitute named Sexy Sally.

I felt like I was the living version of that Meatloaf song, "Bat Out of Hell." I proceeded to engage in a two-month-long party, hopping from bar to bar, bash to bash, for the rest of the summer. Doug went with me to the first two or three dozen parties I crashed, but when he finally snagged a job, he bailed on me—as well as on his parents—and split for the city. I'd never bothered to ask, but it turned out that nineteen-year-old Doug had still been living at home.

Once the school year started, my friends stopped coming around—except for Sarah. She convinced her mom that she had a French tutor and visited me to smoke weed and watch the small black-and-white TV in my room.

I was almost out of money and considering my options, which were really only two: Sell pot for the local dealers or get a job go-go dancing. I was never a good dancer.

One unusually chilly, drizzly day, I sat at the counter of a bar-and-grill near my fleabag hotel and counted out change for a buttered roll and coffee. An old man sitting next to me opened up a flask and poured it into his coffee. It was 10 a.m. and everyone in the place looked like they had nowhere else to go. For the first time since I'd bolted from home, I started to feel afraid. Was this my life?

A few days later, Long Branch filled with sailors on shore leave. I met some of them at the arcade playing pinball and invited a half-dozen over, on the condition that they buy the beer and pizza. Sarah and a few of my school pals came, too. I cranked up the B-52s and it turned into a party. The front desk manager never seemed bothered by the hookers and dealers who came in and out (they gave him a cut, I'd heard), but teenagers and sailors were a combo he just couldn't stomach.

He called the cops.

CHAPTER 5

JAILBIRD

At sixteen, I looked thirty-five. Seriously. When the police showed up to bust my hotel bash they took one look around and decided that possibly-thirty-five-year-old me was trying to corrupt a minor. I didn't want to show them my ID, for fear they would call my parents.

So, they made me pack up my stuff, then hauled me, my suitcase, and my "victim," Sarah, down to the Long Branch police station. I have no idea what happened to the sailors. Jumped ship, I guess.

After the sergeant threatened to throw me in a cell with a hooker named Luscious Lucy, known for stabbing her johns with a nail file and stealing their money, I handed over my driver's license and my parents' phone number.

"Glad to see you're doing so well!" was all my dad said to me when he and my mother walked into the station twenty minutes later. My shoulders fell to about a foot below my waist.

Sarah was picked up by her angry mother, who nearly spit at me on their way out the door. Watching Mrs. Katz drag her shaken daughter away, Mom instinctively stood between her and me with her hands on her hips. For a moment, I felt like a lost cub being rescued by its lioness mother—only this mama lion was wearing a full-length blue housedress and pink slippers.

There was a strange expression on Mom's face, as if she'd woken up from a long sleep only to discover that she was still tired.

We walked to the Volaré wordlessly, and Dad shoved my suitcase into the trunk. I slid into the back seat, assuming we were going home. Just as I was feeling as if I were tunneling back into Alcatraz, I noticed that Dad had driven past the turn-off to our town. He proceeded past the stretch of towns I'd grown up around and kept driving for what seemed like hours.

Afraid to break the silence, I looked at Mom in the passenger seat. The woman who had always looked at me as if I could walk on water refused to turn around and make eye contact. She spent most of the ride crying and digging in her purse. I don't recall her saying a word, and I don't think she ever found what she was looking for.

My dad sat grim-faced and stoic, as usual. If it weren't for the ghostly pallor of his normally olive skin, I might have thought it was like any other day that he was angry at me, which had been most of the time over the previous few years.

After a while, nothing out the window looked familiar. The green trees of Jersey had given way to brown buildings, brown brick walls, and brownish-gray walkways. Everything looked like the artwork of a kid who owned only brown crayons.

I became vaguely aware that my fingers hurt. When I looked down, I realized they were squeezed so tightly into fists that all I saw of my knuckles were white bone.

Finally, we stopped in front of a brown townhouse. It was one of a long line of similar structures running along a busy road dotted with benches that were also . . . brown. I glanced up at the street sign: Eastern Parkway. I'd never heard of it. My dad took my bags out of the trunk and hefted them up the steps to the townhouse, motioning for me to follow. I looked at my mom, who was still crying, still digging in her purse.

When a man I immediately dubbed Redbeard (I would later learn his name was Rabbi Sherba) answered the door, I felt as if I were stepping back in time. Gone was 1981 and hello to 1921 and the world of my grandparents. I stepped into the vestibule as if in a trance.

How could I know then that my parents had begun searching for me shortly after I left the house, calling my friends, the police, everyone they could think of. They had only meant to scare me by threatening to throw me out of the house, but had clearly misjudged their demon child.

A few months earlier, my mother had read an article about Rabbi Sherba in the Jewish newspaper she stockpiled in the bathroom. He was often hired by concerned parents to kidnap their Jewish kids from various cults like the Moonies. According to the article, once the kids were safely in his care, Redbeard expertly deprogrammed the false gods out of them and brought them back to Judaism.

I'd seen the Moonies on TV; they looked like they were having fun.

I had no way of knowing it at that moment, but *fun* was definitely not on the menu for me.

CHAPTER 6

THE VELVET COUCH

My body sunk into the velvet couch as if it were violet-colored quicksand. It made the sweat on my forearms itch like poison ivy. Or was it hives? The more I struggled to straighten myself, the farther in I sank. Frustrated, I gave in and let myself be enveloped in the purple poison ivy.

A buzzing noise made me look up to see what at first glance seemed to be a colony of giant bats. Two blinks later, and I realized it was a half-dozen Chasidic men staring at me, murmuring to one another in what sounded like Yiddish.

Where was Wonder Woman when I needed her?

I guess I was a sight to them, too. I still had the remnants of a tan glowing on my cheeks from my long summer on the Jersey Shore. Punk-rock pink flecked my knotty, sea-worn hair. I still wore the Sex Pistols T-shirt I'd put on a day earlier.

Yesterday. A thousand years ago.

I looked away from them and craned my head toward the stairway. Two children pushed their faces through gaps in the balusters to stare at me, wide-eyed. I guessed them to be about four and six. The six-year-old was a girl.

A bit of dust that my sinking body had displaced seemed to hover in the air like a tiny cloud, then dissipate. It was then that I noticed the smell—mildew mixed with furniture polish and chicken soup. There was also a pronounced smell of body odor, but I was pretty sure that was coming from me.

Maybe Mom was still rifling through her purse; in any case, she hadn't come in with us. Redbeard leaned against the wall near the doorway, talking to my father who, at five-foot-ten, had to bend his head and neck down. This made him look old and short. He nodded as Redbeard spoke. They both looked over at me, then talked some more. My father kept nodding.

On another velvet couch, this one the color of jade, sat a pretty young woman, her head covered in a red scarf. She was profoundly pregnant, and her large belly stuck out all the more as the rest of her sank into the jade vortex.

We were two young women disappearing into nothingness as the Chasids whispered and watched.

"You must feel pretty strange," whispered my jade counterpart in a heavy accent that sounded British, or maybe South African.

"Where am I?"

"You're in Crown Heights."

"What is Crown Heights?"

"It's in Brooklyn." She paused. "You know . . . Brooklyn . . . New York?"

Redbeard looked over at me. "Your parents want you to stay here for a while," he said.

My father nodded at Redbeard one more time, shook his hand, and walked out the door without a word in my direction. Redbeard left the door open so I could watch him climb down the stairs and walk away.

CHAPTER 7

LIFE ON EASTERN PARKWAY

The first morning after I was dropped off, I felt like a slab of cantaloupe dropped into a bowl of blueberries. I stayed in my couch-bed for what felt like days but was probably only a few extra hours.

Hidden under a blanket, I listened as someone—the rabbi's wife, I supposed—moved around the kitchen. I smelled onions frying, which always made me hungry, even on that strange morning. I thought of my mother frying onions to mix into her cabbage and egg noodles—how the cabbage had to be cooked so long it almost disintegrated in your mouth with the soft, brown onions, which were always fried in margarine so they'd be pareve and we could have meat for lunch.

I thought back to what I called the Happy Year, when I was seven and felt invincible. I would come back from playing in the dirt with my best pal Ronny, and Mom would have cabbage and egg noodles waiting. It was a year of winning fights with boys, of being the second-tallest kid in school, of trading Godzilla models for comic books, and of dreaming that I could fly like Superman.

When I was eight, my parents sent all three of their badly behaved children to a private yeshiva in Wanamassa, New Jersey. Most of the kids there were Syrian and all of them came from wealth. They all spoke Hebrew and had known one another since they were four.

I tried playing kickball one day and tripped on the maxiskirt they made me wear, falling face-first into the dirt. That pretty much summed up my yeshiva experience. Yaya, Mendel, and I fit in there about as well as I would in Crown Heights. Luckily, our yeshiva period didn't last long because the principal thought the same thing. After our first year, he called my mother into his office.

"If you love your children, take them out of this school."

Where was that principal now?

I heard Redbeard calling his children to the breakfast table and listened as the older ones were picked up for school. I lay there, breathing in the scent of freshly brewed coffee until the house went quiet, then slowly pulled open the blanket.

The pregnant woman I'd seen the night before was sipping coffee and smiling at me.

"You can't hide under there forever."

"I thought maybe it was just a bad dream."

"No such luck, sweetheart."

I sat up but felt oddly numb, as though ice water pulsed through my veins.

"It'll get better," she whispered. "I'm Lifsa. The rabbi's wife is Bela."

Bela walked into the living room carrying a baby in her arms who looked about a year old. Like Lifsa, she'd covered her head in a red silk scarf. It was stiflingly hot that September morning, and I watched sweat dripping down her forehead.

Bela was a pretty woman whose age I couldn't quite fathom. I found out later she was only twenty-five, but already had six kids. Maybe that's why she looked old beyond her years. "I have challah from last night and strawberry jam and hard-boiled eggs with salt," she said. "There is coffee and juice." Bela spoke with a British accent.

I turned to Lifsa and asked, "Is everyone around here from another country?"

"No," she said, "but the Rebbe does attract people from all over the world."

"The Rebbe?"

"One thing at a time," Bela cut in. "First, eat your breakfast."

Redbeard trotted down the stairs holding a leather brief-case overstuffed with papers. He stopped at the bottom step, turned as if forgetting something, and walked toward my couch.

"The rules are simple," he said quietly, sounding bored, as if he'd made this same speech a hundred times. Maybe he had. He didn't look at me but stared at a picture of an old man with a thick white beard and black hat hanging on the wall behind me. "You will attend *ba'al teshuva* classes at Machon Chana, obey the laws of kashrut while in this home, and come to shul for Shabbos."

"What is Machon Chana?"

"Hebrew school for women," Lifsa interjected.

Redbeard shot her an icy look. "It's the women's seminary," he clarified.

Ba'al teshuva turned out to be classes for secular Jews who were interested in becoming more observant, which I wasn't. At least kashrut was easy; Mom had kept kosher for years—by way of McDonald's fish sandwiches, anyway.

"Great . . ." I said, almost under my breath and meaning anything but. I was back to kickball in a maxiskirt.

"You are free to explore the neighborhood, but you are not allowed to leave it without my permission."

He stepped closer to me, still staring at the old man's picture.

"I will know if you leave. I have eyes everywhere."

He went on to tell me that I was to stay in the Lubavitch community of Crown Heights until I turned eighteen. If I ran away, he was under instructions from my parents to call the police and have me sent to reform school.

When I was eleven years old, I'd seen a movie starring Linda Blair called *Born Innocent*. The terrors she had endured in reform school, including being raped with a broomstick, had haunted me ever since. I'd always wondered why my parents, who had forbidden me to watch films with sex or anything they deemed too "Christian," had let me see that film. Maybe this was why: so I'd be scared straight.

I was broke, underage, underskilled, and lost. I looked out the front window at an endless, impenetrable wall of brick buildings. I didn't see a safe place to run. Even if I were able to break through the ranks of black coats marching by with armloads of books, where would I go?

I took a deep breath and sank as deep as I could into the velvet couch that was now my bed. With zero options I could think of, other than suicide or going home—which, to me, were one and the same—I decided to bide my time and form a new battle plan.

I allowed the rabbi's family to believe that they might bring me around to their way of life. They, in turn, allowed me to sleep in the living room and gave me two hot meals a day. I was to attend Hebrew classes with Lifsa at least three days a week and show respect for the Sabbath from sundown Friday until sundown Saturday.

For the price of a good supper, I had to sit through a lot of long-winded lectures from Redbeard on all the lost souls who were saved because of his tireless efforts and love of the community. No matter what he told me, I could not muster up an ounce of respect for him. He was in his late twenties—barely twelve years older than I—and his life experience had consisted of having a powerful rabbi for a father, studying Torah, and getting married to the daughter of another powerful rabbi. Who was he to lecture me on anything? He couldn't even fathom what it felt like to worry about money.

I was left free to roam the neighborhood but not to leave it without permission or an approved escort. Which meant that I was free to do absolutely nothing but sit on the benches of Eastern Parkway and watch the traffic.

Whoosh! The blue car-service sedans would speed by.

Take me with you, I would beg internally, but it seemed that no one on Eastern Parkway was psychic. They had no clue that I was being held captive in Chasidland.

I remember feeling oddly cold all the time—what my folks would have called chilled to the bone. It was early fall, light jacket weather, but I sat on the benches on Eastern Parkway shivering. Lifsa lent me a down coat that no longer fit over her pregnant belly, but no winter coat could warm me. I was cold from the inside out.

My secret inner shadow, the creature that had spent so many years whispering, *You don't belong,* was quiet. Maybe it was frozen.

"There are unwritten rules in Crown Heights," explained Lifsa as I walked out the door on my third afternoon, headed for a spot on the pedestrian island that was as far from our hub on Kingston Avenue as I could safely go.

"What kind of rules?"

"The goyish white people never go below Classon Street. The *schwartzes* in Bed-Stuy don't cross to our side of Eastern Parkway."

So my new world was apparently divided neatly into white non-Jews, Black people, and . . . us.

"Where do runaway white-girl punk rockers go?"

"Probably to hell."

Lifsa could be funny and seemed to genuinely care about me. She didn't know it, but she was saving me in that moment. She went on to hint at consequences for those who broke the unspoken racial rules. "Stay in the Lubavitch zone, Slovah. Shimmy, the shoe repair guy, walked up Franklin to buy leather and came back with no leather, no wallet, and missing his two front teeth."

"So . . . I'm safe if I stay in the zone?"

"Nobody is totally safe in Crown Heights."

As I followed along the pedestrian island, I picked up my pace and soon found myself walking so fast I was almost running. Where was I running to? I had no idea, but when I grew short of breath and looked up, I was standing near a street sign that read Nostrand Avenue.

I was just a ten-minute trot from Chasidland, but the clean brick buildings with flowers in front of them had given way to out-of-business stores with boarded-up windows covered in graffiti. I looked at the painted board over what used to be a travel agency. It read RAGE. I continued, passing a parked white Cadillac with all of its tires missing.

I remembered watching the nightly news with my parents and seeing buildings burning all over the Bronx. "The landlords can't sell them or rent them, so they burn them," my father explained. "It's worse than Beirut over there."

This wasn't the Bronx, but it didn't look much different from that news footage. Except none of the buildings were actually on fire . . . yet.

The clusters of Chasidic students with armloads of books had morphed into clusters of dark-skinned men openly smoking spliffs and listening to loud reggae music. My feet crunched over broken glass. One of the Rastas in the cluster looked up at me through unruly dreadlocks, clearly astonished. He elbowed one of his friends. "Girl . . . you lost!" he yelled in a heavy accent that sounded Jamaican.

"*Ssss!*" one of the others hissed. He stepped forward and put his hand on his crotch. "Beg you a suck!"

I spun around, my heart beating out of my chest, and fast-walked back toward Kingston Avenue. When I got to it, I saw three policemen on the corner, chatting. I hadn't seen a single cop on Nostrand.

I pushed open the door to Redbeard's townhouse, out of breath and flushed.

"I walked to Nostrand, and all the cops disappeared!"

"Welcome to Crown Heights, sweetie!" said Lifsa.

"But what happened to them?"

"The Lubavitchers vote as the Rebbe dictates, and the cops know it. That buys us a lot of protection."

⋆ ⋯⋆ ⋯⋆ ⋯⋆ ⋯

Redbeard's brownstone was packed, with Lifsa and me sleeping on the two couches in the living room and the rabbi, his wife, and their six kids sleeping upstairs. When you added a weekly array of houseguests camping out two or three at a time in the guest bedroom, and the peers of the rabbi who would come for supper and stay till the wee hours discussing politics and religion, it felt a bit like sleeping in a bus station.

I had just one trait in common with my father: an intense need for privacy. He slept alone in the only room that locked. I'd decorated my bedroom like an apartment, opting for a pull-out couch instead of a bed so that when I closed it, I could pretend the room was my home.

The closest I could get to privacy at Redbeard's hotel was a few minutes in the bathroom or under the blanket.

I slept with my face pressed against the back of the couch, relishing my solitary cave of velvet. If I could have burrowed into the side of the couch like a mole, I surely would have. I always woke to the smell of sautéing onions and stayed hidden under the blanket, clinging to my privacy for as long as my bladder would hold out.

While on the run from my parents and any other authority figures, I'd lived on greasy fried-egg sandwiches and pizza with pickled jalapeños. Making a meal of day-old challah with cream cheese and strawberry jam actually seemed like an improvement. Nobody had ever bothered to tell me about nutrition, and I don't think I'd had a vegetable for two years, unless you count pickles.

On good days, I was given cleaning chores; on bad ones, Bela conscripted me to babysit the children. Cleaning the house was a hundred times better than attempting to entertain the little monsters for hours on end. Not that I was a stellar cleaner, either. I had to ask Bela how to use the vacuum cleaner.

On days when Bela was too busy talking on the phone to notice me, Lifsa and I would go for a walk around the hood, which consisted of roughly seven blocks by six blocks. Lifsa loved visiting shopkeepers and locals. Carrying what surely was an enormous baby, she would waddle penguin-like down the street, shouting hellos and smiling as she went.

Kingston Avenue was the epicenter of the hood, the main drag. Kosher eateries, Judaic bookshops, a kosher butcher, a drugstore, and a gift shop lined the street, as well as one Puerto Rican bodega, to which I was, of course, drawn.

Lifsa alternated between two pregnancy cravings: smoked herring and hot dogs.

When it was herring, we'd stop at Raskin's Fish Market. A Russian man named Shlomo always added a little more on the top for Lifsa after he weighed her container. The place felt right out of the 1920s, with fish sitting out on ice waiting to be expertly cut by Shlomo. I supposed it was quaint, but I couldn't get past the smell.

Lifsa would start munching on the herring as soon as she walked out the door.

"Want some?" she would ask.

"I'm close to puking just smelling it."

"You don't know what you're missing, but the gefilte fish is what they're famous for."

Her other craving could be found at Ess & Bentch, a greasy meat diner. There was a counter for ordering and tables in the back. Lifsa would order two hot dogs, one for herself and one for me, but I'd give her back half of mine after she'd inhaled hers.

Further down the street, on Kingston and Montgomery, was a kosher grocery called Rivkie's. Rivkie's offered the cure for Lifsa's occasional third craving: halvah, a sweet sesame candy. The best version of it is covered in chocolate.

When I finally got up the nerve to ask, Lifsa told me her story. She had been coerced into an arranged marriage by Redbeard and was now waiting for permission from the Rebbe to divorce her husband. I had trouble understanding what she was so happy about under the circumstances, and I didn't know what a rebbe (as opposed to a rabbi) was, but I soon learned.

A rabbi is a learned man who may or may not be the religious leader of a synagogue. A rebbe is a leader of an entire sect of Chasids. I thought that there was only one kind of Chasid, but Lifsa explained there were something closer to twelve, possibly even sixteen, and they followed different rebbes and different rules.

"One of them," she told me one afternoon as we strolled home from Rivkie's, "their rebbe died generations ago, but the members refuse to ever follow another rebbe. So they keep following him like he's still alive." As I gaped, she downed a piece of rugelach in one bite.

She said that another sect, the Satmars, lived in Williamsburg, Brooklyn, and were far more extreme than the Lubavitchers. They wore huge furry hats and dress coats that went out of style two hundred years ago. "They hate the Lubavitchers for being too modern," she said.

That didn't seem possible.

As we walked, Chasidic men would all but cross the street to avoid coming anywhere near me. When they were forced to walk past, they acted like I was invisible.

If I had been invisible, I would have walked away, past the black coats on Kingston Avenue, past the drug dealers and catcallers on Eastern Parkway, past the ugly brown buildings and half-dead trees. I would have kept walking over the distant bridge I dreamed of crossing, and into the bright, colorful lights of Manhattan.

CHAPTER 8

MACHON CHANA

Five days after I'd been deposited in Redbeard's living room, Lifsa dragged me to Machon Chana.

"You'll fit right in! They're all former sinners like you."

"Great . . ."

"The Rebbe loves Machon Chana. He even named it after his mother, Chana."

It was a pretty enough brick building, but the classroom reminded me of *Little House on the Prairie*. The only modern thing in it was the indoor plumbing.

Little House on the Shtetl, I thought.

I wore a torn pair of Levi's, a Blondie T-shirt, and a pair of Frye boots that made a loud clumping noise as I walked in. Fifteen women of all ages, sizes, and forms of proper religious garb populated the classroom. Most were in their twenties, but one woman had gray in her hair.

The teacher, a pale, middle-aged woman in a black wig, looked up at me disapprovingly. Blue veins in her forehead seemed to pop out as she took me in.

"Rabbi Sherba told me you'd be coming. My name is Morah Silverstein. Sit down there," she said, pointing to the empty desk in the far-left corner. "Shalom, class," she intoned.

"Shalom, Morah Silverstein!"

"This is Slovah!"

"Shalom, Slovah!"

"Who can tell Slovah what a *ba'al teshuva* is?"

A gray-haired woman fairly screeched, "*Ba'al teshuva*s are those who come in from the cold of a life of abandon and sin into the warm embrace of *Hashem*."

"Thank you, Chaya," said Morah Silverstein. "Unlike someone like me, who was born into the loving arms of this community."

Chaya was a tall, skinny, awkward-looking woman with greasy hair. She wore a plaid maxiskirt, polka-dot sweatshirt, and sneakers with white socks. The plaid and polka-dot combination was dizzying.

"What do they call *you*?" I asked my new teacher.

"Some call us lifers."

"That sounds like a prison sentence," I said, watching her forehead sprout a blue line. She ignored me.

"Who can tell Slovah why I am wearing a *sheitel*?" she asked, touching her wig.

A woman with a thick French accent piped up, "The hair is very sexy. It may keep the man from praying."

Her name, I learned, was Fagee. She was in her mid-twenties and full-figured, and the scent of her perfume reached me all the way across the room when she waved her arm around. She wore a silk blouse and a clingy skirt that looked designer. The black beauty mark on her cheek looked penciled on, or at least touched up to make it darker. Fagee was not pretty, but there was an air of glamour about her, right down to the jeweled barrette in her brown curly hair.

"Yes. It can be a distraction from prayer," Morah Silverstein said.

"That's why we can't sing where men can hear us. It may keep them from praying," said Chaya.

Another girl—Anya—was a very pretty, black-haired twenty-something from Israel. Her style, if you could call it that, was 180 degrees from Fagee's. She wore an orange cotton dress with a tie-dye print straight out of the 1960s, and completed her hippie look with leather sandals.

"They've obviously never heard you sing, Chaya!" Anya said in an Israeli accent. "That will get them praying, surely."

I took one look at Anya and knew we would be friends. She reminded me of Sarah.

"Slovah! The next time you walk into class, I want you properly attired!"

"Oh. Okay." I sunk so low into my seat, you could barely see my face. I felt as if I were eight years old again and back in prison. The only way I could have felt lower was if Bulldog, my childhood tormentor, stormed through the door and *mooed* at me.

"I've got a jean skirt that's too big for me," whispered Anya.

"I've got some frocks that are too small for me," Lifsa said, patting her belly.

Three days later, I walked into Machon Chana feeling like I was dressed for Halloween. My torn jeans stuck out from under Anya's denim maxiskirt, and my Blondie T-shirt was layered over Lifsa's long-sleeved black cotton pullover.

Morah Silverstein deemed me "passable."

Just what I'd always dreamed of being: *passable*.

CHAPTER 9

THE REBBE

Rebbe Schneerson was the seventh Rebbe and leader of the Lubavitchers, their pride and joy. The great-grandson of the third Rebbe and son-in-law of the sixth, he had been the Rebbe since 1951.

"Why do you all stay here? You should go somewhere safe, like New Jersey!" I said to Lifsa during one of our walks.

"The Rebbe considers the Lubavitch land to be holy," she explained patiently. Where did she get all that patience? "Like . . . it's a birthright of the Lubavitchers. He even said there was something holy about the name Crown Heights."

"The only thing holy about Crown Heights is *Holy shit, it's scary around here*."

"Slovah! *Sheked*! If the Rebbe says it's holy, then it's holy! End of story. He almost never leaves the neighborhood except to visit his father-in-law's grave in Queens."

The Rebbe's shul, which was also the Lubavitch headquarters, was called *770* after its address, 770 Eastern Parkway. I never heard it called by any other name. It was a large, brown, aging building visited by thousands of the faithful each year. They came from all over the world to meet the great Rebbe Schneerson.

His visitors had included the prime minister of Israel, Barbra Streisand, and New York mayor Ed Koch. They came from Russia, the Middle East, Minnesota, Jerusalem, everywhere. They all came to listen to the man many thought was akin to the Messiah.

"He's even buddies with Ronald Reagan, did you know that?"

"Reagan? Why would they be friends?"

"They got chummy after that nutter tried to kill Reagan."

I couldn't deny the energy on the streets surrounding 770. It was explosive. Lubavitchers and Orthodox tourists argued over semantics, the Bible, Zionism, even what kind of car was best. They loved to argue; they lived to argue.

As a *ba'al teshuva*, I was considered a renegade Jew now returned to the old ways. I hadn't, of course, returned to diddly. I had been dragged back, kicking and screaming, by my missionary host. But it was best not to explain that to the lifers.

Born into this protected life, most of them knew little of the outside world, which they viewed as if through a thick wall of distorted glass. I had patience only for the other *ba'al teshuvas*. The lifers reminded me of virgin priests telling sinners not to sin. To me, it seemed that if you were going to knock something, at least have the decency to experience it first. For that reason, I considered myself qualified to knock at least a half-dozen legal sins and another half-dozen illegal ones.

"With other kinds of Chasidim, you can't get in even if you beg, but the Rebbe believes in outreach," Lifsa told me as she devoured her sixth rugelach. "He champions the *ba'al teshuvahs*."

"If he's the *ba'al teshuvah* champion, maybe he could get me my own room."

I was convinced that the neighborhood offered some kind of prize for Lubavitchers who brought in the most non-religious Jews. Maybe the prize was our entertaining company? That would explain why I was bombarded with dinner invitations.

After dinner at a lifer named Silvy's house, while the men stayed at the table discussing "men things" and arguing over Torah, Silvy and her sister dragged me out of hearing distance.

"What is it like going to a rock concert?" Silvy asked as she balanced her toddler under one arm and her baby on her lap.

"You cram in with thousands of people and jump up and down."

"Just like at 770!"

"Not exactly."

"What is it like to date Christian boys?" whispered Shoshana, Silvy's seventeen-year-old younger sister. She'd just been set up to marry the pharmacist's grandson.

"Depends on the boy, really. The ones I dated were kinda rude and . . . a little stinky. But there are some nice ones, too . . . or so I've heard."

"Did you ever kiss one?" asked Silvy.

"Yeah. I kissed a lot of them."

"*Wooo!*" they giggled.

To myself, I thought, *The one I liked kissing the most was a girl.* How would they have felt, I wondered, hearing about Cindy Butler?

"What about you two? What have your lives been like?"

"I went to school at Beth Rivkah," said Silvy. "Then I got a *shidduch* with Eli. We had a big wedding—over six hundred people! Now I have Sarah and Rivkah, and I hope a boy on the way. I am praying every day for a son. I want at least three sons!"

"Why do you want so many babies?"

"The Rebbe reminds us of the first mitzvah in the Torah: Be fruitful and multiply."

"How about multiplying, like, once, or maybe twice instead of thirty-five times?"

The girls seemed perplexed by this.

"Haven't you ever done anything wild?"

Shoshana stared blankly. "Wild?"

"Yeah, something wild and free. No? Okay, how about something bad? Haven't you ever been bad?"

"Shoshana, tell her about the carob."

"You tell her. You tell it better."

They huddled closer to me, nervously stealing glances to make sure the men were still at the table.

"When Shoshana was five," Silvy said just above a whisper, "she chewed up a carob bar and spit it in her underpants!"

"Yes," giggled Shoshana. She was beaming with excitement. "Then I didn't have to go to school. *Ema* thought I had the poo-poos!"

"You rebel! What did you do with your free day?"

Shoshana's smile faded. "I studied and helped *Ema* clean the house."

"But now we laugh every time we see a carob bar," Silvy chimed in, trying to keep up the festive mood. "And we never told *Ema*."

"Ladies, there's hope for you yet."

<hr />

Bela carted me, Lifsa, and her children to 770 on Friday nights and Saturday mornings. When it was time for the Rebbe to speak, she would hush even the baby.

"*Sheket*! The Rebbe! The Rebbe!"

I felt claustrophobic in the glassed-in upper floor, what we called the women's tower, pressed against hundreds of Slavic and Israeli women, seated (if you could find a seat) on hard wooden bleachers. The younger women craned their necks to see the Rebbe down below, while the older ones contented themselves in just hearing his voice. Often, one or two would faint from the heat.

Being shut up in that tower while the men moved about freely in the open air below outraged me. I wondered repeatedly— sometimes out loud—why the men were not shut in the tower while the women danced and sang below.

I thought of the *Ms.* magazine I'd left on my bed for Mom to find. "Women's Lib" felt like a battle cry in New Jersey. I looked down at the dark green maxiskirt Bela had given me. It was impossible to summon up any woman power in a green maxiskirt.

"How could such a pious man as the Rebbe want his women to practically suffocate above him?"

"*Shhh,*" Bela whispered.

"The men are not to be distracted by us. They are here to pray," whispered Lifsa.

"What are *we* here to do, die of asphyxiation?"

"*Shhh* . . . that's not *tzniut,*" whispered an old Russian woman wedged behind me.

Equal rights was not a popular topic in shul.

An elderly woman seated on a bleacher near me farted loudly.

"I feel right at home now," I whispered to Lifsa.

"*Shhh,*" Lifsa hissed, nodding in the direction of the Rebbe. "It's like God is talking."

To be *tzniut*—modest—I was not allowed to sing out loud when men were present. I was to cover myself from collarbone to calf and never wear pants. I was to learn the customs, go to synagogue, and marry a man I didn't know, whom I would grow to love. I was then expected to have somewhere between six and twelve children and physically touch no male other than my husband and sons—not even in a handshake—for the rest of my life.

The no-touching part seemed fine—I wasn't longing to touch a man—but being turned into a baby factory, well, I found this less than amusing.

But the Rebbe did interest me. There was something compelling about him, like a cult leader or a modern-day prophet. It probably started with the picture Redbeard always stared at when he spoke to me.

A swarm of Chasids flapped around the Rebbe as he strode through them, calm and majestic. It seemed as if he heard nothing but the gentle beat of his very own drum. Amid the sea of yarmulke'd men beating their chests as if to pack his every word into their hearts, he remained tranquil, sitting in his special, throne-like red chair.

At night, after I'd prepared my bed-cave on the couch, I'd sit staring at his face. The deep, mournful eyes framed in dark circles reminded me of Omar Sharif.

I never heard the Rebbe give a speech in any language other than Yiddish, although I was told he spoke many languages and had many college degrees. The women near me would whisper translations: "He's asking us to do more mitzvahs," they'd say, or, "He wants us to be more positive."

The Rebbe's speeches, when not on Shabbos, often lasted for hours and were piped through speakers hanging from the ceiling and out on the street. If you were lucky enough to snag one, low-power radio transmitters offered simultaneous translation into English or a variety of other languages.

Awestruck Lubavitchers who couldn't fit into 770 gathered by the hundreds around the speakers outside. A single word from the Rebbe could send shudders through the masses inside and cheers from the blur of blue and gray on the street—followed by a distant purr from the homes along Eastern Parkway tuned in to the live radio broadcast.

He talked of children and how they were the future. He said that he dreamed of Jewish children carrying a message of unity and peace forward for subsequent generations. He spoke of the Messiah and what we must do to prepare for Him. He told jokes and whispered messages that only the old rabbis seemed to understand. They would answer with a bend of their knees as if they were praying, or a rocking on their toes. His eyes twinkled from above his Santa Claus beard as he bent forward, using the podium to steady himself, and sent out a breathless stream of Yiddish.

While I was aware that I was being sucked in, I could not fight my curiosity. The Rebbe's soft, pale, brilliant eyes peering out from that mass of white fur attracted me. I had the sense that, in this community where I was mostly treated as invisible, the Rebbe might somehow *see me*.

He was the *ba'al teshuva* champion, and I needed a champion.

It didn't matter what translation the women whispered to me. I was hearing my own: "You can make it. You can do it. Don't give up. Never give in."

CHAPTER 10

THE REBBE'S WINE

My first *farbrengen*, or celebration, came just before the High Holy Days. These were occasions for gathering around the Rebbe's table to eat, sing, and hear his words of wisdom, and they were usually for the men—but this was a special one. It was just for women, and we were invited downstairs at long last, to the large, open main room. The man room. Maybe the Rebbe had heard me after all.

I stood on a long line of about seven hundred women of all ages, and we slowly made our way toward the Rebbe for a blessing.

Everyone was giddy with excitement, chattering away. I tried to sort out the strange mish-mosh of languages. I picked up bits of Russian, French, and Yiddish, but they all melded together like language soup.

"Sometimes he gives everyone a dollar with his blessing," whispered Lifsa.

"They say the moment he looks into your eyes, he knows everything about you," purred Fagee in her inimitable accent. "I hope he does not see that affair I had in Brussels."

"I'm just glad the girls get a chance for once," I said, a little too loudly.

"Rossi! The Rebbe is a total woman's libber," whispered Anya from behind me. "Didn't you know? He's big on the education of women."

I looked at the long line of gray-faced ladies in their wigs, pregnant and clutching babies, and thought, *Right . . . total women's libber.*

A portly woman in a crooked brown sheitel turned to me. "He believes women have the holiest mission of all—to save the Jewish people."

Fighting the urge to reach out and adjust her head covering, I said, "Let me guess. This is the whole 'be fruitful' thing, right?"

She seemed stunned. "Yes! It is a woman's holy mission. Her true calling."

I turned back to Anya. "What were you saying about women's lib?"

Three hours later, I finally stood before the Rebbe. He seemed smaller than I'd expected, but there was clearly something special about him. I couldn't deny it.

Is this what it is like to meet a prophet?

For what felt like hours but was really only seconds, he looked at me—or rather, looked into me. His blue eyes seemed wet and kind as he smiled. They almost twinkled. All I thought was *Santa Claus.*

I didn't know what to say. Out of my mouth spilled, "Hi, Rebbe!"

I should have asked someone exactly what one is supposed to call this man.

He smiled and seemed on the verge of laughing, then pushed a small shot-size cup of wine toward me and said something in Hebrew.

I guessed this was my blessing, and, as if in answer to my questioning face, he nodded his head. I didn't know what I was supposed to do. He said something else. This time it sounded

Yiddish. I think he was joking about me to the man behind him. He smiled and then nodded his head again.

The women near me screamed, "*Drink it!*"

Nervously, I downed the shot of wine in one gulp, nearly choking. Not knowing what else to do, I said, again a little too loudly, "Thank you, Rebbe!"

He smiled. His soft blue eyes twinkled again. I felt my heart skip.

As I snaked my way through the throngs of women and out of 770 onto Eastern Parkway, I was in some sort of daze. After three hours of waiting in line, my stomach was rumbling, and I became vaguely aware that I was hungry. I noticed a lot of the women nibbling on small brown cakes and thought that I should find out where they had gotten them—but I was still captive to the feeling, the strange sensation of the Rebbe staring into my eyes.

As my friends and I headed across the street, I noticed a group of women huddled together by a tree. They were looking at me and whispering to one another.

"What's with them?" I asked my patient friend. "Did I screw up that badly?"

"Sweetie, not only did you get more time with the Rebbe than almost anyone else, but you got blessed wine!"

"Wasn't that the point? To get some blessed wine?"

"Idiot, he was doling out bits of honey cake today, not wine!" yelled Anya.

"Maybe he took one look at me and figured I needed a drink."

Anya laughed. Fagee looked angry. "You Americans are so stupid! He is Moshe Rabenu! He is like Moses! It is like *Moses* gave you a cup of wine!"

"Okay, okay, calm down. It's not like he parted the Red Sea or anything," I said. "Maybe you can ask Moses to get me a pastrami on rye. I'm starving!"

Fagee slapped me on the shoulder.

"You don't understand how special you are. The Rebbe blessed you. That is forever."

As we marched to the kosher pizza place, the women we passed whispered and stared at me. It was as if my little moment with the Rebbe had been broadcast on the news: "Runaway punk rocker blessed by Holy Man."

I tried pretending it wasn't a big deal, but after that day, Bela didn't have to drag me to 770. I wanted to see him again.

I thought of his blue twinkling Santa Claus eyes.

Maybe he really had seen me.

CHAPTER 11

SHABBOS

I woke one morning to find the house filled with the smell of meat and onions. I looked at the clock. It was 9 a.m.

I walked into the kitchen to find Bela sautéing madly in two frying pans.

"Are you cooking a cow for breakfast?" I asked.

"It's cholent," Bela said, "For Shabbos."

"We can't turn the oven on and off on Shabbos," said Lifsa, jumping in with an explanation, as usual. "We leave the oven on warm from Friday night to Saturday night. The cholent can sit in there forever."

No response seemed necessary, so I poured myself a cup of coffee and sat down next to her as she cut potatoes. Bela laid the onions and beef cubes she'd been browning in a large roasting pan, then covered them with red beans. Lifsa handed her the bowl of cut potatoes, and she tossed them in, too.

"So . . . the whole dinner goes in that one pot?"

"That's cholent," Lifsa said, "a buffet in a pan. Didn't your mother ever make it?"

"We're Jewish," I said, "but not *that* Jewish."

The phone rang in the living room, and Bela wiped her hands on her apron as she went to answer it.

"She's fine . . ." I heard her say softly. "Yes . . . yes . . . It's too early to tell. I'll tell him."

"She's talking to your mother," Lifsa whispered.

"How do you know?"

"She's talked to her a few times, and she always sounds angry when she does."

Bela walked back into the kitchen and said, "Your mother wants to talk to you, Slovah."

I shook my head, but Lifsa slapped the top of it. "She's still your mum, dum-dum!"

I trudged into the living room, a feeling of sinking dread in my stomach.

"Hi, Mom."

As soon as she heard my voice, she started crying. "What else were we to do?" she said between sobs.

"I don't know, Mom. Something."

"Slovah. You were just too wild for us." She sounded out of breath. "Are they feeding you enough?"

I started to laugh. Not *Are you safe?* or *Are you frightened?*

"Yes, Mom. They feed me *too* much. I'm getting fat."

"Good," she said, sounding relieved. "I was worried."

I wanted to smash the phone against the wall. *That's* what she was worried about!? I felt a pain in my back and realized I was hanging my head so low my chin was pressing into my collarbone.

"Your sister Yaya met a nice boy at the JCC named Donny Silberstein."

"That's great, Mom."

"He has a younger brother."

"*Mommm . . .*"

"Slovah. Don't fall for a Chasid. They make terrible husbands. The wives raise the babies and still have to work to support the family while the men study all day."

"You picked a strange place to send me if that's what you're afraid of."

We talked at each other for a few more minutes . . . then I muttered something about having to go help with Shabbos, and we said our goodbyes.

I walked back into the kitchen.

"You look befuddled," Lifsa said.

"*Befuddled*. I think that's going to be my new word."

As she and I sat and peeled garlic, I filled her in on the phone call in whispers.

"If you hate it here so much, why didn't you just tell her so?" she asked, blunt as always.

I thought about Sandy Hook Beach. The last time I was there, I'd sat around a bonfire with Mag and Webs. Webs was playing guitar and singing "Lola" by the Kinks. I heard the rough Jersey ocean crashing onto the shore and Webs's raspy voice. I sat so close to the fire that later I discovered tiny burns from the embers on my denim jacket. Small price to pay for heaven.

"Because right now, I hate her more."

"Ladies, stop whispering! I need you to go to Rivkie's before they close. I need eggs for the cholent."

"You throw eggs in there, too?"

Bela and Lifsa just looked at me and shook their heads like I was hopeless.

● ·· • ˙ ·●····● · ··

On the way to Rivkie's, Lifsa and I passed four women begging in front of 770. Whenever a Lubavitcher passed, they'd hold up their paper cups, which were already overflowing with cash.

"Wow, they are raking it in!"

"*Tzedakah*—you know, *charity*—is a big deal around here. The Ramban felt it was a true sign of righteousness."

"The Rambam?"

"I'll explain later."

Lifsa bought a dozen eggs and a chocolate-covered halvah bar that she broke in half for us. Probably not so nutritious, but I couldn't have imagined anything tastier for breakfast than dark chocolate and sweet sesame.

That evening, Lifsa took me to Friday night services at 770, and I was shoved into the tower behind her. She looked so pregnant, I worried the heat might make her burst. Luckily, an old Russian woman with her hair in a turban gave Lifsa her seat, and I managed to shimmy in next to her.

The men below sung what must have been their favorite tune. I had already heard it a dozen times.

"We want *Moshiach* now / We don't want to wait!" went the refrain.

The Rebbe did not sing, just pounded his fist in rhythm. The more he got into it, the louder they sang.

"Doesn't the world have to end for *Moshiach* to come?" I asked Lifsa.

"*Shhh*," said the old Russian woman, who was suddenly unhappy that she had offered Lifsa her seat, given the kind of company she kept.

Lifsa fanned herself with her hands as sweat dripped from her black wig.

"Maybe I could ask the Rebbe to let the women come downstairs where they keep this thing called air," I half-whispered near her ear.

"*Shhh*!" hissed the old Russian woman.

"Slovah, be quiet. You'll get us both in trouble," said Lifsa.

"Good," I said. "Maybe *Moshiach* will come then."

"*Shhh*!" The old woman was turning red.

"*Ba'al teshuva*!" Lifsa said, well above a whisper.

The woman shook her head but didn't say another word.

At the end of the service, Lifsa took my arm and dragged me downstairs and out onto Eastern Parkway.

"Why did you say *ba'al teshuva*?"

"Honey, being *ba'al teshuva* explains everything from drinking to apparent insanity. After all, we've just come in from the cold."

"I can do insanity. Watch this!" I stuck my tongue out and did a little crazy dance.

"Stop it, you nutter! We're right in front of 770! You've got to learn to button your trap! I've been waiting six months to see the Rebbe. Don't screw it up for me, or I'll never get my permission to divorce my ass of a husband."

"I never heard you curse before."

"You bring it out in me!"

We found a bench on Eastern Parkway and sat in the breeze. Fall was coming.

I closed my eyes and let the wind caress my face. In my mind, I traveled to where I heard the waves and the seagulls, the laughter of my pals as we nestled together in towels on Sandy Hook Beach a hundred years ago.

Lifsa jolted me back. "It was an arranged marriage, a *shidduch*. We met at the airport."

"The airport?"

"It's a common first date place around here. You go to the airport and watch the planes take off and land."

"Thrilling. Where do you go for your second date—the train station?"

"It was nice, actually. We were married three months later, and I was pregnant a month after that."

"So . . . what went wrong?"

"He was always drunk. Pretty soon, he started beating me. I was afraid he would hurt the baby."

"You need permission to divorce *that*?"

"You need permission for everything around here."

"If the Rebbe really is like Moses, he won't want you to be with that jerk."

"I don't think he will . . . but he only meets people twice a week, on Sunday and Thursday. It can be a long wait. I heard he even turned away President Kennedy once!"

"Holy shit!"

"Well, there's nothing holy about shit, but yeah."

⁕ ⋯ ⁕ ⋯ ⁕ ⋯ ⁕ ⋯

I had to admit, the Rebbe seemed uniquely qualified to carry his message of peace and forgiveness. He had no children but was said to embrace the Lubavitchers as his family. He'd been born in Russia at the turn of the century and lost family in the Holocaust, yet there seemed to be no trace of bitterness in his eyes, only a sorrow that bordered on joy, and the sense that he was always remembering and hoping at the same time.

He moved me.

The way the community worshipped him, though, and asked him for permission to travel, to use birth control, to divorce, to have surgery . . . all of that scared me to death. I wondered if it scared him, too.

CHAPTER 12

MASHEY'S HOUSE FOR SHABBOS

"Hello, my little sunflower!" Mashey exclaimed in her Russian accent as she gave me a rib-crushing hug. Just five feet tall and thirty years old—though she looked fifty—she was stronger than any woman I knew. I had assumed that, like many Lubavitch women at any given time, she was pregnant, until Lifsa said, "No, sweetie, she's just fat."

Mashey's strong, calloused hands and the checkered scarf (or *shmata*, as she called it) tied around her head made her look like a peasant woman accustomed to field work. She was always laughing. The fact that she was usually drunk probably explained it.

"Why do you always call me your little sunflower?"

"Because you came to us just a few months after the *Birchas Hachamma*."

"The *birka* . . . what?"

"It comes around every twenty-eight years, when the sun completes its cycle. It just happened in April."

"That makes sense. I'm a Leo after all. Fire sign."

"We don't follow the zodiac. That's a goyish thing."

"There were thousands of people in the street in front of 770 for the Rebbe's sun blessing!"

I wondered what the hell she was talking about—then looked up and saw the reason for her proclamation: Yoseph, Mashey's eight-year-old son, had just appeared at the top of the steps, his long black *payot* dangling in front of his ears.

"Hey! I thought Lubavitchers didn't have *payot*!" I said, figuring that I'd never understand the rules of this place.

"They don't, but he likes them," said his proud mama.

Overhearing the exchange, Yoseph chimed in, "Rechamim has them, and he's Lubavitch!"

"Rechamim also doesn't do his homework. So don't be like him. Go back to your room and study!"

As Yoseph ran back down the upstairs hallway, he shouted, "*Loshon Hara!*"

"What's that mean?" I asked.

"Oh, it means *gossip*. You're not supposed to talk behind people's backs."

"You love to gossip!"

"That's right, baby. I'm a bad Jew! Come, let's drink some vodka before the men come home."

The men were Mashey's husband Shamul, her brother Shimone, and her sixteen-year-old son, Jacob. They were spending the day parked near Union Square in what was called the "Mitzvah Tank." It looked like an old ice-cream truck turned into a Lubavitch-converting machine on wheels. They would call out to passersby, "Are you Jewish?" And if the person said yes, they'd offer Shabbos candles to the women, or to help the men pray.

"That's got to be a thankless job," I said, sipping the vodka and orange juice Mashey had made for me.

"I think of them as firefighters—fighting the fires of assimilation—and yes, it is very thankless. But it gets them out of the house so I can drink vodka and cook dinner with you."

"My mom talked about goy fire, too."

"Goy fire! I like that," she said. "Now, tell me what an uncircumcised penis looks like. It must be disgusting."

"It is kind of gross, actually."

Mashey poured more vodka into our juice.

"If anyone asks, it's just orange juice."

Mashey finished frying the schnitzel and placed it on a platter, then wrapped the whole thing in aluminum foil. She dumped the boiled, sliced carrots in a bowl and tossed them with chopped dill.

Looking over at the foil-encased platter, I asked, "Why do Jews eat so much chicken?"

"It may come from the Ramban."

"That Rambam guy again."

"The Ramban! Rabbi Moshe ben Nahman. He was one of the greatest rabbis ever. He taught healthy eating, which was very unusual eight hundred years ago. He said chicken was better to eat than other animals."

"Cheaper, too."

"Yes, that too."

Yoseph came running down the stairs.

"*Ema! Ema!* I've got a present for you!" he handed Mashey his two *payot*, which he had clipped from his head and wrapped in a wad of toilet paper.

"Yoseph . . . what have you done!? Those curls were so cute!"

"Now I'm Lubavitch!"

"Oy, Yoseph," she said, shaking her head and smiling with one side of her mouth. "Slovah. Pour me more of the . . . *orange juice*, will you?"

"Yes, ma'am."

When Yoseph had skittered from the room, I turned back to Mashey and said, "So if Lubavitchers don't have *payot*, who does?"

"The Satmars in Williamsburg. They hate us."

"I heard that," I said. "'Cause you're too modern, right?"

"Crazy, right? I mean . . . we're not that bad!"

We were sharing a belly laugh at the irony when the door opened and in walked Mashey's husband Shamul. He was only a few inches taller than she, and twice as fat. He was red-faced and seemed even more giddy than we were. His son and brother-in-law looked flushed as well.

"What's up with you all?" Mashey shouted at them, as if trying to bring them to their senses.

"Jacob met his first transvestite!" said Shamul. "He didn't know whether to give him Shabbos candles or wrap him in teffilin."

In New Jersey, I'd been a regular at the midnight showing of *The Rocky Horror Picture Show*. Tim Curry singing "Sweet Transvestite" was the highlight of the show for me. I knew every word to that song and sang it all the time.

"I gotta go to this Union Square!" I announced.

"Bring a gun," said Mashey as she set the table.

CHAPTER 13

PIZZA AND HUMMUS

Mr. T. was a sweet old man who lived in a small house next door to my family's home in Rumson. Figuring he was lonely and bored with his life of watching wrestling on television and petting his fat tabby cat, I started visiting him after school my sophomore year. He was more than happy to stockpile Marlboro Lights, Michelobs, and Snickers bars in exchange for my company. I don't suppose my parents were very excited about this relationship, but, figuring I was just spending time with a lonely old man, they never said a word.

When Mr. T. mailed me a check care of Rabbi Sherba for a hundred dollars, it felt like a million bucks. I have no idea how he got my address and couldn't have cared less.

The only problem was the nearest bank was on Utica Avenue.

"Walk quickly but calmly. Show no fear and go as close to nine a.m. as you can. Utica will be busy with commuters then," Lifsa explained.

"So, no cops there either—just like on Nostrand?"

"What can I say? The Rebbe has a lot of clout, so we get all the protection." She looked at me sternly. "Be careful! There have already been, like, eighty murders in Crown Heights just this year. They call the police station on Utica *The Alamo*. Some nudnik even painted it on the wall there."

As I walked along Eastern Parkway toward Utica, a station wagon crawled past me stuffed with young Chasidic men holding baseball bats. They pressed their faces to the window and stared.

I remembered the civilian patrol Lifsa had told me about. "They are holy," she'd explained. "If anyone is getting mugged, they teach them a lesson from the Bible: Thou shalt not mug!"

I felt comforted by their presence, though from my brief glimpse they seemed barely more than children, with their peach-fuzz chins and pale skin. Still, as a group they seemed intimidating. If they'd asked before they drove away, I would have appreciated an escort to Utica.

I walked for twenty minutes—well out of the safety of Chasidland—before getting to the bustling main thoroughfare. I saw a large bank on the corner, and on my way over to it, I passed a store that had a Dry Cleaner sign in the window. When I looked inside, all I saw were two men sitting behind a counter smoking. One of them was writing in a notepad. There were no racks of dry cleaning, no hangers, no laundry, not even a cash register. What were they doing in there? I made a mental note to ask Lifsa about it.

On Utica, the graffiti popped up just as it had on Nostrand. The visible police presence consisted of two cops leaning against a brick wall drinking coffee. But, just as Lifsa had predicted, Utica was jammed with commuters rushing toward the subway. I figured there were far too many people around for anybody to try and mug me.

Once inside the bank, I saw that it was enormous, with cathedral ceilings and bronze-trimmed tellers' windows. It reminded me of a 1940s movie I'd seen once, in which machine gun-toting gangsters had held up a place just like it.

I found a sign that said "New Accounts" and waited on a line behind five other people. After about ten minutes, I made my way to the desk of a harried woman in Jheri curls. She took my ID and Mr. T.'s check and, after asking me a bunch of questions, opened a savings account for me.

"How long will it take to clear?"

"It's out-of-state, so . . . about a week."

I felt my stomach rumble. There went the extra cash to pick up a slice of pizza and a Coke on the way back to Bela's.

I thanked her and made my way back out through the big doors onto Utica. As I walked toward the corner, I saw three teenage boys hanging out in front of a deli. They were Black—like everyone else on the street but me—and one of them wore a jogging suit the color of the sky. When a young woman with a very large rear end squeezed into very small pants passed by, they all had something to say about it.

"Shake it, mama!"

"Yeah, baby!"

One of them who had turned his baseball hat around backward whistled, and when he did so, I noticed that one of his two front teeth was capped in gold. When the boys noticed me, they elbowed one another, then stepped out in front of me, preventing me from passing.

"Where you going, Blondie?" Blue Jogging Suit taunted.

"Got any money, bitch?" Gold Tooth said.

A man wearing a suit and carrying a briefcase swerved around them and headed for the entrance to the subway without even slowing down.

So much for safety in numbers.

When I thought about the moment days later, I realized I hadn't acted out of bravery so much as feeling like I had nothing left to lose.

"DO YOU REALLY THINK I'D FUCKING BE HERE IF I HAD ANY MONEY!?" I shouted.

The boys looked at the bizarre creature standing in front of them in a Cheap Trick T-shirt over a long-sleeved red turtleneck . . . and started to laugh. "Crazy bitch," one of them muttered as they parted and let me pass.

•·····•·¯•·..•·· · ·

At this point, my savings had dwindled to $400. I'd spent the rest on lunch and quarters for the pay phone outside the deli. Each time I made a call, it cost me a dollar. I'd called Cindy Butler three times and left my new number, but she never called me back. Figuring maybe four would be the charm, I tried again. Her mom picked up the phone.

"Honey. You're a big improvement over the dipshits my daughter dates, but I think you have to give up on her now. She's not ready to embrace her sapphic side. Find someone who appreciates you."

Click.

I didn't know what *sapphic* meant but I got the message.

I called Sarah.

"Man, what happened to you," she shouted, "getting taken away like that? Getting carted away just blows!"

Sonya grabbed the phone. "Don't your parents watch the news? Bedford Stuyvesant, Crown Heights, these are bad fucking neighborhoods!"

I heard Sarah wrestling the phone back.

"Honey . . . I'm just so sorry about what they did to you."

I closed my eyes, listening to Sarah's soft voice alternating with Sonya's loud one. For just a moment, I was not standing in the middle of Kingston Avenue at a pay phone, but sitting on the Calvin Klein couch in their warm living room, listening to Todd Rundgren while Sarah danced in front of the window.

Sonya woke me up. "Those Rumson preppies are throwing some wild parties this year."

It was finally senior year, and I was missing it. Missing what might have been the most fun year of my teenage life. I hated to admit it to myself, but given what had happened, I really wished I had taken a thousand deep breaths and graduated when I was supposed to, in 1982. I needed another year of childhood.

The idea of being worried about nothing but grades and parties felt like a visit to Disneyland.

•··•˙˜•...•· ··

My theater pals, Mag and Wolf, were the only friends I had who actually offered to visit me in Crown Heights, probably because they were older and independent from their parents.

Wolf had moved to Manhattan to work at Vidal Sassoon. I couldn't imagine anything more glamorous than living in Manhattan and working at Vidal Sassoon.

"Dear . . . they're just a bunch of queens like me!" he said when I complained about the Chasids. "Only I'm way better dressed."

Sonya, Sarah, Wolf, and Mag. They were my touchstones; all I had left of what I called civilization. The rest of my pals had been drifting away since the moment I left home.

When I walked along Kingston Avenue, the dozens of Chasids I encountered scurried along as if in a rush. Their energy seemed electric, somewhere between ecstatic and nervous.

"Why are they always hurrying?" I asked Lifsa.

"If you had ten kids you'd be rushing around, too!"

At home, there had always been noise. My mother preferred screaming to speaking, and my father only spoke in a loud growl. My sister hummed constantly except when she was complaining, and my brother whined. Out of self-preservation, I'd cultivated an ability to crawl into a quiet place inside my brain and daydream.

"Bombs can go off," my mother used to say, "and Slovah won't hear a thing."

Here, surrounded by Chasids chattering in Yiddish, I

reverted to my old ways. I accessed my inner cavern and drifted as far back into the depths of it as I could. I was alone in this community, an impostor going through the motions. Except for the Rebbe, who crept into my thoughts often, I was only feigning interest in the Lubavitch way of life. I was buying time, hoping my next move would appear before me like a miracle. Wasn't that what you were supposed to hope for in a religious community: a miracle?

When I stepped out of the protected Chasidic universe, I felt even more alone. The old women who clustered together on benches along Eastern Parkway, cracking peanuts out of their shells, eating them, and tossing the shells into piles at their feet, looked at me like I was lost or crazy. I felt a bit of both.

The Rasta men on the corner smoking spliffs looked at me like I was lunch.

The teenage boys dancing around blaring boom boxes looked at me like I was a narc.

I hadn't realized how important music had been in my life until it was taken from me. Blondie, the B-52s, the Ramones, Led Zeppelin, Pat Benatar . . . the soundtrack of my teen years had been replaced with "We want Moshiach now."

"Double Dutch Bus" wasn't exactly rock-and-roll, but I couldn't help walking close enough to listen to the kids singing it. The tune was catchy.

"What you looking at? Nothing for you to see here!" growled a boy wearing a black knit ski hat.

There didn't seem to be anywhere that I belonged.

＊･･･＊･＊。･･･＊・・

When Anya found out I'd been paying for the bagel and cream cheese with a slice of onion and tomato that I ate for lunch at the dairy deli, she introduced me to a second-floor cafeteria that you would only know about if you knew about it. It was like having the secret password for a speakeasy.

"We're here for lunch," Anya said to the man at the door.

There were long tables lined up one after the other, and at each table sat Chasids, mostly students, chatting away while they ate. The men and women sat at separate tables. Stacks of small booklets that Lifsa had once explained were called *benchers* were stacked up on each one. According to what she'd told me, after you were done eating, you were supposed to read the *bencher* and say your after-meal prayer.

There were also sinks for washing your hands before the meal. You were supposed to pour a cup of water three times over your right hand, then three times over your left. I never bothered with all that cup-pouring, just washed my hands the old-fashioned way, to the obvious disapproval of the Chasids standing behind me in the washing line.

The food speakeasy offered a simple, free lunch to any Jew who needed it: sliced challah or rye bread, sliced salami, and pickles with mustard. The food filled my stomach, but all that salami left me thirsty and constipated. When Fagee was paying, which was almost always, I opted instead to meet the girls at the kosher pizza place.

Fagee had enjoyed her life in France. She'd been something of a bad girl, having affairs with married men, drinking every night. She may not have been on a crash course to greatness, but she was having a lot of fun. One day, as she sat in a French café hungover from too much wine the night before, she opened the paper and read about the Rebbe.

"It was like a message from God," she said. Fagee decided to turn her life around and left Versailles for Brooklyn.

When she told me all this, I pretended to ponder it as if it were a sane decision, then said, "Leaving France to come to Crown Heights . . . *hmm* . . . I might not call that the best choice."

"It was for the Rebbe, silly girl. I love this man."

Anya had come from Tel Aviv for similar reasons, and I couldn't fathom how anyone would leave the Holy Land in search of spirituality. Wasn't Israel the epicenter of all things Jewish? Anya had gotten hooked when she'd spent a weekend at a Lubavitch Chabad outside of Tel Aviv. She'd gone home and immediately talked her parents into sending her to the Rebbe.

"How often do you get to pray with the Messiah?" she asked.

"Do you really believe he's the Messiah?"

Anya twirled a strand of her long black hair, looked at me, and her whole face seemed to smile. "Probably not, but you know . . . *just in case.*"

The little sign on our table at the pizza shop read, Israeli pizza, falafel, french fries, hummus, tahini, Coke, Diet Coke, iced tea, and coffee. I'd learned quickly that Israeli pizza was more white than red like the Italian version, with a lot less sauce.

I loved sauce.

The plastic tables were filled with twenty-something Chasidic men and women, many smoking cigarettes, and lots of teenagers. Strollers and toddlers were there in force as well.

"Doesn't *Hashem* mind if we smoke?" I asked.

"You would think so, but no one has told us not to yet," Anya said, taking a long drag off what looked like a joint but was really a hand-rolled Drum cigarette.

At the back of the place, a thick red-velvet curtain covered the opening to a backroom. I watched as an old Chasidic man with a white beard grazing his belt walked immediately to the back, where an Israeli counterman parted the curtain for him.

I craned my neck to try and see what was in that room. I could make out boxes of sodas and dry goods, but the curtain fell closed before I saw anything else.

"What do those old men do back there?" I asked.

"Who knows, who cares?" said Fagee.

"I heard Shula got a *shidduch*!" said Lifsa, downing a slice of pizza covered in hummus and pickles.

"Jesus, Lifsa, have that baby already!"

"Did you know Jesus was a Jew?"

"A fucking *shidduch*! Why must I marry for the *hope* of love? I want to marry for love!" said Anya.

"I want to marry for sex!" announced Fagee, nibbling at her falafel with tahini sauce.

We all cracked up.

"Sex is overrated," Lifsa said. "I'd rather have a good *caca!*"

"Eat salad!" shot back Fagee. "I always tell you! It's the baby that is keeping you from shitting!"

A group of women in sheitels looked over at us and whispered. I realized one of them was Bela and waved at her. She nodded but did not come over.

"I don't think Bela likes me," I said quietly.

"Do you like her?" Lifsa asked.

"Good point."

A few days later, a few of us decided to meet again at the pizza place. When I got there, Shula was sitting with Anya and Fagee. She had just gotten engaged to the Chasidic banker we'd heard about. Rich and religious, he was considered a good catch. Shula wore beautiful boutique dresses, as Fagee did, and was also French but not as heavily perfumed. She was very pretty, with green eyes and thick red lips.

"I love the way he smokes," she said dreamily. "He kind of does a *shhh, shhh, shhh* as he blows out the smoke. How could I not love this man?"

"You think you love him because he doesn't inhale his cigarette smoke?"

As we talked, an old Chasidic man with a cane walked to the back and was ushered through the curtain by the same counterman.

"Do you ever notice that those old rabbis walk in there but they never come out?" I said. "What do they do, kill them in there!?"

"Of course, Slovah. Everyone knows the pizza place is a rabbi recycling factory," Anya joked. "The old ones go in. They get chopped up into the hummus, and the new ones come out the back door."

"Shit!" exclaimed Fagee. "I am eating hummus! Now I have to think of that old man chopped up in my pita!"

Anya dipped her finger in Fagee's hummus and put in her mouth. "The hummus is pretty chunky today."

"*Aakkk*, I will never eat again!"

CHAPTER 14

THE RED CURTAIN

Walking along Kingston Avenue in the afternoon felt like stepping into one of the old movies my mom liked to watch. Even the signs had a vintage look about them: Weinstein's Hardware, Crown Cosmetics, Crown Bagel. Underneath the name on the Crown Bagel sign it said, "It ain't just bagels."

This was the backdrop to my new life. The scurrying Chasids completed the look. I was not walking down the street in 1981. It was 1941.

Behind the counter at Weinstein's was a Chasid sporting a long, black beard, *tzitzes*, and a yarmulke, wearing a sweatshirt, jeans, and a tool belt. I'd always assumed they all looked the same: black coats (longer ones on the Sabbath), books under their arms, pale faces, and scrawny, unexercised bodies. The tool-belt Chasid looked like he'd just finished doing pushups.

At the kosher pizza place that afternoon, as Anya, Fagee, and I nibbled at our food, I told them about the strange case of the Chasid in a tool belt.

"Lubavitchers have toilets too, you know," said Fagee. "Someone has to fix them—we can't give all our money to the goyim."

"I just didn't know they grew macho Chasids," I said.

"Macho? Well, did you give him my phone number, for heaven's sake?" Anya joked.

As we chattered on, a Chasidic man who looked about eighty walked in. He shuffled past our table and into the back room, with the assistance of the counterman.

"I can't take it anymore!" I announced. I waited until the counterman was ringing up an order and shot past him through the curtain. There, behind the boxes of soda, flour, and plastic cups, sitting on the floor on cushions around a large bong, were three pious-looking old men. One was in mid-inhale as the water in the bong gurgled; another blew smoke out of his mouth. The air smelled of really good pot, the kind I'd had to pay double for in New Jersey, with exotic names like Sinsemilla and Maui Wowie. This wasn't like the cheap, home-grown stuff I'd sold in pink wrappers.

The men looked up at me, clearly astonished. One of them started to giggle and that triggered the rest of them into fits of laughter.

The counterman raced in and stood between me and the old men, as if protecting them.

"Get out, get out!" he growled at me.

Not knowing quite how to react, I saluted the group of giddy old men and walked back to our table, shaking my head and laughing all the way.

"Those old geezers are smoking really good weed back there!" I said triumphantly.

"Well . . . marijuana, it is kosher, you know," Fagee purred. "I think it just has to be blessed."

CHAPTER 15

DANNY

"We must always remember," my mother would say just after she lit the Shabbos candles in the faux gold candlesticks she had gotten free for opening a Christmas Club account at the local bank, "your Great-Uncle Moshe suffocated to death in the train on the way to Auschwitz. The Nazis didn't even have a chance to send him to the gas chambers. There were so many Jews shoved into that train car that he died of asphyxiation." Ignoring the horrified looks on the faces of her children as she served the meal, she said, "Eat your chicken before it gets cold."

One year, I bought a squeeze bottle of fake vampire blood at the local five-and-ten-cent store and poured it on my sister Yaya's least-favorite Dawn doll. She cut her hair off to complete the look. We'd overlooked the fact that the disfigurement was permanent, and that Dawn would forever be consigned to the role of concentration-camp victim.

"You can never trust a goy," Mom told us often. "When Sedane, your cousin-three-times-removed, was being taken away by the Gestapo, she threw her baby to her best friend and neighbor as they dragged her off. That *shiksa* friend tossed the baby back to the guards, who machine-gunned it."

"*Mom*! I'm trying to eat!"

"That's what happens when you trust a shiksa. Don't even get me started on the boys. All they want is one thing. If you want to find a nice boy you can trust, look for the yarmulke!"

* * *

One afternoon at the pizza joint, a tall, clean-shaven young man wearing a yellow T-shirt and matching yellow yarmulke walked up to me. He flashed me a wide, silly smile and said, "I'm Danny, and I've been watching you for a while. You're just what we need around here." Then he let loose with a high-pitched, girlish giggle that made it impossible to not laugh, too.

"Are you Lubavitch?" I asked, noting his lack of Chasidic attire.

"My family is, but I'm . . . something else."

There was something about his childlike face and that yellow yarmulke that made me warm up to Danny immediately.

"Would you like to sit with us?"

Fagee elbowed me. "Slovah. If one of your rabbi's spies find out you are hanging out with boys, there might be some problems for you."

"*Slovah*, huh . . ." said Danny.

"My name's Rossi, actually. Slovah is my Jewish name."

I kicked Fagee in the shin and slid over, making room for my new friend. He immediately pulled out a pack of Drum tobacco, rolled four cigarettes, and passed them around.

"I like him already," Anya laughed, grabbing the cigarette.

"I don't want to get you in trouble with your rabbi. Let's grab an elephant beer at Hector's," he said.

"What is an elephant beer, and what is Hector's?" I asked, raising an eyebrow.

"Follow me."

Without a word, I left Fagee and Anya and followed him out of the restaurant.

"Be careful," Fagee called after us.

Danny led me down the street to the Puerto Rican deli and opened the door for me. "Hector, this is my new friend Rossi!"

"*Si*, the lady who is always getting change for the phone."

Salsa music was blaring. Hector, about thirty with a handlebar mustache that made him look like Sonny Bono, was dancing behind a bulletproof glass wall by the register. He wore a button-down shirt that was unbuttoned so low I could almost see his navel. I counted three gold chains against his hairy chest. "Dan the man, you're classing the place up with this blondie!" he shouted.

"*Qué pasa!*" came a voice from the back of the store. A man in his sixties with a pronounced beer belly emerged, wearing a shirt that was both flowered and striped. Like Hector's, it was unbuttoned extravagantly to showcase several gold chains sparkling against his furry chest. His Sonny Bono mustache was white.

"This is Uncle Pete," said Hector. "He owns the joint."

Uncle Pete bent down, took my hand, and kissed it. "Welcome, *mamita*."

Danny went to the deli fridge and returned with two beers the size of oil cans.

"This is an elephant beer." He flipped one open and handed it to me.

"I'll be wasted if I drink that."

Hector did a little salsa dance. "Party time!"

Danny pulled two milk crates out from a corner they shared with a broom and mop, and we sat on them, drinking, and watching Hector dance. I felt oddly comfortable. My breath slowed; my body relaxed. How long had it been since I felt relaxed?

Periodically, a Lubavitch man would walk in and slide a five- or ten-dollar bill into the turnaround in the bulletproof glass. Hector would take the money and spin out a small manila envelope in return.

"What the fuck?" I said after one of the Chasids had left with his little parcel.

"He's got ten old cans of tuna fish on the shelves and some potato chips that are two years past stale. Do you really think he's making a living on groceries?"

"The chips aren't that bad. I bought a bag yesterday," I said.

"Mi'ita, blondie!" shouted Uncle Pete. "I'm gonna be a rich man, selling nickel and dime bags to the rabbis! Yeah, baby!"

"Why don't they buy from all those Rastas on Franklin?"

"*Mami*, if those rabbis go out of the free zone, they don't have the cops or the patrol to protect them. Only the ones with real *cojones* go out there. You know . . . big machos like Danny Duck over here."

As we laughed over that, a petite Chasidic man with a short black beard walked in. If I'd seen him from behind, I might have thought he was a twelve-year-old boy. He slid a twenty to Hector and got back two packets.

"*Toda raba*," he said to Hector.

"*Toda rabbi* to you, too, *papi*!"

The little man turned and smiled at me, then looked over at Danny. "Who is your friend, Daniel?" he inquired.

"This is the famous Slovah Rossi."

"Just Rossi thanks," I interjected.

"Nice to meet you, Famous Rossi. I'm Yehudah."

I started to put out my hand but quickly put it down. "Sorry. Forgot the no-hand-shaking thing."

He nodded and smiled. "We have shaken hands with our souls."

I watched him as he walked toward the door, then turned back and said, "The word on the street is you're a little *meshuga*."

I laughed. "*Ba'al tshuva!*"

"*Zay gazunt*." He bowed his head. "We need a little more *meshuga* around here." With that, he departed.

"I like him," I said to Danny.

"Yehudah? Yeah. That little guy is a big macher around here, but he's not bad. He's one of the few Lubavitch muckety-mucks you can hang with."

Danny pushed a five-dollar bill into the turnaround.

"Right, Mister Macho. Let's hook the lady up!"

Hector pushed back a small envelope and Danny's five.

"This one's on me—for La Rubia!"

I opened the bag and saw a tight little ball of pot. I put my nose to the bag. It smelled sweet and pungent and gloriously familiar.

"Feels like home," I sighed.

"We can light it up out back."

I took a big swig of beer. It tasted terrible, but I loved the rough feeling of it rolling down my throat into my stomach. I let out a loud burp.

"Classy!" said Danny, following it with three belches of his own.

"What's with all the Chasids smoking pot? I saw a slew of old rabbis sitting around a hookah thing in the back of the kosher pizza place."

"You went back there? I'm surprised Shimi didn't shoot you. He's very territorial about his old rabbis."

"But what gives?"

"A lot of the Lubavitchers I know get stoned and then go *daven*. They feel it puts them in a mystical state for prayer."

"Damn. Who knew the hats-beards-coats were stoners? Wow!"

"Is that what you call them?"

I was halfway through my beer and feeling pretty giddy. "Hey, Danny, you wanna help me get ten grand?"

"Oh, yeah. Who do I have to blow?"

"*Woo! Mi'ita!* Not in my store!"

"No one! My mother promised me that if I ever married a Jewish boy, she'd give me ten thousand dollars! You could be my fake husband!"

"That's a lot of dough. What would you do with it?"

"Get the fuck out of here, of course!"

"Of course!"

We sat there on those milk crates talking until the sun went down. Turned out Danny Cohen came from a highly respected religious family that was what they called *Cohanim*. This meant he was descended from the tribe of Israel that were priests. *Cohanim* were not permitted to go to cemeteries and were regarded as dwelling in a higher spiritual realm than other Jews. They were not permitted to marry women who had slept with non-Jews.

That put a stake into my ten-grand plan.

It had never occurred to me that there was anything special about the name Cohen. Growing up, I'd associated it with cheap things like Cohen Optical, where my family shopped for cheap glasses.

Danny had grown up über-religious but had shaved his beard sometime around his nineteenth birthday. He still lived at home with his parents and sister but went to Manhattan every day to work as a commercial artist. Once away from the prying eyes of Crown Heights, all hell broke loose.

"I like to hang out near the West Side Highway and Christopher Street, where all the gay bars are. It's wild over there!"

"Are you gay?"

"*Naaahhh*," he said, "I just like to party!" Danny elbowed me in the side. "How 'bout you, Blondie? You seem like you have a little AC/DC side?"

I thought of Cindy Butler. I wanted to tell him. But this wasn't the cozy little Barn Theater. This was a Puerto Rican deli in Crown Heights.

"I've, um . . . dabbled."

"Yeah! The dabbler!" Danny shoved his fist in the air as if in celebration.

Was this something to celebrate? I wondered.

It occurred to me, as we sat there and got to know each other, that Danny was more of a prisoner than I was. I would be able to leave the community when my sentence was up—the minute I turned eighteen and didn't have to worry about getting shipped to reform school. Danny might very well be stuck living his fake, dual life for the duration.

"I think you should have two elephant beers, Danny."

"Yeah! Party time!"

I came back to Redbeard's house a bit loaded, but it turned out I was the least of his problems. As I walked in, I heard a loud argument taking place in the kitchen.

"I'm not going to try again! He's a monster!" Lifsa shouted.

"He said he has been praying, and it will not happen again," Redbeard spoke, adopting his most soothing tone.

"Lifsa. Everyone deserves a second chance," Bela pleaded.

"Yes. Maybe next time, he can do it better and kill my baby!"

I tiptoed upstairs to wash up.

. . . .

For supper that night, Redbeard recited the blessing over the challah, then cut off a piece, dipped it in a bowl of salt, and put it in his mouth. Then he passed the bread basket and salt around. No one spoke until we'd all completed the ritual.

I'd never eaten salt with challah before. "What is the significance of the salt?" I asked. "Is it like the saltwater for tears on Passover?"

"Everything around here is like tears," Lifsa said.

"The significance," interjected Bela, "is that we want to make a blessing over the tastiest challah, and dipping it in a little bit of salt makes it taste even better."

"I like my challah sweet—like a husband should be!" Lifsa grumbled.

I helped Bela spoon peas into a bowl, and we passed it

around the table along with roast chicken, cucumber salad, noodle kugel, and Persian rice. The younger children had gone to bed, but the twin girls and oldest boy sat staring at their father as if awestruck. Lifsa sat next to me and played with her peas.

"Eat something," Bela said. "You're eating for two."

"I'm not hungry."

Redbeard sat up in his chair and cleared his throat, and we all instinctively stopped eating. "The Rebbe talks about forgiveness. It is the first thing I tell Jewish girls and boys when I start to teach them how to leave their past behind and embrace *Hashem*. Always forgive. To forgive sets you free from the bondage of hate."

"You never said that to me," I said, feeling my cheeks grow hot from the beer.

"No? Well, then, I'll say it now: Always forgive."

"Would you forgive Hitler?" asked Lifsa, with tears in her eyes.

"Some things are beyond forgiveness. But only *Hashem* can judge."

"More chicken?" Bela asked, trying to lighten the moment.

I felt a rumbling in my chest. "I don't forgive my parents for sending me here."

"You will," Redbeard said without looking up as he filled his mouth with chicken.

After dinner, Lifsa said goodnight. Since there were no Shabbos guests, she went upstairs to sleep in the guest bedroom.

"I'll miss you, couch buddy," I said.

She smiled and kissed the top of my head.

I sat up in the living room and played with the twins—Rachel and Leah—and little Moshe.

"Totty said you like music," Moshe said.

"The kind I like is called New Wave, kinda of what punk rock became when it started making money."

"Punk?" the twins said together.

"How do you dance to it?" Moshe asked.

"You just jump and down like a crazy person. It's called slam dancing. It's easy. Watch."

I sang "God Save the Queen" by the Sex Pistols, trying to do my best Johnny Rotten imitation.

"The queen, like Queen Esther?" Rachel asked, clapping her hands. "She saved the Jews!"

"Well, okay then. Esther, Queen of the Jews!" I continued jumping up and down like a pogo stick until the children joined in. "God save Queen *Estherrr*. The Queen of the Jews!"

We looked like a living room full of giggling grasshoppers.

I remembered dressing up for Purim as a child and thinking of it as a fun day of playing and marching around in costume: Jewish Halloween but without the candy. Yaya would not consider dressing as anyone but Queen Esther; Mendel demanded to be the good and brave Mordecai; and I was more than happy to be Haman, the villain. I drew a beard and mustache on my face and clipped on red devil horns. I didn't mind being evil if I got to be a boy.

"It's punk Purim!" I shouted as I swung Moshe around.

Bela darted out of the kitchen with a look of horror on her face.

"Rachel, Leah! Don't you have homework to do!?"

She swatted the girls' behinds, and they ran up the stairs with their brother close behind, still hopping.

"I'd prefer if you didn't teach my children how to dance, or to sing when men are in the house! Thank you!"

"Fun isn't allowed in your religion?"

"It's your religion, too, sweetheart," Bela said angrily. "You could learn a lot from Queen Esther. She used her female power to save the Jews, not to corrupt their children."

I looked at Bela dumbfounded. *Female power?*

The next morning when I crawled out of my couch cave, I saw a line of suitcases by the door.

Lifsa, fully dressed, was sipping a cup of coffee.

"I've been waiting for you to wake up so I could say goodbye before I leave."

"Leave?"

"I'm sorry, sweetie, but I'd rather go back to my parents in South Africa than live another day with that monster."

"But, Lifsa! What am I gonna do without you?"

Lifsa started to cry as she sat down on the velvet couch next to me. She let her face fall on my shoulder, and I petted the back of her wig. It felt hard, like acrylic.

"I'll write to you," she said. "I'll send you pictures of the baby when he comes."

"He?"

"Yes. And he's a big boy, too. Gonna be a fighter, not like his mom."

"You're a fighter, Lifsa. Look what you're doing right now."

"Yeah, well . . . we'll see."

I helped the driver take Lifsa's bags to the car and watched them slowly pull away. She blew kisses to me out the back window until the car disappeared.

She'd been my first friend in Crown Heights, and I knew I'd never hear from her again.

CHAPTER 16

MOVING OUT

It wasn't hard to convince Redbeard to let me move out. I'd never seen Bela happier than the day I took my duffel bag and suitcase out from behind the couch.

"Try to do some good with your power, Queen Esther," Bela murmured.

Rather than helping me with my bags, Redbeard just watched as I struggled to get them out the door and down the walk to the hired car that was waiting.

"I expect you to check in with me once a week," he said sternly. "Remember, I know everything that happens in this neighborhood."

As I glanced back at the house, it seemed like I'd spent years camping in that living room. But it had been only two months. I was using the few hundred dollars my parents had sent to move into a large apartment with Fagee, Anya, and Chaya—the older girl who'd always kissed the teacher's ass at Machon Chana.

My new home was just five blocks from Redbeard's. After a five-minute car ride, I found myself standing in front of a three-story brick building that had once been painted white. Most of the white had long since chipped off. Ours was a sprawling three-bedroom apartment on the top floor, and I was to have the smallest bedroom.

I threw my bags next to the mattress on the floor of the windowless cubby and closed the door. I can still remember the ecstasy of that sound, the rub and click as my very own bedroom door shut behind me. It was an old apartment, in terrible shape, but that didn't matter to me. Its wooden floors were scratched and worn and its front windows—one of which had a crack held together by graying masking tape—looked out over the hubbub of Kingston Avenue, letting in every bit of noise. In the kitchen was an old gas stove spattered with what looked like dirt but turned out to be rust.

The apartment was ruled by Chaya, the actual leaseholder. Polka-dot-and-plaid Chaya was as eager to impress the elders in the community as she'd been to impress the teachers at school. She was more than eager to lecture *ba'al teshuva* girls who didn't conform to what she felt those elders wanted. She kept a tzedakah can in her room and filled it with change to give to the poor. After she left for work, I would pick enough change out of it to buy a buttered roll from Hector.

I didn't have much patience for Chaya, who looked to me like a huge ostrich, clumsy and awkward. If only she really were an ostrich, she would stick her head in the sand and give us all a break. "You can't eat dairy!" she'd say when I nibbled on a slice of cheese from the fridge. "It hasn't been six hours since you ate meat!" It didn't take long for me to figure out why Redbeard had so readily agreed to my moving here; I'd exchanged one warden for another.

Anya and Fagee were my salvation. Fagee had the large bedroom near the front. Anya could manage only a half-share of the rent, so she slept on a cot in Fagee's room. A few nights a week, she would take a break from Fagee's snoring and crawl onto my mattress. "Just this once," she would beg each time, but I didn't mind. I loved falling asleep to the soft purr of Anya's breathing.

It was Fagee who introduced me to one of my few pleasures during that time: chocolate sandwiches. If ever there were anything sinful, it was a breakfast of strong coffee and a roll filled with nothing but chocolate. My palate would never be the same.

At one point, Shula came to stay with us for a few weeks, and we laid out a bed for her in the living room. Chaya or no, we were bent on finding ways to have fun. Thankfully, Chaya could find no rule against Jewish women drinking kosher wine in the privacy of their own home, much as she tried.

On Sunday nights, our apartment filled with just-past-adolescent women, some in the first stages of the *shidduch*, some still missing Levi's and boys. We would sing loudly and out-of-tune with the radio and laugh as we consumed horribly sweet kosher wine from coffee cups.

Sometimes, if I drank enough wine, I almost felt happy.

During the week, we gathered at the pizza shop and smoked cigarettes, comparing our rage at submission and double standards and poking fun at the pot-smoking old men as they went through the red curtain.

"Want some potato chips and chocolate with that!?" we'd call out.

I didn't have much money for art supplies, so I used the walls of my bedroom as my canvas and painted murals of powerful, muscular women with long wild hair, their arms thrust in the air as if in victory. "Wishful thinking," I called it.

"These are self-portraits, you know," Fagee said.

"Holy shit!" I replied, looking at the blond Amazons flying over my bed. "If only."

Redbeard didn't call or visit, not even once. Not that I minded; I didn't check in with him, either. I figured he was keeping tabs on me through Chaya the Narc. All the same, I knew my parents mailed him a check every month to look out for me. I'd seen my mother's unmistakable handwriting on an opened envelope in the pile on his desk and pulled out a check for two hundred dollars. The memo line read, "Keep my Slovah safe."

CHAPTER 17

MANHATTAN

One afternoon, I climbed down the stairs into the subway station at Kingston, stealing glances at every hat-beard-coat I passed. Would one of them turn me in to Redbeard? I hung my head low as I bought two subway tokens, then hopped on the 2 train to Manhattan.

I'd never ridden the subway. It was covered in so much graffiti, you could hardly see the metal walls underneath. The seats were filthy. One of them was cracked. Litter covered the floor and if you couldn't find a seat, there were only filthy straps to hang on to. As the train pulled out, I heard a rough metal-on-metal screeching noise. The train vibrated, the screeching continued, and I wondered if the thing would even make it to my stop.

I looked around and saw that, other than two Chasidic men holding piles of books and talking in Yiddish, I was the only White person on the train.

I watched each stop go by, planning to go all the way to Seventy-Second Street in Manhattan. At Franklin Avenue, two Jamaican men hopped in and took over a bench at the end of the car. One of them wore a T-shirt that had the Jamaican flag across the chest.

One of the Chasids looked up at them.

"*Ah, wah da dem*!?" said one of the Jamaican men to the other, and they laughed.

The Chasid looked down, back at his books.

By the time we got to Seventy-Second Street, about an hour later, I was giddy with excitement and terrified at the same time. I braced for the sound of sirens and the police coming to drag me off to reform school. But this was New York in 1981. The police were busy with far more pressing matters than a runaway teenager.

I saw a bright corner eatery with "Gray's Papaya" in flashy letters. It offered hot dogs and papaya drinks and was bursting with customers of every skin color and style of dress, all waiting shoulder-to-shoulder for the cheap combo of two hot dogs and a drink. A Puerto Rican kid on a skateboard rolled in, sporting a foot-high blue Mohawk. In New Jersey, someone might have thrown a beer bottle at him. In Crown Heights, they would have gawked in horror. But in Manhattan, they just made room for him at the counter.

I kept walking, following the directions Sarah had given me, and wound up at a posh-looking building with a doorman.

"Yes . . . ?" he said, scrutinizing me thoroughly. I clearly didn't look like someone who had any business at a swank Upper West Side apartment building. Well, at least I wasn't wearing my crazy *ba'al teshuva* garb, having ducked into the first diner I saw and changed into torn jeans and a motorcycle jacket in the bathroom.

"Katz in 10B, please," I said.

He called up, then nodded. "Tenth floor."

Sonya and Sarah flew out of their dad's apartment and tore down the hall to meet me. I felt dizzy. My eyes welled up. They looked so young and beautiful. It felt like a million years had passed since I had last seen them, though it had been just six months since I'd run away from home, and three since I'd been carted out to the Chasids. But I wasn't the same person anymore, and we all knew it.

Sonya had bleached her hair platinum and was dressed in what she called her "Marilyn" look: vintage cocktail dress and pumps. Sarah wore an oversized Todd Rundgren T-shirt and a pair of jeans. They were teenagers, pretty much just as I had left them. It was my eyes that had changed. I didn't know what I was exactly, but I knew I wasn't a teenager anymore.

"Think of this weekend as a vacation; you sure need one," Sonya said.

"Dad's away with his new girlfriend for three whole days," said Sarah. The place is all ours!"

That night, I took the longest bubble bath of my life. Submerged in the lavender-scented bubbles, I felt the fear that had wrapped itself around my throat and threatened to strangle me loosen and dissipate.

"What's it like out there?" Sarah asked as we sat in the living room. I was wrapped in a borrowed bathrobe, and they were both in pajamas.

"Like hell with matzo balls."

"Is it really?"

"Yeah. It's kinda terrible."

"Why don't you go home?"

I remembered back to the day I'd come home from school to find my mother sitting at the dining room table holding the notebook I'd filled with poetry. Half the poems were about Cindy Butler, but luckily, I'd thought to remove the pronouns. I usually kept it in my school bag, but that morning I'd been running late and had forgotten to stuff it in.

Mom was tearing the pages out of the book one by one. "Eight years of Hebrew school and I get a slut! No decent man will ever want you! You're soiled goods!" she growled as she ripped, flipped, and ripped again.

I looked into Sarah's pleading eyes. "Harriet and Marty's House of Torture is even worse," I said.

I ate smoked salmon canapés that Sonya had dolloped with Grey Poupon mustard and sipped Chardonnay from a large balloon-shaped glass. I'd never held a glass that big; I was terrified I'd break it. Looking out the window at the skyline of Manhattan, I let out my breath for the first time in half a year.

Sarah cozied up next to me on the couch and draped her legs over mine. I'd always loved the way she smelled—like Breck shampoo. If there was such a thing as heaven, surely it was this apartment at this moment.

"Were you scared?"

"I was too scared to be scared."

⁕⸳⸳⸳⸳⸳⸳⸳⸳⸳⸳⸳⸳⸳⸳

They took me for a walk around the Upper West Side, past bars, little cafés, and lots of takeout joints. In front of a place with takeout chicken, a bunch of teenagers stood around a boom box blaring Blondie.

"Now, this is where I belong!" I announced.

"Yeah, you do, honey," Sonya said. "All the cool people belong in Manhattan."

But after I had luxuriated through Friday and Saturday, the dreaded Sunday arrived.

Sonya made me a fried egg on toast with Grey Poupon. "We put it on everything," she explained.

"Can I stay?" I asked, near tears.

"Oh, honey, I wish, but Dad's coming back, and we have to go to school," said Sarah, putting her head on my shoulder.

"I'm so sorry you have to go back to that bullshit!" Sonya added.

I put on my long pullover, then a Talking Heads T-shirt. My denim skirt was layered over zebra spandex pants.

"*Ewww!*" Sonya shouted.

"Don't rub it in."

The girls walked me back to the Seventy-Second Street subway, and the closer I got to the station, the lower my head hung. I felt like a steer going to slaughter.

"Dad's giving us the place again in three weeks!" Sarah called out as I went through the turnstile.

"Something to live for!" I shouted back, not kidding in the least.

The train was packed, and I felt comfortable surrounded by the mass of many colors and backgrounds. There was no seat, so I grabbed the strap that hung over a businessman reading his paper. The strap felt greasy. I switched to another one, not much better.

By the time we pulled into Nevins Street in Brooklyn, I'd found a free spot on the bench across from a Russian-looking man with a hairy chest and the obligatory big gold chain. Oblivious to the litter and crowd, he sat there reading a newspaper. Then, just as the train pulled out of Nevins, a long caramel arm reached in through the open window and snatched off his chain. The man jumped up and yelled, "What the fuck!" but there was nothing he could do; the train was already moving, screeching as it picked up speed.

That Russian cursed all the way to Grand Army Plaza, then got off along with the rest of the remaining business commuters. The only ones left on the train were five teenage boys with a boom box blaring "Super Freak" by Rick James, and me. One of them looked me over as he screamed the lyrics.

After all those years of working hard to be shocking, I suddenly wished I blended in. I sat staring at my feet.

I closed my eyes for a moment and let my tongue taste the roof of my mouth; the flavor of Grey Poupon lingered.

CHAPTER 18

THE METAL ETCHINGS

Chaya picked up her tzedakah tin one day, shook it, and let out a screech. "Has anyone been taking the tzedakah?" She stormed into the living room where Anya, Fagee, and I sat around a folding table drinking coffee.

"I borrowed fifty cents for breakfast yesterday," I said.

"That's tzedakah for the poor!"

"What am I? A millionaire?"

Chaya went into her bedroom. We heard her clumsy leather shoes as she trotted down the hallway and then the stairs to Kingston Avenue.

"You know she's gonna go tell the rabbi," Anya said.

"I'm broke. Isn't that what tzedakah is for?"

"Apparently not, sweet girl," said Fagee. "It's for *other* poor people, not the ones you live with."

I nodded as I fanned my hand under my nose. Fagee's perfume was overwhelming, but it failed to cover the body odor underneath. I never said anything to her about this, just stayed near the window when it was too many days past her last bath.

Anya wasn't so demure. "Is it a French thing, dear? The whole perfume instead of bathing?"

"What are you trying to say?" Fagee replied, lifting an eyebrow.

"That you smell like shit, dear—but the perfume is lovely."

I snorted so hard, coffee came out of my nose. Figuring I better change the subject, I said, "I need to get some kind of a job. I can't keep taking Chaya's tzedakah."

The next day I saw an ad in Anya's *Village Voice* for a salesperson. "No experience necessary," it said in boldface. *That's me*, I thought.

I called the number from the pay phone outside Uncle Pete's and was delighted when the woman who answered gave me an address near Union Square. I'd been dying to see that place ever since Mashey's son had met a "transvestite" there.

I called Redbeard from the pay phone, and when he picked up I said, "I've got a job interview. In Manhattan." He hadn't busted me for going to Sonya and Sarah's, but I didn't want to push my luck.

I expected a long lecture, but all he said was, "Fine. Give part of what you make to tzedakah. I hear you owe it." He hung up the phone.

Fagee put her arm around my shoulder. "I knew she'd tell him."

• • • • • • • • • • • • •

Two days later, I got onto the subway again and emerged in the middle of Union Square Park. It looked more like a refugee camp than a place to relax, I thought. Homeless people camped out everywhere, sleeping under makeshift blankets. A garbage can was on fire, surrounded by formless men warming their hands. One of them would drop something into it and the flames would shoot up and dance wildly.

Everything was covered in gray-and-white pigeon shit, even the people. I wandered near some older teenagers break dancing, executing robot-like moves and spinning around on broken cardboard boxes. They had a bucket for change near them, but there was only a quarter in it. I stopped to watch one of them spin around on his butt with his feet in the air, and almost immediately a dark-haired man called out, "*Hola, mami!*" His friend chimed in, "*Hola, Rubia!*" and started whistling.

I kept moving.

Growing up, parks had meant little children playing and baby carriages. There were no children in this park. No baby strollers except for the one a homeless woman was pushing, filled with her belongings. On the top of the pile was a doll with no arms.

It was eleven a.m., and every bench seemed to be occupied by either a sleeping homeless person or a drunk. I saw a young white guy with no teeth shooting a needle in his arm. One guy I passed was wearing nothing but a big garbage bag tied with a rope belt. He had so much snot dripping down his nose that it looked like a yellow faucet.

The grass was half brown. There were broken bottles and litter scattered around. I stepped around a pile of dog shit, only to come upon a rat eating a piece of a hot dog bun. It didn't even budge as I walked by.

By the time I got to the east side of the square, my heart was beating so hard I thought I might faint. I craned my neck to look above the doorways of the buildings until I spotted the address of the one I was looking for, then hurried inside.

The artwork that lined the waiting room walls looked like it had been painted on sheets of metal. Two of the pieces depicted the globe, and the rest were landscapes. A young man with a bushy beard sat on one of the office chairs looking through a newspaper. A bicycle leaned against the wall.

"I'm here for the job interview . . ." I said in his direction.

"Ask her," he replied in a heavy Cockney accent. "She's in charge 'round here."

I walked over to a young woman sitting behind a desk. She wore wire-frame glasses and a ponytail, and she was dressed like a secretary, in a skirt and buttoned-down shirt.

When I introduced myself, she said, "Listen, it's not much of a job interview. You see the art on the walls?"

"Yes."

"Those are metal etchings. We'll give you five of them to sell; they go for twenty bucks each. If you sell them, you keep half the money. If you never come back, you got five free metal etchings for making the trip over here. If you come back and keep working, we'll also give you twenty bucks a day—but only the first week. After that, it's commission only."

"What if I sell them for more than twenty bucks?"

"Ah, I like 'er already!" shouted the bearded guy. "My name's Stew, love. What's yours?"

"Rossi."

"I'm Justine," said Glasses Girl.

"This job is bollocks," Stew said, "and everyone knows it. The metal things are rubbish. But the coffee 'ere is free."

"Cool. Well then, I'll just grab a cup."

I walked back out caffeinated, lugging a large portfolio under my arm.

I tried stopping passersby on Fourteenth Street, but they shot past me without slowing their pace. I walked into one of the stores that didn't have boards over the windows. "Would you like to look at some beautiful art?" I asked the guy behind the deli counter.

"Get the fuck out before I call the cops!" he shouted.

By five, my feet were burning, my arms hurt from carrying the bag, and I'd sold nothing. The closest I came was an old woman who felt sorry for me and gave me a dollar. I just about crawled back to the office.

"Sorry."

"Nobody sells the first week," said Justine. "Here's twenty dollars. Come back tomorrow and try again."

"Chin up, love. I'll buy you a beer, if you like," said Stew, who was still sitting in the same spot for some reason.

"Thanks, but I have to get back to my neighborhood before dark."

"Where do you live?" Justine asked.

"Crown Heights."

"Yeah, honey, you better go."

I caught the 4 train and found a seat next to a fat woman with two kids. When I changed over to the 2 train at Nevins Street, I instantly felt like I wore a sign on my forehead that said, "Yeah, I'm White, go figure."

The door between my car and the next one slid open, and six young Hispanic and Black men walked in. At first, I thought they were some sort of gang, like out of *The Warriors*. They strutted rather than walked and were all wearing red berets and white T-shirts that read "Guardian Angels." As they passed me, one of them nodded. They settled at the end of the car, their eyes constantly in motion.

When we reached Franklin Avenue, two Rastas got on. One of them said something in Jamaican slang that sounded like "blood clot" and laughed. When they saw the red berets staring at them, they stopped talking and sat down.

·····•····

I made $110 bucks that first week—five payments of twenty dollars each, plus the proceeds of one sale. I'd sold an etching to Fagee, who liked the globe. I gave back the other four pieces and promptly quit.

"Let's stay in touch, love," Stew said. "I'll come visit your flat."

Fat chance.

But sure enough, he showed up a few days later. It turned out he was Jewish and had always been curious about the whole Chasidic thing. When Chaya came home from work that night to find Stew having coffee with me and Fagee, she just about turned purple.

"Men are not allowed in this apartment!"

"But he's Jewish," I said.

"I don't care! This is not *tzniut*!" She clomped into her bedroom and slammed the door.

"What's with 'er?"

"I think this is what happens when you are thirty-five and have never had sex," Fagee answered.

CHAPTER 19

THE BILLY-CLUB BOYS

Things went along smoothly enough for a couple months. Mom shipped me a care package every few weeks: Tam Tam crackers, peanut butter, and StarKist tuna packed in water. My favorite were the cans of Chef Boyardee ravioli.

Chaya wouldn't let me put the ravioli in the cupboard.

"That's not kosher!" she screeched. "Get that *treyf* out of my house, or I'll throw it out."

I hid the ravioli in my closet and when Chaya wasn't around, I'd sit on my mattress and eat the stuff cold out of the can. It was just little cheese pouches in tomato sauce—what could be so bad?

I decided that to keep the peace, I'd check in with Redbeard once a week. Every few weeks he'd insist I visit him in person, but thankfully, those visits were short—as if I were just something he needed to check off his "to do" list.

"Are you still going to classes at Machon Chana?" he asked during one of our chats.

I knew he knew I'd stopped going.

"I'm not big on school."

"If you don't change the course you're on, you won't be big on anything," he scolded, then sat back in his office chair and scratched his beard. "It is a blessing to have children. If you don't get your act together, you'll never be a mother."

"I don't want kids."

"How can we preserve the Jewish people if we don't have children?" he said angrily. "Now, drop these letters in the mailbox on your way out."

And just like that, the visit was over.

· ··· · · ·•··· • · · ·

Shula got married and moved out. There must have been two hundred people crammed into the basement of one of the yeshivas for her wedding. After the service under the chuppah, Shula and her chain-smoking husband walked up the aisle arm in arm. It was the first time they'd touched. They were led into a private room and the door was closed behind them.

"This is the first time they have been alone together," whispered Fagee.

"I hope he stops smoking long enough to do a decent job of screwing her."

"He has to. The law says he must satisfy his woman."

"The law?"

"He must keep her happy in bed, so she keeps having babies."

"Of course."

They strung a curtain up in the middle of the main room, and the men danced and sang on one side while the women danced and did not sing on the other. Fagee, Anya, and I grabbed hands and twirled one another around the floor.

"I never liked dancing with men, anyway," I whispered to Fagee, admiring the way Anya's long, dark hair spread out like a fan around her shoulders as she spun.

"Promise me you'll never cover your hair!" I shouted at her.

"If I ever do, I'll get a *sheitel* so sexy it will give the boys heart palpitations."

And the girls too, I thought to myself.

Chaya started putting in overtime at her job as a secretary, so we had peace until she came home at seven. I sometimes invited Danny over for one of the wacky meals I concocted out of Mom's care packages. Stir-fried Hebrew National salami and spaghetti was his favorite, but he had to eat fast and get out by 6:30, before the warden came back. One day, Chaya came home an hour early. When she saw Danny sitting on the couch sharing a joint with Anya, she flipped her feathers. She'd managed to overlook the fact that Fagee had abandoned prayer books for fashion magazines, but this! Danny was the second boy I'd brought home, and pot, too! This was just too far beyond *tzniut*!

Chaya moved out, but not before calling the Lubavitch landlord and telling him that the girls who remained were entertaining men with no chaperone.

Fagee, Anya, and I celebrated our liberation from Chaya, along with Christian New Year 1982, with Chef Boyardee and cheap champagne drunk from coffee cups.

"Ding dong, the witch is dead! Happy New Year!" we shouted at the stroke of midnight. Dizzy from champagne, Anya tumbled onto my mattress next to me and stared up at the ceiling. I curled up next to her. "Anyata. Do you think I'm a bad person? I scared Chaya out of her own apartment."

"You're a sweet kid who thinks she's a hundred-and-five." Anya kissed me on the forehead. "There's nothing wrong with you. If there was, the Rebbe never would have given you that wine. Just remember that. Always try to remember that."

I closed my eyes. "Thanks, A."

One morning in January, about three weeks after Chaya left, I woke up freezing, my breath making white steam when I exhaled. I got out of bed, pulled my coat on over the nightdress I'd stolen from Bela, and walked into the hallway. I put my hand on the radiator. It was ice cold.

As I stood there trying to figure out what to do, the door crashed open so forcefully that shards of wood flew into the air. One large piece narrowly missed me. The door had been smashed in half, and three large Hispanic men with billy clubs barged into the apartment. I have no idea why I focused on this, but the first guy had the number 1952 tattooed on his forearm. *Was it the year he was born? Was it the last thing I would see before I was murdered?*

He smashed his club against the wall and Fagee's framed Monet print of flowers crashed to the floor, the glass shattering.

"Get the fuck out!" he bellowed.

My heart was beating so hard my chest hurt. I tried to talk but could hardly get the words out. "Whaaa . . . WHAT?"

Fagee and Anya appeared in their nightgowns, still rubbing their eyes, and jumping foot to foot on the cold wooden floor.

The three men walked through the apartment, smashing at the walls with their clubs. 1952 flung the coffee table Anya had rescued from the street and lovingly painted blue. One of the legs broke off as it landed. Fagee's teacups scattered in pieces on the floor.

"Get the fuck out!"

Suddenly, a middle-aged Lubavitch man wearing a brown yarmulke appeared in what was left of the doorway and the three goons settled down. The Chasid walked past them and stood in front of the three of us, now huddled together out of cold and fear.

"I don't understand," said Fagee. "We are paid up on our rent."

"By order of the landlord, you must now leave," he proclaimed. "We will give you until the end of the day to get your things together and go."

"But . . . but . . . why?" stammered Fagee.

"The lease-holder is gone! So you're gone, too," said the Lubavitcher.

"But where are we supposed to go?" I asked.

"This is not my problem."

"We need more time!" demanded Anya.

"These gentlemen will be back at five. For your own sake, don't be here."

He walked out. The men with clubs followed him, but 1952 stopped at the doorway, looked at me, and licked his lips. "*Vuelvo enseguida.* I really hope you *are* here when I get back."

We didn't know about things like tenants' rights and so, facing a clubbing, we abandoned our beloved *ba'al teshuva* pad. I couldn't help thinking about my mother's refrain: "You can trust a man wearing a yarmulke. If you get into trouble, look for the yarmulke!" *Not this time, Mom.* Our pious, yarmulke-wearing landlord, who went to shul and davened every day, had forced three young women, one of whom (me) was only seventeen years old, into the street in the freezing cold with our belongings in garbage bags. Would his henchmen really have beaten us? I would never know, but I was quickly learning that men in yarmulkes can do terrible things. It was a lesson I would relearn many times in the year ahead.

Standing in front of the brownstone that had been our home, I was dimly aware of Chasidic women with grocery bags and book-toting teenage boys bundled up in winter coats pushing past us. For them it was just another Wednesday.

Fagee had promised to lend me a pair of gloves, but I had forgotten to ask for them. I was losing feeling in my fingers.

My chest felt like it was filled with ice. Where would I go? Who could I call? I felt as numb as my fingers. Being badass was easy in a safe, quaint little town in New Jersey. In this strange place, there was no room for badass. There was only getting by.

It would be years before I would fully recover from the shock of that day. Teeth chattering, adrenaline racing, stomach churning, fingers turning blue as I clutched the few possessions I had hastily shoved into garbage bags, I stood immobile. I wanted to crawl into one of those bags myself—at least I'd have been a little warmer.

Party mode had been replaced by survival mode.

CHAPTER 20

HOMELESS

I later heard that there were more than 1,800 murders in New York City in 1981. It was not a very good time to be homeless.

Standing on the street, for one fleeting moment I pictured my warm bed in Rumson, my lava light doing its cool, goopy thing and illuminating my room in an eerie green. I could almost feel the mountain of soft pillows I loved to dive into. Then, like a record screeching under a fingernail, I remembered my parents.

Slovah! You're grounded for life! my mother screamed in my head.

Nine months had passed since I'd first run away from life with my parents. I couldn't go home.

My friends and I made some quick plans and took turns at the pay phone. Fagee went to stay with her cousin in Boro Park. Anya moved into the girls' dormitory at Machon Chana. I didn't want to do either of those things, and I certainly didn't want to go back to Redbeard. I'd thought of calling him, but I could just hear him saying, *I know everything that happens in this neighborhood.*

I thought of calling my mother, to whom I'd spoken only once since I'd been delivered to Crown Heights. Again, it hit me: The only thing worse than being homeless was going home.

I ended up calling Danny, who listened to my tale of woe and said he had an idea. His pal Sheky from yeshiva worked as a doorman. He lived with his wife in a one-bedroom on the outskirts of the neighborhood. He said he'd find out if they could take me in, at least for a while.

I stood waiting for the pay phone to ring. When Danny finally called back, he told me his friends would make room for me on their couch, but only for a few days. He came by in his sister's black Oldsmobile, and we piled my bags in the back. His best friend Izzy was in the front seat smoking a spliff.

Izzy was about five-foot-two and wore a black-and-white-striped yarmulke. Unlike most of the men in the area, he lifted weights and was very muscular. He liked to wear tight T-shirts to show off the results. In the winter, he wore a red down jacket that seemed to mold itself around his sturdy frame. His face was shaved except for a handlebar mustache, making him look more Mexican than Polish. He spoke so fast that it was nearly impossible to keep up.

"You know nothing happens around here without Sherba knowing about it," Izzy said. "No way those Spics came to scare you out without him knowing. I mean, he knows everything around here. Probably paid them himself. I went to school with that prick. Did you know that? Yeah, we're the same age. He was a little prick then; he's a little prick now. No way he didn't know about this. He probably paid them himself. Little prick."

As we drove to Sheky's, Izzy took out a prescription bottle and opened his pocketknife. He put the tip of his knife into the bottle, pulled it out covered in white powder, and snorted it up his nose.

"No wonder you talk so fast."

"I'm a busy man. That's why I talk so fast. Keep up, baby."

Sheky's goyish wife Nancy had cemented his status as a castaway in Crown Heights, but he'd gone to school with

Danny and Izzy, and they were only too happy to hang out at his place, smoking weed and making fun of the religious kids they'd known in yeshiva.

Nancy answered the door, her brown hair disheveled, and her pregnant belly protruding under a black, oversized men's T-shirt. It was four p.m., but she looked like she'd just woken up.

"Come on in," she yawned. "Sheky's in the bedroom rolling a joint."

Danny put my bags near the couch, and I sat down. Unlike the velvet couch at Redbeard's, this one looked like brown leather but felt like plastic. It squeaked when I sat.

"Back on the couch again," I said, and hung my head as I sunk into the cheap upholstery.

"It's only for a few days," Danny said.

Izzy sat at the glass-topped dinner table, cutting lines and snorting them with a rolled-up dollar bill.

Sheky came out of the bedroom. He was a skinny, petite man with a peach-fuzz mustache that made him look twelve. "Sorry about what happened. That really blows."

"Yeah. I hear that a lot."

"Do you think Sherba did this to her?" asked Danny.

"Oh, yeah," Izzy chimed in while Sheky took his turn snorting. "That little prick—you remember he was always a prick. I'm so sure that prick did this. Little prick!"

"He's a rabbi! He wouldn't do that!" I said.

They all started laughing. "Dream on, little sister," Danny said.

"Let's go to Bed-Stuy. I'm running low," Izzy announced.

"Not in my sister's car," Danny said. "I'll come out and the tires will be gone."

"Right, your sister's car. Well, big man, how about you stay in the car with Sheky, with the motor running, and I'll run in and score," Izzy said, grinding his jaw as he spoke.

After a few days at Sheky's, I felt my brain go foggy from all the pot and elephant beer. One day, I heard Nancy and Sheky fighting in the bedroom.

When Nancy emerged, all she said was, "Sorry, sweetie, you have to go."

I called Mashey.

. ...

When Mashey opened the door, she immediately threw her arms around me. "I can't believe this happened to you! Let's have some vodka and talk about what you're going to do."

We sat at her kitchen table, drinking our usual concoction of vodka and orange juice, and eating crackers with whitefish salad and Persian pickles.

"I can only keep you for the weekend," Mashey said. "My mother-in-law is coming to stay. You could go to the dorm at Machon Chana . . ."

I shook my head.

"Sherba's house?"

I looked at her in horror.

"Home?"

I made the cutting-my-own-throat motion. Seeing that Mashey was out of ideas, I said, "I'll figure it out."

The morning Mashey's mother-in-law was scheduled to arrive, I left my suitcase with most of my things in Mashey's basement and put a few days' worth of clothes into a duffel bag. I called Danny to pick me up.

"Where to this time?" he asked as I climbed into the car.

"I got a place for a few days," I said, lying. I'd decided to have him drop me off at the building in Manhattan I felt most familiar with: Port Authority Bus Terminal on Fortieth Street and Eighth Avenue. I'd taken the Academy bus there from Red Bank a few times; once when I'd visited my pal Sandy in the hospital after a car accident, and once to go to a Devo concert with my theater gang. I'd marveled at the thousands of punk rockers surrounding me that night, and the overwhelming sensation of belonging. If this was New York City, I wanted a piece of it. In New Jersey, I'd been spit on just for wearing a Sex Pistols T-shirt.

As Danny and I pulled up to the bus station, I saw a slew of dive bars and triple-X adult video shops. Crowds of people rushed past homeless beggars on their way to wherever.

Danny found an open spot and eased over to the curb. As we sat with the motor idling, we heard a loud ruckus and turned our heads to see two prostitutes fighting on the corner.

"I'll kill you, Lacreesha!"

Nobody seemed to mind or notice. Everyone just walked around them.

"Be careful," Danny said. "Don't put anything in your pocket. They slice them open with razor blades."

"Got it," I said, not sure that I did.

"Call me if you get into trouble!"

I hopped out of the car and decided not to turn back and look at Danny or I might lose my nerve. I pushed my way into the station, through a crowd of commuters who were coming out. I had no idea if I was going to catch a bus back home or just walk around and wait for a miracle to happen.

A man with no legs shot by in a wheelchair shouting, "Spare change!" He had a piece of cardboard taped to his chest that read "Vietnam Veteran Please Help."

I had tried to put on my toughest outfit that day: beige cowboy bandanna around my head, Rolling Stones T-shirt, leather jacket, Levi's, and Frye boots. For some reason, I'd thrown my *ba'al teshuva* outfit into the duffel bag in case I needed it.

I slid into a chair at the counter of a coffee shop and counted out four quarters. The waitress brought me a cup of coffee and a buttered bagel. I must have sat there for two hours, nursing that coffee, and tearing little bird-sized bits off the bagel.

The waitress, a middle-aged woman with spits of gray in her hair, seemed to feel sorry for me.

"Let me get you a refill, honey. It's no charge here."

"Sorry I've been here so long."

"Oh, honey, you see that old drunk over there?" She pointed at an old man at the end of the counter. "He's been here since yesterday."

After another hour, I felt my bladder burning. I left her an extra quarter and went to the public bathroom. There was a homeless woman bathing in one of the sinks as I walked in. She had taken off her top and was using paper towels to wash her armpits.

The first booth I tried had a floor covered in toilet paper and none on the roll. The next one had a large turd floating in the toilet. Finally, I found one that was passable.

When I came out, the homeless woman looked at me. "Got any change, sweetheart?"

"No. Sorry."

"Fuck you!" she screamed and started throwing paper towels at me. "Fucking cunt!"

I took the stairs to the lower level where the bus to Red Bank loaded. I looked at the line of people getting ready to go home. They all seemed bored.

How I would have loved being bored.

I thought about them traveling to some little house in New Jersey, where they'd take a hot shower, eat dinner, turn on the TV . . .

Red Bank was only a ten-minute drive from Rumson. It would be so easy.

You are never allowed to associate with that slut ever again!

Go to your room!

You're grounded!

Or . . . not so easy.

After the bus pulled away, I tried to keep my head low and not make eye contact with anyone. I passed two scroungy young men sharing swigs from a pint bottle of amber liquor. One had a bandanna wrapped around his head that looked like mine except it was red. Red Bandanna whistled at me.

I kept walking. The two guys started following me, whistling, and making hissing noises. None of the commuters standing around waiting for their buses said a word. They just buried their bored faces in their newspapers like nothing was happening.

I saw a blond, good-looking cop leaning against a wall. He reminded me of Steve McQueen. As I approached him, the two men kept walking.

"Can I help you?" he asked, sizing up the situation.

"I think you just did."

He looked at the men walking quickly away. "They're nothing. Are you waiting for your bus?"

"I'm, *um*, just killing time."

"There's a lot of that going on around here. Follow me."

"Where?"

"There's a safe place to hang out where nobody bothers you."

"Okay."

I followed him out the door to the inner lot where the buses parked. He led me past three parked buses, along a wall with no windows. I didn't see any sort of office or hangout; just a hidden, dark area behind the parked buses.

When he turned around, his zipper was unzipped, and he was holding his penis in his hand.

"Just put your mouth right here," he said.

"No . . . um. . . no, ah . . . thank you . . . I, um . . . have a husband," I stammered.

"So what!? I have a wife!" He reached for my head, and as I jerked it back, my bandanna slid off. I backed up, almost tripping, turned and ran away.

I called Fagee from the pay phone upstairs.

"A cop just showed me his dick!" I said, out of breath.

"Get over here now! I have a place for us!"

I felt my heart skip a beat.

To this day, I can't remember how long I was homeless in Port Authority. It may have been one day or three. What I vividly recall was the taste of metal in my mouth.

Fear has a flavor. Three decades later, I still harbor a secret fear of homelessness. Every time I pass someone curled up in a dirty blanket on the street or in a park, I do not raise my eyes and pretend not to see him, as most New Yorkers do. I take a moment and say silently to myself, "There but for the grace of God . . ."

At one point, I owned two apartments and a house. It didn't keep me from worrying that one missed payment might land me back in the basement of Port Authority.

As much as Crown Heights had been my prison sentence, the simple fact was that I had nowhere else to go. I didn't want to wind up with the hookers I saw pacing the street outside. I didn't want to live like the toothless old ladies I saw dragging their possessions in a multitude of shopping bags.

And anything was better than going home.

CHAPTER 21

THE BA'AL TESHUVA
SARDINE CAN APARTMENT

Always the social butterfly, Fagee had lined up a place for us to sleep, at least for a few weeks. I was back in a living room again, but it was better than sleeping at Port Authority.

The basement apartment had two bedrooms with two girls in each; Fagee was in one of those. Two additional girls slept on cots in the living room. For me, Fagee had bamboozled a cot in a cutout area against the wall of the dining room. There was a Japanese folding screen in front of it that made it almost feel private.

"Your hands are so cold! I just made lentil soup. Eat!" Fagee said as she led me to the kitchen table.

Her bedroom-mate Raquel, a skinny, pale twenty-one-year-old girl with greasy black hair and pimples, extended her hand to me. "Did a cop really show you his *shmeckel*?"

"I told everyone," Fagee said.

I sat down and ate the soup Fagee thrust in front of me. I'd been hungry for so many hours that my stomach had gone past the growling stage into some sort of numbness.

"We got you the best non-bedroom bed!" Fagee said excitedly.

When I'd drained the soup bowl down to the faded flower pattern at the bottom, I walked behind the screen, dropped my duffel bag, crawled under the white sheets and cotton pink blanket, and closed my eyes. Everything smelled clean, like cotton and flowery laundry detergent.

I must have fallen asleep instantly, because the next thing I heard was the clamoring of six girls fighting over the Mr. Coffee. I started to sit up, but my head felt like it weighed a hundred pounds. I let it sink back into the pillow.

Sometime later, I opened my eyes to see Fagee sitting on the foot of my cot with a worried look on her face.

"You must really be allergic to penis. You've been sick since the bus station."

"I must be gay," I said, trying to make a joke out of it.

Fagee wasn't laughing. "I wish you'd told me you had no place to go. I would have begged my cousin . . . I would have—"

"*Shhh*. It's okay, Fagee. I'm okay. Just a little tired."

I stayed in bed for five days, getting up only to eat Fagee's soup or use the bathroom. Hidden behind the screen, with blankets tucked all around me, I let whatever strange sickness I had succumbed to take over. I thought of Cindy Butler's lips. They tasted like Newport cigarettes and orange-flavored Chapstick. I thought about my mother and tried remembering the last time I'd felt anything but rage for her. I came up with a week when I was ten years old. I'd stayed home from school, sick with the flu, and Mom had sat by my side, nursing me with chicken-noodle soup and Lipton tea loaded with honey. I flashed to the billy-club men smashing open our apartment door and shattering Fagee's beautiful china. I envisioned the cop pulling out his dick, how white it looked against the dark blue of his uniform.

I felt weak and numb. I sank further. If this were death knocking on my door, I felt ready to let him in. I heard the girls trotting around, smelled coffee and simmering soup. I kept my eyes gently closed. Death wouldn't be so bad. At least I wouldn't have to go back to New Jersey.

When I finally emerged from my cocoon, the girls were sitting around the table having dinner. They looked up at me and started to clap. "*Baruch Hashem!*" Fagee yelled.

It occurred to me as I came back to life that Redbeard must be aware of what happened to me. Lifsa said he knew everything about everyone in Chasidland. And yet he hadn't attempted to help me, despite the fact that he'd continued accepting my parents' checks. Truthfully, I was grateful for having been spared the sermons that would surely have come with his assistance.

My parents were clearly as oblivious to my plight as they'd been to my drug use under their roof. *As you used to say, Mom, "What you don't know won't hurt you."* If she'd known the details of my ordeal, surely it would have caused her some pain.

Nothing to do but move forward, I told myself.

One afternoon, I heard Danny's voice outside the brownstone, yelling, "Can Rossi come out and play!?"

That was all the landlord's wife, Mrs. Fishman, needed. She hadn't liked the sight of me from the moment I'd dragged my garbage-bag luggage into the house (having left my only suitcase in Mashey's basement until I knew for sure where I'd be landing).

Good girls have suitcases.

She came downstairs and banged on the door, so flustered that she'd pulled her wig on backward. "No fraternizing with boys in my house!" she shouted, wagging a gnarly finger in my face. After just a few weeks of sleeping dorm-style with seven women, I was on the verge of being tossed out by yet another supposedly pious family.

Fagee counseled me to put on my most pious outfit: denim maxiskirt, long-sleeved sweater, no makeup, hair in a ponytail—and no rock-and-roll T-shirt—and visit the owner of the stationery store on Kingston Ave. Doing my best to appear demure, I managed to convince the old man to rent Fagee and me the apartment above a nearby drugstore for $250 a month. I had an actual lease! No one could throw me into the street again.

I put two dollars in quarters into the pay phone outside Uncle Pete's.

"Hello?"

"Hi, Mom."

"Slovah! Are you okay? Your father and I have been worried sick about you!"

I thought to myself, *Now you're worried about me?* But I hadn't exactly been forthright about my circumstances.

It took every ounce of self-control I had not to explode, but I didn't want to fight. "I'm fine, Mom. I finally got my own place."

"All by yourself?"

"No, no . . . don't worry. I'll be living with a nice Jewish woman I met at Hebrew class."

"*Shana madelah.* That's wonderful. Give me the address, I've got coupons for you."

"These little stores don't take coupons, Mom."

"The Chasidim are smart. I'm sure they use coupons somewhere."

After a few more pointless exchanges, I got off the phone shaking my head. She really didn't have a clue where she'd sent her *shana madelah.*

Accessed by private stairs from the street, the apartment was a big two-bedroom with double-sized windows that looked out onto the hustle-bustle of Kingston Avenue. There was an eat-in kitchen with a skylight that would have let in a lot of sun if it hadn't been covered in pigeon shit. If you didn't count four milk crates pushed together to make a table and two mattresses on the floor, the first piece of real furniture I ever owned was an itchy Scotch-plaid couch that Fagee found on the street. We coerced Danny into hauling it to our place in his sister's station wagon, and he roped Izzy into helping him drag it up the stairs.

"I gotta get at least a blow job for this," Izzy announced, horrifying Fagee. Then he plopped himself on the couch and lit up a joint. "Who's gonna party with me?"

"It's too early, Izzy. We've got shopping to do," I said.

"You made me drag this couch up the stairs, and you're not even going to give me a kiss?"

I leaned down to kiss him on the top of the head, and he grabbed me and forced his tongue into my mouth. I wriggled in his grip until he let go.

"Not cool! Izzy, not cool!"

"Come on, Izzy, let's leave the girls alone," Danny cajoled.

Izzy pulled himself off the couch and stormed down the stairs. "See what happens the next time you ask me for a favor!" he called back over his shoulder.

⁍ ··· ✱ ·•✱•···•✱ ··

Once we'd settled in as best we could, I called my parents and asked them to bring my Radio Shack stereo and a box of albums from New Jersey. They showed up in Dad's Datsun pickup truck with the requested items, along with a small black-and-white television, a TV stand, and several grocery bags loaded with Hebrew National salami and hot dogs, two almost-stale Entenmann's coffee cakes, a box of Tam Tam crackers, three cans of Nescafé instant coffee (marked "three for a dollar"), a dozen cans of tuna fish in water, a large supply of McDonald's ketchup packets, and two loaves of stale Wonder Bread.

This was the first time my parents had visited me since I'd left home nine months earlier.

"Would it have killed you to move somewhere with an elevator?" Mom huffed as she mounted the final stair. Under her coat, she wore a blue housedress and pull-on slippers. One of her socks was pink, the other red.

My father, wearing his denim winter coat with the white sheepskin lining and a ski cap, seemed shorter than I remembered. The gray in his sideburns seemed new, too. He made several trips up, first with the television and then the stand. Fagee and I carried the smaller items.

Once the car had been unloaded and locked up, we gathered in the kitchen, Mom on a wooden chair and Dad leaning in the doorway.

"We called Rabbi Sherba every week to find out how you were doing," Mom said.

"What did he say?"

"He said we were driving him crazy," Dad said.

"I hope you stopped sending him money. He hasn't checked on me once."

"Harriet! I told you!"

"Pish posh! He said he was monitoring you from afar. He has his ways."

"*Uh-huh*. Those *ways* haven't done squat for me."

"Make your father some coffee. Have you met any nice Jewish boys?"

I heard Fagee, who had closed herself in her bedroom, start laughing.

"Not a one, Mom."

"When are you going to make your mother happy and marry a nice Jewish boy?"

"Or at least a boy," Dad said under his breath.

Unable to resist the family fun unfolding in the kitchen, Fagee came out and introduced herself. When my mother realized she spoke French, she started yammering happily in French, too.

"Slovah," said Fagee, "you didn't tell me your mother spoke French!"

"Yeah . . . she loves *kvetching* at me in four languages: English, Yiddish, German, and French."

My mother smiled widely as she chattered away in the language she had loved since college French Club in 1946 but rarely had the chance to speak. Meanwhile, I boiled water and made my father and myself black instant Nescafé with one Sweet'N Low, and the two of us settled on the living room couch.

"Are you okay?" he asked, sipping carefully.

"I think that's the first time anyone has asked me that since I got here."

"So?"

"I will be."

We sipped for a few minutes in silence, listening to my mother and Fagee. When Mom cackled with laughter, I thought about how long it had been since I'd heard that sound.

"You know . . . we looked for you."

"When?"

"When you ran away. We looked for you."

"I thought you threw me out!"

"No. Never. We might have grounded you for life, but we'd never throw you out."

CHAPTER 22

SEX

I'd arrived in Crown Heights with a dirty secret: I had no idea if my hymen was intact or not. When I was fifteen, my first boyfriend David had plied me with beer and tried to jam himself inside me. When I felt a sharp pain, I pushed him off.

I never let him try it again.

A year later, I was grappling around with Billy in Marvin's boyfriend's basement, but I had no idea whether rough-and-ready Billy had broken my hymen or not—only that it hurt like hell when he tried to jackhammer his way in.

Then there was the drunken night at the Tideaway Rock Lounge in Long Branch, when I'd let a man named Mike who'd been buying me drinks all night lead me upstairs to his hotel room. When he tried to push himself inside me, it hurt so much I screamed.

I decided to take a break from the whole sex thing, but that didn't keep me from going out. There weren't a lot of punk bands around the Jersey Shore, but I latched onto one called Jade that played in a bar in nearby Sea Bright. Jade's lead singer was a tall guy named Wayne. He had long hair bleached platinum and wore leather pants. He took a liking to me, and we started dating.

One day, Wayne and I were hanging out in his basement apartment at his mom's house. When he pulled off his leather pants, a twelve-inch monster hung from his crotch.

"You're not gonna put that thing in me!" I yelped.

"Actually, I'm not," he said softly, and proceeded to attend to every part of my body with his tongue. "Fucking is just for boys who don't know how to make love."

Anything I'd done with boys up till then had been about as pleasurable as a root canal. The oral sex I'd enjoyed with Cindy Butler in the back seat of my parents' Volaré was a whole different story—a hot and sweaty one. This felt a lot like that.

"Wow," I exhaled. "It's like . . . you're a girl."

"That's right, darling."

⁕•⋯•⋯⋅⋅⁝⋯⋅⋅⋅⋅

Izzy knocked on my door one Sunday afternoon.

"Wanna come out and play?"

While I didn't like Izzy's incessant cocaine-induced chatting, I was broke and really tired of eating salami, pizza, and falafel.

"Um . . . okay. But only if you take me out to eat. I'm starving."

"It's time you tried roti!"

"Is that like rigatoni?"

He just rolled his eyes, said, "Get in," and drove to a West Indian takeout joint on Nostrand Avenue. When we walked in, reggae blared from a speaker on the counter. The song faded out and the radio announcer cooed, "Yah, man, and that was Rita Marley and the Melody Makers!"

Bob Marley had just died but his widow and children were continuing his legacy.

"The oxtail roti is the best," said Izzy.

"Oxtail? Like, *tail*? Gross!"

"It's beef; you'll like it."

I watched as the counterman filled up something that looked like a cross between a pita and a flour tortilla with something that looked like beef stew. He rolled it up and wrapped it in aluminum foil, then handed it to me. It felt like it weighed two pounds.

"Holy shit, Izzy, this is like a small baby!"

"Come on! I got a six-pack of Red Stripe at my place."

Izzy drove to a row house about ten blocks from where I lived.

"It's my parents' place," he explained. "I live in the basement."

Another basement apartment at mom's. Oy.

"Aren't you, like, twenty-three?" I asked.

"Hey, baby. It's free rent!"

Izzy had his own entrance at least, but the place was like a cave—even after he scurried around turning on various lamps. There was a hot plate and fridge against one wall, and a small bathroom across from it. In the center of the room was a king-size mattress dressed in a burgundy blanket covered in questionable stains. The place smelled like cigarettes and stale beer. The only decor was a rifle mounted on the wall.

Izzy closed the door, then double-locked it with a key.

"I never saw anyone use a key to lock their door from the inside."

"Keeps my dad out."

"What's with the rifle?"

"Bad neighborhood."

Izzy pulled the Red Stripes out of the fridge, and we settled onto two beanbags on the floor with our takeout. He immediately began to shove the soggy, gooey roti mess into his mouth. I unpeeled a few inches of foil from around my own and took a small bite. It tasted like nothing I'd ever tried. The texture was reminiscent of my mother's slowly simmered goulash, but this meat was something else: spicy, sweet . . . a treat for the mouth and nostrils simultaneously. It was so good I started to tap my feet, almost dancing while I ate it.

"What is this taste?" I asked when I came up for air.

"You never tasted curry before?"

Curry! I even liked the sound of it. I munched away happily but, try as I might, I could only finish half before I had to put the thing down and lean back.

"You gonna finish that?"

When I shook my head, he slammed it into his mouth in four bites.

"Jesus, Izzy!"

"There's not a lot of Jesus around here, baby."

He rolled a joint and took a deep drag, then handed it to me.

After just two hits, I felt spectacularly wasted. "What is this stuff?" I asked but the words came out like my mouth was lined with cotton.

"It's the good stuff from Bed-Stuy!"

Izzy jumped up and proceeded to show off his best karate moves and kicks for my benefit, then said, "Check this out!" He pulled open a drawer to reveal an extensive collection of pocketknives.

"What are you so afraid of?" I asked, but my cottonmouth made it sound like *War ya afray av?*

"Hey, baby. I'm only five-foot-two. I used to be an even littler squirt. When I was in yeshiva, the older boys were always trying to get into my ass."

"Literally?"

"Yes, baby." He swatted his own butt. "They wanted a piece of this. I learned how to fight pretty fucking fast." He slammed the knife drawer shut, walked over to me, and got down on his knees like he was going to pray. "Now come to bed, baby."

I wasn't even remotely attracted to Izzy, but I was feeling loose from the pot and beer. I let him lead me to the mattress. As I sat on the corner of the bed, Izzy kicked off his boots then pulled down his jeans. But when he turned to face me, I got a full-blown case of the giggles. Izzy had the smallest penis I'd ever seen! It couldn't have been more than a half inch. It looked like a thumbnail sitting on a thick mound of black pubic hair. The only things about him that were large were his testicles.

"I'm so sorry, Izzy!" I choked out, trying hard to get a grip. "It's . . . it's the pot."

I knew from the little experience I'd had with David, Billy, and Wayne that penises could double, even triple in size when aroused. The thing was . . . that little thumbnail I'd seen seemed fully erect. I had a feeling it was about as big as it was going to get.

I imagined most girls would find this tiny member disappointing, but I felt relieved. Considering Izzy's muscles and fondness for martial arts, I'd been afraid his dick might be Wayne-sized. "Hey, baby. It's not the meat. It's the motion!"

I agreed to have sex with Izzy and his thumbnail, and it didn't hurt one little bit. In fact, between the effect of the pot and my basic lack of interest, I could hardly tell it was inside of me. I tried distracting myself from Izzy's irritating grunts and thrusts by closing my eyes and thinking of something else. My old friend Wonder Woman materialized, which was nice, but within minutes I'd fallen into a deep sleep.

Izzy's "What the fuck?" woke me, and I could tell I'd been snoring.

"Sorry," I said quietly.

Izzy barely spoke a word as we got dressed, and his uncharacteristic silence persisted all the way back to my place. As I was about to get out of the car, he went to kiss me, but I turned my head, so he got my cheek.

"Why don't I come up, and we can try again?" he whined.

"*Nah.* I'm good."

"Baby, baby, please. I need to get off!"

"How romantic."

As I started to shimmy out of the car, Izzy grabbed my arm. I looked down at his filthy fingernails making red dents in my forearm and growled, "Let me go, Izzy."

"You gotta at least jerk me off!"

"Let me go or I'll scream my fucking head off!"

The second he released my arm, I jumped out of the car.

Just before Izzy sped away, he rolled down the car window and yelled "Dyke!"

I climbed the stairs, my bionic hymen doubtless still intact.

CHAPTER 23

ROBBY

One warm spring afternoon eleven months after I'd run away, as I was walking to Uncle Pete's to get change for the pay phone, the "civilian patrol" drove by. I counted about ten men in the station wagon this time, two holding baseball bats, and one a hammer. I saluted them.

When I heard giggling behind me, I turned to find a young man—more of a boy, really—watching me. He had red hair, pink freckled skin, and blue eyes. He wore tight designer jeans and a blue down coat, a look so at odds with what I'd become used to around the neighborhood that I had to wonder if he'd been teleported from another planet.

"I'm Robby," he said, holding out his hand.

"I thought I was the only non-Chasid White person in town."

He looked at my denim skirt. "You're not one of them?"

"I'm in disguise."

"Me, too, honey, I'm dressing down. Way down. Normally I wear eyeliner to bring out my blue eyes!"

Could it be that I had found not only another White person who wasn't religious but a gay one? I thought of the Barn Theater in Rumson, of Matthew and Wolf; I'd missed having a gay boy pal, someone who wasn't just biding his time until he could get in my pants.

Robby, who reminded me of Peter Pan, turned out to be twenty-three though he looked sixteen. When I asked him what he was doing in Crown Heights, he explained that he had answered an ad in *The Village Voice* that said, "Artists: renovate your own home." Since he couldn't afford Manhattan, he'd decided to take advantage of the landlord's offer to fix up a dumpy apartment while he lived in it rent-free.

Naturally, we became instant best friends. It turned out not only was Robby gay, but he was also more promiscuous than anyone I'd ever met.

"Cops are my favorite. I love a man in uniform!" he'd say.

One day, after Mom sent a care package with enough food in it to feed Pittsburgh, I called Robby. When he picked up, I screamed, "Get your ass over here! I've got food!"

Less than five minutes later, Robby plopped himself on the Scotch couch, heaved a dramatic sigh, and said, "Girlfriend, you would not believe what I did last night!"

"*Shhh!*" I said and pointed to Fagee's closed bedroom door.

"I am French!" Fagee yelled. "Do you really think I have never met a gay man before!"

"Fagee, come out! I've got Hebrew National hot dogs, macaroni, and a can of beans. I am thinking frank and beans à la pasta for supper."

"God! You Americans, with your disgusting food!"

I placed the low coffee table I'd rescued from the garbage in front of the couch and suddenly, everything seemed perfect. I had a real living room with a couch to watch TV from, a table to lay my feet on, and friends to watch with. I even had an ashtray for the center of the table, an amber antique glass thing with indents for the cigarettes—another street find. When I'd brought it home, it was so dirty I didn't know it was amber until Fagee washed it off.

"It's like we're the Brady Bunch!" I announced when Fagee finally emerged and plopped down with us.

As we sat squished together on the couch—me in the middle—watching a *Happy Days* rerun, I beamed with pride. I took a half-smoked joint out of the ashtray, lit it up, and passed it to Fagee. "Take two tokes of this and that 'disgusting food' will taste like four-star cooking!" I told her.

"Now, girlfriends," said Robby, who'd been waiting impatiently for a commercial so he could regale us, "let me tell you about the ménage à trois I had last night!"

"So French!" Fagee proclaimed.

CHAPTER 24

RAQUEL

"**R**aquel needs a place to stay," said Fagee one morning over chocolate croissants and Nescafé. Fagee never revealed the source of her income, but always seemed to have money for my favorite decadent breakfast treat. This was lucky for me because, after putting aside money for the gas and electric bill, I had to count out pennies to buy groceries. I'd been rationing Harriet's last care package as best I could, but there are only so many ways to cook Hebrew National hot dogs.

"Raquel? Where would we put her?" I asked.

"She can take half the living room—on the wall behind the couch."

"Shit! I love our living room!"

"She'll chip in a hundred a month."

"Okay!"

Raquel arrived with two suitcases stuffed with clothes, a *siddur*, and a grocery bag full of meat and vegetables.

She took off her coat and hung it on the rack on the landing, revealing a plaid maxiskirt and a striped long-sleeved shirt. *Another ostrich*, I thought to myself, as she set a bag of groceries on the table.

When Raquel opened the fridge, she looked shocked. "Oh my God!" she said.

"What? What?" I came rushing over, expecting to see a rat chewing on the celery sticks.

"Hebrew National is not kosher!"

"Yes, it is! My mother keeps kosher, and she sent it!"

"My rabbi says it is not kosher!"

"So don't eat it, Raquel," Fagee reasoned.

Raquel put her groceries in the fridge but kept them in the bag so they wouldn't touch the *treyf.*

Fagee had acquired a single futon mattress from Shula's chain-smoking husband, and we'd set it up against the wall behind the couch for Raquel. Fagee had then hammered hooks into the walls at each end of it and run a clothesline across, then draped a sheet over the clothesline. It wasn't exactly private, but it was private enough.

That night, even with my bedroom door shut, I heard Raquel reading aloud from her siddur.

Does this bitch ever sleep?

I was sitting on the toilet the next morning reading *The Village Voice* when I heard a murmuring sound outside the door. When I opened it, I almost knocked Raquel over.

"Were you just talking to me?" I asked.

"No, I was praying."

"Why on earth were you praying outside the bathroom door?"

"I was doing the *Asher Yatzar* for you since you used the bathroom."

I started to laugh. "You were saying a bathroom prayer for me!? Are there separate verses for Number One and Number Two?"

"Yes," she said, dead serious. "Which prayer do you want?"

"I don't want any prayer! Leave my bathroom activities alone!"

Three days later, Fagee and I were sitting on the couch drinking sweet kosher wine from coffee cups.

I hung my head. "I wish Anya could be our roommate," I said. "I miss her."

"Shula turned the basement into a guest room, so Anya has a free place to stay until the baby comes."

"Then what happens?"

"Then the mother-in-law moves in."

"Then can Anya move in with us?"

"Maybe. Maybe Shula, too. Have you met the mother-in-law?"

We heard Raquel open the front door.

"Be nice to her," Fagee whispered.

Raquel fairly danced into the room, her pale skin flushed. "I met a girl named Shoshana who met the Rebbetzin today!"

"How nice," Fagee said, pretending to be impressed.

"Is that the Rebbe's wife?" I asked.

"Yes!" Raquel squealed and squeezed in between us on the couch, smelling of body odor and bubble gum. "Shoshana went to the Rebbe's house, rang the doorbell, and the Rebbetzin actually opened the door! Chaya Mushka!"

"What, they don't have a butler?"

"*Shush*, Slovah," said Raquel, giving my leg a swat. "Rebbes don't have butlers. Anyway, she offered Shoshana cookies and juice."

"What did they talk about?" I asked.

"She told Shoshana to learn Yiddish. So I am going to start classes tomorrow!"

"Did . . . she talk about anything else?" I was actually curious what a woman married to a prophet might be like.

"Shoshana said she was so elegant. How do you say *elegant* in Yiddish?"

I was on my last hundred dollars. I called Mr. T and asked if he could please send me another check, but meanwhile, I was living on care-package crumbs and the free-lunch cafeteria.

The morning after Raquel had chattered on about the Rebbetzin, I opened the fridge and . . . whatever food I had left was gone!

It can't be.

I wiped the morning dew out of the corners of my eyes and looked again. It was gone, all right. The fridge shelves were covered in aluminum foil and laid out on them—meat on one level and dairy on another—were Raquel's kosher groceries.

When she came home from Yiddish class late that afternoon, I was waiting for her.

"*Gut morgen!* That means good morning!" she announced.

"*Ayin kavin yan!*" I responded. "It means *go shit in the ocean*! How dare you throw out my food!"

"How can you purify your soul if your food is *treyf*?"

"It was kosher enough for my mother, so it's kosher enough for me."

"You're welcome to eat my food. I'm going to make chicken meatballs."

"I don't want your fucking chicken balls!"

When Fagee came home, she found me smoking and sulking in her bedroom.

"*Q'est-ce que c'est?*"

"The bitch threw out my food."

"*Sheeeet.* I'll go talk to her."

When Fagee walked into the kitchen, she found Raquel busy cooking the chicken balls in tomato sauce.

"This is not your apartment, Raquel. You cannot throw out other people's food."

As I listened to their voices, I crossed over to my own room and took a seat on the windowsill. I loved to smoke and blow the rings out the open window and watch the way Crown

Heights changed at night. From the safety of my perch, the night world opened before me. The lights of many businesses went out; the Chasids rushed home; and when no one was left on the street, the feral dogs came out in packs. Mutts, a German shepherd, and a few pit bull mixes fought with one another and dug through the garbage bags. They were a motley crew of dirty, scarred, and ragged creatures, much closer to wild than the polished pedigree pets I'd known in Rumson with names like Bobo and Fifi.

I'd first discovered the wild dogs when I was walking home from Mashey's a bit too late one night. When I saw a pack of them digging through the trash, I started to run, and they ran after me. Then I heard a voice coming from a window and looked up. It was Yehudah, the tiny Chasid I'd met at the deli months before. "Walk, don't run! Show no fear, and they will leave you alone."

"Thanks."

"Be careful. We need *mishigas* around here."

I forced myself to slow down, and when the dogs caught up to me, I made myself as tall as I could and kept walking determinedly toward home.

They backed off. Castaway pets or born in the trash, I didn't know, but I never ran down the street in Crown Heights again.

A knock on my door brought me back to the present.

"Yeah?"

"Can I come in?"

"Yeah."

Raquel walked in looking at her shoes. "*Zay moykhl!*"

"Gesundheit."

"It means *I'm sorry*."

"How 'bout the twenty-three bucks for the groceries you threw out?"

"I don't have any money right now, but I can give you a blessing."

"Great."

Raquel waved her hands in circles around her and then put them over her eyes. She mumbled something in Hebrew.

"Am I gonna be rich now?"

"No, but you will have a lot of children."

"Lovely, just what I need. If you ever throw my food out again, you'll have to move. Consider this fair warning."

•····•·˙•˙•···•˙ · ·

Raquel's apology wasn't going to fill my stomach till Mr. T's check came—but I had an idea for cash. I painted a sign on the doorway outside reading "Art Lessons." Above the mail slot on the bottom of the door, I painted "Messages."

One morning a Lubavitch woman knocked at the door.

I hung my head out the window.

"My children need to learn to be creative!"

"Sounds good," I said. "Come on up and we'll talk about it."

She dropped off her four-year-old son and three-year-old daughter the next morning for what was supposed to be a one-hour lesson. She didn't come back for four hours, and when she did, she was wearing a new wig.

The three-year-old had tried to eat the finger paints, and the four-year-old had shit his pants. The smell was so bad I thought I'd vomit.

She handed me twenty bucks and said, "Same time tomorrow?"

"I'm booked for the rest of the year."

I went to the grocery with the twenty and bought a box of lasagna noodles, a jar of Ragu tomato sauce, a pint of cottage cheese, and a loaf of Italian bread. With the change, I bought some wine coolers from Hector.

I knew there must be far better ways to make lasagna than with Ragu and cottage cheese, but that was the recipe I'd grown up on, and I needed to eat something familiar. The best part of Mom's lasagna was eating it cold for breakfast the next day.

As it baked, the noodle concoction sent a familiar aroma through the apartment that made my mouth water and inspired Fagee to emerge from her hideaway. I cut out two squares, one for each of us, and opened the wine coolers. But even as we ate it, I was already anticipating the real delight: morning leftovers.

I opened my eyes at seven a.m. to the sound of Raquel and Fagee arguing.

"No, Fagee, the morning washing is right, left, right, left, right, left. You only do three rights, and then three lefts over bread!"

"All this washing, Raquel. I will have no skin left on my fingers when I am done!"

I heard Fagee leave first, and then Raquel trotted down the stairs.

Lasagna time.

I bounced out of bed and flung open the refrigerator and there, to my horror, was an open space where my lasagna had been.

"Raquel! Raquel!" I screamed out the window, but she was already gone. I rode my fury and rumbling stomach as I packed all of Raquel's belongings into her suitcases. What didn't fit, I shoved into a pillowcase. Then I went to the big central window in Fagee's bedroom, the one with a view all the way down Kingston Avenue, sat down, and waited.

A few hours later, I saw my soon-to-be-ex roommate trotting along with an armful of books. "Raquel! Raquel!" I shouted waving my hand side to side.

She looked up at me, confused at this unusual show of friendliness.

"Raquel! *Gay avek*! *Gay avek*! That means *Get out*!"

I opened each of her suitcases in turn and upended it out the window, watching as a flurry of underwear, jackets, skirts, and stockings floated gently to the street. Caught in a breeze, her white bloomers danced in the air for a moment before landing like a bird on a fire hydrant. Then I tossed out the suitcases, which landed with a thud on the sidewalk.

It was as if life on the street came to a halt. Chasids stood motionless, staring at Raquel's clothes spread out on Kingston, as she raced around collecting them.

I closed the window and double-locked the door, knowing she had only the key to the bottom lock.

I scrounged together enough change to go shopping and made another lasagna for dinner that night. After Fagee and I had eaten, we sat on Raquel's futon and drank the rest of the wine coolers. I felt pretty damn blessed after all.

CHAPTER 25

WHEN MOM TRIED STABBING THE MAGNOLIA

One Erev Shabbos—Friday night—as the Lubavitchers were rushing to get their chores done before sundown, Magnolia came careening down Kingston Avenue shouting, "Rosalinda, I'm here from Jersey! Start the party!"

The six-foot-tall, broad-shouldered person in a fuchsia mini-dress and red vinyl go-go boots was quite a sight to the Chasidim. I'd known she was coming, but seeing her on Kingston Avenue was quite a different thing. I hung my head out the window to watch as Mag plowed through the sea of black-and-white suits. It was a sight to behold.

I cranked up Blondie on the stereo, and when she walked in, she grabbed my hands—her coat still on—and we started dancing around the apartment like two crazy kids.

"Rosalinda, your apartment is fabulous—in a shabby chic kind of way."

"Mag. Only you would find the beauty in this place."

"Are we staying in or going out?

"I've got beer and lasagna and my French roomie is in Boro Park for Shabbos."

"In it is! Fabumond!"

Mag pulled off her go-go clothes and changed into a pink lace nightie with matching panties.

"Ain't I pretty?" she sang, twirling like a little girl.

I heated up the remaining lasagna, and we ate it on the couch, chasing it with elephant beers. Mag draped her long legs over my lap. "Rosalinda. It must be love that brought me here, 'cause this place is for the birds!" She pulled her legs down, leaned over, and kissed me on the lips. "But you're worth it."

I looked at her. The kiss hadn't stirred up anything inside me. I thought about the heart-racing, face-burning sensation I'd felt when Cindy had kissed me. My face was cold. My heart was quiet.

I knew Mag had had affairs with several of the Barn Theatre gang, men and women both. I'd always known the offer was on the table, but had never felt attracted to the tall, screeching Amazon. Still . . . her adoring eyes and soft smile warmed me. The last time I'd seen Mag, I'd been dancing with my eyes closed on the balcony of the Monmouth Arts Center while the punk band Shrapnel cranked it below. She reminded me of whatever it was I used to be.

I kissed her back.

She took my hand and led me to the bedroom.

We crawled under the covers and kissed—not the hard, passionate kind of kissing I'd done with Cindy, but soft, slow, careful kissing. *How can someone so loud be so delicate?* I thought. I closed my eyes and felt Mag kissing my ear, my neck, my breast. She reached her hand down between my legs.

"Be careful. I may be—I'm not sure, but . . . um—"

"What's wrong, sweetie?" she whispered.

"I may be a . . . virgin?"

"*May* be? What does that mean?"

"When guys have tried, it has always hurt, so—"

She kissed me and gently began to push her finger inside. "Honey. It only hurt because you weren't interested. Trust me when I say, that is not the case now. At all."

We fell asleep curled up in each other. We were both so tired and drunk we forgot to kiss goodnight.

·····•·····

When the sun came shining in through the big Kingston Avenue windows, I got up and made a pot of coffee. I couldn't stop smiling.

"I had to choose between eggs and beer, so it's bread and coffee for breakfast!" I chirped when Mag came in the room. She'd thrown a pink frilly robe over her nightie and cinched it at the waist with her pink vinyl go-go belt.

We tore apart big hunks of Italian bread and dipped them in our coffee.

"Rosalinda, dear. I just want to mention . . . You are a lot of things—sexy, fun . . . smart . . . brave . . . but you are certainly not a virgin."

"How do you know?"

She started to laugh. "How can someone so tough on the outside be so naive on the inside? Honey, I was way, *way* up in there."

I thought of the myriad sexual encounters I'd had. With the exception of Wayne, who had never entered me, and Izzy, who'd been so small that he couldn't possibly have made a dent, they'd all been painful.

"I wonder who broke it?" I said.

"It doesn't matter, sweetie. You clearly weren't enjoying the ride."

As I pondered Mag's words, I heard banging on the door downstairs and ran to the window. My parents were standing outside with bags of groceries.

"Mag, it's my mom and dad!"

"Shit! Your mother hates me."

"Get dressed! Hurry up!"

"Coming!" I yelled out the window. "Give me a minute!"

I crept down the stairs as slowly as I dared, and when I finally opened the door, my mother pushed past me, leaving my father to struggle with the door and most of the packages.

"Would it kill you to live somewhere with an elevator?"

"Mom, you should have let me know you were coming."

"What, I need an invitation!?"

Ahead of me, Mom climbed quickly, holding the railing as she went. When she reached the top of the stairs, she saw Mag pulling her skirt over her slip, her ample cleavage filled with bits of Italian bread.

"Hello, Mrs. Ross. Nice to see you again!"

Mom stood immobile and slack-jawed for a moment, as if she had suddenly frozen into a block of ice. Then she came to and strode past Mag into the kitchen.

My mother was convinced that the evil plague that had possessed me, which had built the wall between us, was somehow linked to the masculine-looking creature she'd seen smoking in her yard one afternoon—the same creature who was here now, brushing breadcrumbs from her breasts.

"Mom, isn't it nice? Magnolia came to visit me all the way from New Jersey!"

Not knowing exactly what to do, Mag wisely retreated to the bedroom to put more clothes on. I heard her stomping around and the sound of the alarm clock falling to the floor.

Mom found a small steak knife in the dishwashing rack, sat down at the kitchen table, and began sawing away at the semi-frozen Entenmann's cake she had brought. I could almost hear her thinking, *This evil creature planted a seed in my daughter.*

Suddenly, she thrust the knife into the air and, in an eerie, shrill voice, cried, "*I'll kill you, Magnolia!*"

Mag emerged from the bedroom fully dressed with her bag slung over her arm. She took one look at my mother waving the knife around and sidled toward the front door. "Rosalinda, your mother seems to have gone nuts. Love you! Call me!" With that, she sped down the stairs as fast as her long legs would carry her.

My mother flew to the doorway, still brandishing the knife, and hobbled down the steps after her, screaming, "Stay away from my *shana madelah!*"

As I stuck my head out the window, Mag raced down the street past the horrified Chasids. My mother, moving faster than I had ever seen her move, was a block behind her, waving the knife side to side, screaming, "Stay away from my daughter!"

My father came in with the last of the grocery bags and dropped them on the kitchen floor. He nodded wordlessly, took an apple out of one of the bags and ate it, core and all, in four bites.

I sat down on a milk crate, dumbfounded. When Mom finally came back, twenty minutes later, I asked, "Mom, what were you going to do . . . murder my friend?"

She was out of breath, her face crimson and covered in sweat. She put the knife down on the table.

Out of her mouth came, "Do you want another bite?"

"Of what, Mom!? What are you talking about!?"

She banged both of her fists against her chest. "Of my heart!"

I shook my head.

"Marty, we're not wanted here!" she announced, then grabbed her purse and headed toward the stairs again.

"Goodbye!" My father grunted before following her.

I sat at the dinette in front of the massacred cake. I broke off a piece and put it in my mouth, but it was too stale to eat, so I spit it into the garbage.

What the fuck was that?

Years later, it was still hard to believe all that had really happened, but it had. If Mom had caught up with Magnolia, would
she really have stabbed her with a dull steak knife? I'd like to
think she wouldn't have gone that far, but, having looked into
her eyes in that moment, I knew she was capable of such a thing.
She would have gone to jail, I suppose. Or maybe she'd have
gotten off on grounds of temporary insanity.

The episode certainly validated what I'd always suspected:
Under the right conditions, Mom was full-blown cuckoo. I'd
long suspected that she was more than just "eccentric." Over
the course of my childhood, I had occasionally caught her
talking to my Aunt Roslyn, who was quite dead at the time.
But homicidal? This was a whole new level of crazy.

CHAPTER 26

DANNYVILLE

Danny decided he wanted to give me a tour of where he hung out when his family thought he was working late, so he borrowed his sister's car—a blue Cadillac—and drove me into Manhattan. He parked near Sheridan Square and led me down Christopher Street.

I'd never seen anything like it. Every ten feet was a gay bar with blaring disco music. The street itself was so crowded with preening gay men that cars could hardly get through. It felt like the after-party for a parade, but it was just a Wednesday night in the West Village.

At the end of Christopher, we turned right on West Street. In the shadow of the West Side Highway, some seriously macho-looking guys in leather had congregated around two bars, one called Badlands and the other The Ramrod. The double R on The Ramrod sign was designed to look like a cattle brand. Apparently, this West was wild.

"Come on!" Danny said, pulling me along behind him. I wore a sweatshirt with a hood, which he told me to pull over my head, I guess to hide my womanly features. Then he smuggled me into a joint that was so dark all you saw were the floating orange tips of lit cigarettes. In this murky world, my identity was safe.

I loved the way I felt, wading through the dark past jumbles of shadowy figures. It was like floating in a black ocean. As my eyes adjusted, I realized that one dark form consisted of two men fucking.

I was a seventeen-year-old runaway from the sticks trying really hard to be a thirty-five-year-old New Yorker. "Cool," I whispered to Danny, and gripped his hand a little tighter.

When he said there were glory holes in the back of the bar, I asked if he meant urinals. Of course he laughed his ass off.

"One guy sticks his dick in the hole on one side, another guy puts his mouth on it on the other," he explained.

"But what if one guy is really ugly?"

"When the lights are out, a hole's a hole."

As we pushed our way through the bar, I accidentally stepped into the light illuminating the cash register. A huge muscular man with a bushy handlebar mustache and no shirt yelled, "Get out! Get out! No girls allowed."

Without a word, Danny maneuvered me back out onto the street and around the corner to Badlands. "We can shoot pool in here," he said. He went off to grab a couple of beers while I racked up the balls.

As we played—pretty badly—a man slammed his beer down on the bar. I looked up in time to hear him yell, "Fish!"

Another man took the cue: "Fish!" And then the whole bar erupted into chants of "fish, fish, fish, fish!"

Danny and I looked at each other, downed our beers, and left.

Back on West Street, we ran into a thirteen-year-old blond boy turning tricks on the West Side Highway.

"Meet Blondie," said Danny. "I took him in for a while."
Whatever that means.

"Hi, honey!" the sweet-looking kid said, giving Danny a peck on the cheek. "Nice to see you! I'm *sooo* busy tonight, honey."

A half-dozen Hispanic boys fluttered nearby and seemed to be on call to run errands for Blondie. "Go get me some cigarettes!" he said to the one who seemed to be the oldest but couldn't have been more than sixteen.

"He brings in the money. The others don't," Danny explained. I still had a million questions I'd probably never ask.

Danny and I hung out for a while and watched the action. A half-block from where we stood, two men in leather chaps openly jerked each other off. Suddenly, a station wagon full of Chasidic men pulled up to Blondie, and the one in the front passenger seat rolled down his window and waved him over.

Blondie sent one of his assistants to the window first. The kid talked to the Chasid for a few minutes, then came back and whispered briefly to Blondie.

Blondie strutted over to the window and leaned against the car door. "Hi, honey! How you doin' tonight?"

"Are they trying to convert him?" I asked Danny, sending him into yet another fit of giggles.

"Yeah, sure," he said, laughing.

I realized the men wanted to *hire* Blondie. I gaped as they haggled.

"Come on," said Danny, and led me across the West Side Highway to a concrete slab near the water where we could sit and watch a group of Black gay men—two in drag—dancing to a boom box blaring Donna Summer.

A tall, skinny young man with an Afro done up in bright pink curlers elbowed his friend and pointed in my direction. "Look, Shanelle. It's a dyke!"

"I'm not a dyke. I'm bisexual!" I shouted back.

"Yeah, baby! I hear you. Twice the chance of a date on a Saturday night, right?"

I saw a line of rotting old piers and dock houses in the distance and wanted to explore them, but Danny shook his head. "Those are pretty dangerous at night," he said. "Lots of crazy cruising, trans hookers, drugs . . . you name it."

Dangerous? I felt safer among these disco-dancing gay boys than I had ever felt in Crown Heights. Nobody was interested in me, and nobody seemed to be concerned about the kind of gay bashers they surely would have faced in South Jersey. These people were just letting it all hang out—sometimes quite literally.

"We can come back in the daytime, if you really want to check it out," Danny said.

"Yeah. Cool."

* * *

A week later, I ran into Danny at Uncle Pete's. "Can we go to the West Village again, Dan? That was so wild!"

"Have you read the paper this week?"

"No, I never read the paper. Why?"

"Everyone's talking about this 'gay pneumonia' thing that's going around. It's really bad, they say. Sounds like it's contagious."

"What the fuck? A gay disease? How is that even possible?"

"I don't know, but I'm not going back there till they figure it out."

I could still hear Donna Summer singing in my head, from the center of what had seemed like the greatest party in the universe. I didn't know it was about to be last call.

CHAPTER 27

FREE TO BE YOU AND ME

Spring was in full bloom and suddenly the brown of Chasidland seemed covered over in flowers. Everything and everyone seemed to be celebrating: the trees, the sky, the children.

For months, I'd walked by the barbershop on Kingston and seen the barber sitting alone, reading a paper. I'd wondered how the poor man stayed in business. Today, one year since I'd run away, the shop was packed and there was a line of impatient, shaggy-haired Chasids extending out the door and down the block. I'd learn later that the Lubavitchers don't cut their hair from Pesach to Shavuos, roughly April till June.

I was getting thrillingly close to the freedom bell of my eighteenth birthday, when my parents could no longer control where I lived.

I opened the large windows in the bedrooms and the small dirty one in the kitchen to let a cross breeze flow through the apartment. A piece of tissue paper danced on the chipped tile of the kitchen floor as I opened a can of fruit cocktail, mixed it with a packet of McDonald's mustard, and poured it over a baking dish that held three pieces of raw chicken breast. I opened the hot oven and slid it in.

Anya watched in amusement. "And what the hell do you call this creation?"

"*Chicken à la fruit,*" I declared.

"I think you're a little '*chicken à la fruit*,' dear."

"True, but I gotta say, I really like this cooking thing."

I poured two cups of coffee and sat down on the couch next to Anya. I looked into her dark eyes, noting how exotic she was.

Like Cleopatra.

"Anya, I've got something to tell you."

"What?"

"I'm . . . um . . . I'm pretty sure that I'm . . . well . . . bisexual."

Anya smiled. "Me, too."

"What!?"

"Oh, Rossi. All Israeli women are bisexual. We go into the army at seventeen and come out *sabra*."

"*Sabra?* Is that *dyke* in Hebrew?"

"No, silly. *Sabra* means *cactus*—thorny on the outside, soft on the inside. We get tough *way* too fast and too young, so what can we do but . . . you know . . . turn to each other?"

"All Israeli women?"

"Well, all the ones I chum around with."

There was nothing thorny about Anya's outside. Looking at her in her saffron Indian gauze dress and leather sandals, it was hard to imagine Anya carrying a gun. I'd never heard her talk about the army before.

"What was the army like?" I asked.

Anya put her finger to her lips. "It took six months in a Buddhist monastery to forget what it was like. Why do you think I came here?"

"To pray with the Messiah?"

"To be cleansed by him."

Anya put her hand on my cheek. It felt warm and soft—not the least bit sabra.

"Remember what I said. There's nothing wrong with you. The Rebbe blessed you. He knew who you were. He knows everything."

"Then he knows that every time I put on a maxiskirt I'm lying."

"Yes, I suppose he knows that, too."

I leaned my head against Anya's shoulder and sighed, "Thou shalt not lie."

•···•·¯•...•··

A few days later, I began putting away my pretense of religious acceptance. I had never been a follower anyway, and in this world of same-same, standing out felt like a badge of honor. Having my own apartment and listening to Anya's words had given me chutzpah.

Once my mind was set, it all happened quickly. On Monday, I put away the Salvation Army maxi skirts that had been my "camouflage," and by Wednesday, I was back in my favorite torn jeans and safari-print spandex.

My friends watched with a mix of fear and admiration. Some of the timid girls ended their friendships with me; others circled me in awe. I became their voice—perhaps even their inspiration—and a walking message that joy and pride can be felt while wearing zebra stripes.

One afternoon, I walked to Mashey's house for a visit. When she answered the door, I expected her to hug me and kiss me on both cheeks, like she always had. Instead, she hung her head.

"I'm sorry, Slovah. It's not good for the children."

"Mashey? Your kids love me, and so do you. We're friends. Who cares if I'm wearing pants?"

She shook her head. "We have a reputation to uphold. I'm so sorry." She shut the door.

I met Anya and Fagee at the kosher pizza place.

"Mashey doesn't want to be friends with me anymore."

"What a coward!" said Anya, and proceeded to cluck like a chicken.

"You know . . ." said Fagee, "the rabbi is not going to like it when he finds out you are wearing jeans again."

"What's he going to do, have me arrested?"

"I wouldn't put it past him."

I grabbed a slice of pizza out of the box, folded it, and took a bite. All I tasted was sour cheese. I longed for tomato sauce and oregano.

"What's done is done. I threw that fucking jean skirt in the trash. Sorry, Anya. I hope you didn't want it back."

"Not after you got your period all over it. Didn't your mom ever tell you about tampons? Sanitary pads are a mess."

"She said I'd lose my virginity if I used a tampon."

"Um . . . isn't it a bit too late for that?" Anya said, making Fagee shout "*Merde!*" and laugh so hard she tipped over her iced tea.

A group of Lubavitch mothers and kids gathered around a nearby table openly stared at me, leaned in to whisper, then stared again.

I waved at them.

Fagee elbowed me in the gut. "Don't ask for trouble. We have to live here!"

I sat back and looked out at the little village that didn't seem a bit like it belonged in New York City. A teenage boy sped toward me on a bicycle, looking like he'd popped out of a Norman Rockwell painting until he passed, and I saw the yarmulke with a Star of David bobby-pinned to his brown hair.

A mother dragged a cranky toddler along, pleading with him to walk faster. Finally, she picked him up and his chubby red face unclenched into a smile.

I smiled, too. Maybe I could be happy . . . but how?

"Excuse me."

I emerged from my trance to find a freckled teenage girl standing over me.

"My friends and I . . ." She pointed to three other teenage girls at a booth waving. "We just wanted you to know . . . that we think you're really cool."

I stood up and hugged her. "Thank you!"

One of her friends gave me two thumbs-up.

"I know you're with your friends, but would you mind sitting with us for just a few minutes? I mean . . . you're our hero."

The moment felt like something close to joy.

"Sure. I'll come over in a few," I said, my cheeks warming to pink.

I turned to Fagee and Anya. "I'm going to sit with those cute little teenyboppers for just a few minutes. Be right back."

"Rossi?" said Fagee. "It might interest you to know that you're a teenager, too. Those girls are probably your age!"

I looked at them again; they seemed so young. One of them had a bag with a tiny teddy-bear keychain hanging from the zipper. If you took away the maxi skirts and long-sleeved shirts, they wouldn't look so different from my old classmates, now enjoying senior year at Rumson Fairhaven High School.

I felt old enough to be their mother. Probably looked it, too.

"Kind of a hard pill to swallow, eh?" Anya asked.

"Yeah."

CHAPTER 28

MACDOUGAL STREET

I found a letter in my mail slot from my old school pal, Jeni Webster—Webs—the one who had introduced me to community theater.

> *Girl, am I ever going to see you again? I'm coming to New York in two weeks, and I want to see your sorry ass. I miss you.*
> *Love,*
> *Webs*

With Fagee's guidance, we made plans to meet at a café on MacDougal Street, in Greenwich Village. When I got off the subway at West Fourth Street, I felt like I was stepping into a movie I'd seen once, in which everyone wrote poetry, smoked cigarettes from long holders, and said things like "Far out, man."

Macdougal consisted of a row of cafés, one after the other, occupied by college students (from nearby NYU, I guessed), some long-haired hippie types, and lots of arty types. I actually saw two men wearing berets and sipping coffee out of tiny, doll-sized cups. I think they were speaking Italian.

And there was Webs waving to me from an outdoor table at Café Reggio.

"Isn't this cool? It's like stepping into a Jack Kerouac book!"

"Who?"

She rolled her eyes and ran over and hugged me.

"We have to have a cappuccino. This is the place that brought them to America!"

"Isn't that just a coffee with steamed milk for twice the price?"

"Oh, honey, it's a lot more than that."

I let Webs order for us.

"Two cappuccinos with cinnamon, and two chocolate cannolis, please."

The foamy concoction was so delicious I had to close my eyes as I drank it. "This is *not* my dad's Sanka," I sighed.

"Wait till you try the cannoli."

I bit into the cylindrical pastry and super-sweet creaminess filled my mouth. It was almost too much. I winced.

"Now, sip your cappuccino. It's like a chaser."

Webs was right. The sweet cannoli, strong coffee, and cinnamon mixed in my mouth like poetry.

"Holy shit! I want to have this every day!"

"Stick with me, kid!"

Webs looked much as she had the last time I'd seen her: same beautiful face and long dirty-blond hair. The extra thirty pounds she'd put on was in all the right places. She was still garbed in typical Rumson preppy style: light-pink sweater over a white button-up shirt. The only difference was that she'd traded in her Lee jeans for a pair of Gloria Vanderbilts. "Ain't they swank?" she said when she saw me admiring them. "Lower East Side, half price!"

That was a corner of the world I was familiar with. I'd grown up going to Orchard Street once a year and cringing as my mother haggled with every Yiddish-speaking vendor. She'd bought my leather bomber jacket there for fifty bucks, down from a hundred. I had to admit . . . it was still my favorite possession.

Like the girls at the pizza place, Webs suddenly seemed at least ten years younger than I felt—but that didn't mean my style had changed. I was wearing torn jeans, my Blondie T-shirt, and the ever-present Frye boots—probably the same outfit I'd had on the last time she'd seen me. It was what was inside me that had changed.

"Don't you sleep anymore?" she asked, searching my tired face.

"Yeah. With one eye open."

"How the fuck could they send you to Crown Heights?"

She came around to my side of the little café table, leaned down, and put her arm around my shoulder. She kissed my cheek, and I let my head fall against her. The smell of cigarettes and Jean Naté washed over me. For just a moment I was back in Webs's bedroom, listening to her sing as she strummed her guitar to a Jackson Browne song.

She settled carefully back onto her little chair and leaned her elbows on the table. "None of us knew what happened to you. You just disappeared. I went by that dump in Long Branch, and the manager said you'd checked out. I finally went by your house and your mother gave me your mailing address. She also gave me a message for you."

"Really?"

She reached into the back pocket of her jeans and pulled out what appeared to be a small white square. When I opened it up, I realized it was a folded index card. My mother loved index cards.

Slovah, I asked your German friend Jeni to give this to you. She seems very nice for a shiksa.

Always remember your great-, great- and many greats grandfather was a prominent rabbi during the

Spanish Inquisition. He was burned at the stake by Queen Isabella for refusing to eat pork in front of his congregation. If you ever eat pork, you'll smell your ancestors burning. This I know. Remember, too, no matter what, your mother loves you.

I've been writing a poem. I don't know if you like such things, but here is how it starts: People being what they are, I'd trade them all to buy a star.

Love,

Mom

PS Here are some coupons for a free salad bar at Wendy's. Do they have Wendy's in Brooklyn?

I let Webs read the note.

"Oh, dear lord!"

"You can't make this shit up!"

Sitting there in front of Café Reggio, filled with sugar and caffeine, the two of us cackled like schoolgirls. And for the first time since I'd run away from home, I felt like one.

CHAPTER 29

THE CHASIDIC DOUBLE DATE

One night, Fagee scammed a couple of Chasidic guys into taking us to a jazz club. I'd never been to anything like it before; my idea of a club was slam dancing and Mohawks.

Luckily, Fagee warned me what to expect. "It is totally *glamorrrousss*," she purred. "You must wear black and only black."

I pulled on my black spandex pants, black V-neck T-shirt, and my black denim jacket.

The only thing that wasn't black were my Frye boots.

The place was like a scene out of a Humphrey Bogart movie, all style and crystal, with trays of champagne and martinis going everywhere, and in the middle of it all was a jazzy little trio fronted by a lady singer who looked like a human hourglass. I could have closed my hands around her waist. Her breasts, by contrast, poured out of her midnight-blue cocktail dress, lush and deep cocoa. I don't remember a thing Fagee or the human meal tickets had to say that night, but I can recall every curve of that woman and the dry fruity taste of champagne drizzling down my throat as I traced her up and down with my hungry eyes.

It hadn't occurred to me that, while I was drooling over the singer, the Chasids were drooling over us. Fagee, bless her soul, only had eyes for the champagne.

"Where am I?" I asked as the second round of bubbly was poured. I felt as if I had been transported to another world.

"This is Soho," said the Chasid who'd been designated "mine." "You are at the Greene Street Café."

He had checked his black hat when we arrived but retained the uniform of a formless black suit and a yarmulke. His beard was relatively short, so that if you didn't look closely, in the dark, he almost looked like any other businessman. Later, he would explain that while Lubavitchers are not allowed to trim their beards, they are allowed to burn them off. I was too entranced by the entertainment to listen to the gory details of the process.

Fagee's "date" was shorter and fatter and clearly hadn't learned to burn his beard.

• ··· • ˙ ˙ ˙ ··· • ˙ ˙ ˙

The men had booked a fancy town car with a driver to impress us, and when we were done at the café, we drove up the West Side Highway into Harlem. There, I feasted my eyes on beautiful old buildings, still majestic with their layers of graffiti and broken and boarded-up windows.

We scuttled across town to the FDR and skimmed down the East Side, looking out at the East River as we headed for Wall Street to see what big business looked like when it was deserted.

We cruised into the South Street Seaport and watched the first flickers of sunrise peeking above the river while the fishermen settled into their workday. The air smelled like rotting fish, but I didn't mind one bit. One of them waved at my happy, dreamy face. I held up four fingers, too awestruck to make them wave.

Finally, as the sun showed itself in full, we drove over the Manhattan Bridge, down Flatbush Avenue, made the large circle around Grand Army Plaza, sped past the Brooklyn Museum, onto Eastern Parkway, and all the way back to Crown Heights.

It felt like going back to prison after a furlough—or what I imagined that to feel like. I could still taste the champagne, still hear the sultry, ebony singer crooning the Billie Holiday song: "Ain't Nobody's Business If I Do."

Billie sounded like my kinda woman.

I sensed our escorts getting nervous as the streets grew familiar and we passed people who might recognize them. They hunched over, clearly trying to keep a low profile as the car pulled up to our flat.

Fagee and I looked at each other and smiled and the two men got out of the car to walk us to our door.

"Can we come in?" asked Fagee's date.

"I'm sorry, but . . . we are very tired," she said.

When my date leaned in to kiss me I made sure he got my cheek—a move I seemed to have perfected.

"But we took you out on the town," Burnt Beard whined. "Maybe we can just come up for coffee?"

"Thank you for a wonderful night," I said, as I took my keys out of my pocket and fumbled with the lock.

Burnt Beard put his hand on the door. "At least a blow job or something? We spent a lot of money on you ladies!"

Fagee's eyes and lips narrowed into slits. "That's not *tzniut*!" she yelled and slammed the door in their stunned faces.

Days later, I saw her date walking down the street with his friends. He did the "you are invisible" walk around me, but as he passed, I said in full voice, "Thanks for last night!"

He hurried off, horrified, as his friends stole glances back at me in my jeans and T-shirt.

"Go buy a razor!" I shouted after him. I wasn't an expert on the rules, but I felt fairly certain that trimming one's beard was not as bad as trying to score a blow job from a seventeen-year-old.

CHAPTER 30

BRINGING THE FUN ON
KINGSTON AVENUE

L ife on Kingston Avenue could be challenging, but it was not without its little amusements. There was a man I called the "Shabbos Roller," a Chasid with a black beard so long it nearly touched his knees. He kept up with the pre-Shabbos rush of errands by lacing up a pair of roller skates and racing through the neighborhood at full speed, his wondrous beard trailing behind him like a flag.

"Yahoo!" I'd shout as he whizzed past.

"Good Shabbos!" he'd call out, flashing a smile.

Then there was the "Tzedakah Belcher." Tzedakah—charity—must be offered by observant Jews, preferably every day. In a frigid city riddled with crime, I don't know why word didn't get out among the homeless that all they needed to do was find their way to the Chasids and say they were Jewish. The Kingston hood was filled with down-on-their-luck Jews who were fed, clothed, and housed by the community. In normal parts of the city, when a tattered, dirty man approached begging for money, most people turned away. But in the Chasid zone, all a man had to say was "tzedakah" and the religious dug into their pockets and handed over their change.

One rotund, formerly homeless man spent so much time devouring free meals at Ess & Bentch that his deafening belches could stop your heart a half-block away. The man clearly had an issue with Schnitzel.

"Better than yesterday!" he'd say after every ear-splitting eruption.

⸱⸱⸱⸱⸱⸱⸱⸱⸱⸱⸱⸱

Not all Jews were purely *frum* (pious), of course. The red-curtain bong-tokers and West Side Highway cruisers were ample evidence of this. One day at the pizza place, I dumped a pile of Fritos corn chips on a plastic plate and handed it to an old man as he shuffled toward the back.

"For after!" I said.

"Thank you," he replied, bowed his head, and took the plate behind the curtain.

⸱⸱⸱⸱⸱⸱⸱⸱⸱⸱⸱⸱

Getting a package from my mother was always an adventure. Along with the Tam Tam crackers, cans of tuna fish, kosher beef sticks, and stacks of useless coupons sometimes came women's underwear large enough to fit three people inside. But what always sent Fagee into hysterics were the accompanying notes.

> *Slovah,*
> *I got the tuna fish on special at Uncle Henry's auction. There is a check for thirty dollars in the socks. Don't tell your father. He thinks I spoil the children. There are coupons for free McDonald's hamburgers. You can order them with everything but hold the meat, then you get*

a nice lettuce and tomato sandwich for free. Honor thy
father and thy mother and marry a nice Jewish boy.
Preferably one with a job, not like your sister. She is on
her fifth deadbeat in a row. Where did we go wrong?
Love,
Mom.

Eventually, she discovered FedEx and started sending stuff
with freezer packs. One day, it was Empire kosher fried chicken.
The freezer packs had thawed by the time the care package
arrived, but the chicken was still cold so I figured it wouldn't
kill us. I planned a feast of spaghetti and chopped chicken and
called my friends to come over.

Danny showed up with a large Russian Chasid sporting a
bushy red beard. He looked a bit like a grizzly bear or a wres-
tler. Or a wrestling grizzly bear. Robby's contribution was two
bottles of red wine and his B-52s album.

I placed a large bowl of my spaghetti-chicken-ketchup mix
on the table and yelled, "Come and get it!"

"*Ahhh*," purred Fagee, "this is . . . how you say? . . . *fine
dining*!"

"This is how your say *free*, you dingleberry."

"What is *dingleberry*?"

"You don't want to know," joked Danny as he passed a joint.

Robby put the B-52s album on and started to dance, shaking his hips side to side in his tight Jordache jeans. I knew the
music well from my Jersey days and started to sing "Dance
This Mess Around."

The Russian put his plate down and started to dance, too.
He was trying to emulate Robby, shaking side to side to terrible
effect, so he gave up and started dancing behind him. Soon,
he was grinding his crotch into Robby from behind, and they
danced like that until the song ended.

Robby whispered something into the Russian's ear, then said aloud, "I'm gonna show my new friend my renovation." He winked at me, and the two of them ran down the stairs.

I shook my head and grabbed the Russian's still-full plate and gave it to Danny, who just about inhaled it.

"What's with all the gay Chasids?" I asked him when he came up for air.

"They're not gay . . . We just . . . They just . . . Well, growing up, you're not allowed to touch a girl, and then you're crammed into these all-boys yeshivas, and puberty happens, and . . . shit happens."

"Ah . . . *sheeet* happens," Fagee said, stoned out of her gourd.

"Everybody knows about it. But all that is supposed to stop when you get married. Some of the men just can't forget that the hottest times they ever had were with boys."

• ··· • ' ~•···•· · ·

Robby came back a few hours later, plunked himself down on the couch, and said, "That bear almost broke my bed!"

When I'd opened the door for him, I'd found a rolled-up paper scroll with a rubber band around it that someone had shoved through the message slot. When I unrolled it, two hand-rolled drum cigarettes fell out. It was a note from Anya.

> *My sweet rock-and-roll sister. I don't care for sloppy goodbyes. By the time you read this, I'll be on my way back to Israel. Remember what you promised me. God doesn't make mistakes. You are perfect, just as you are. Love, Anya.*

Sitting on the couch next to Robby, I lit one of Anya's cigarettes. It smelled sweet, like Anya. I walked into the hall and looked back, watching Danny and Fagee cracking up as Robby imitated the Russian man dancing like Frankenstein's monster.

Our parties had been little islands of fun in an ocean of shit, but now Lifsa, Shula, Mashey, and Anya were gone. I remembered their faces, the way they'd listened intently to my every word and offered advice from deep in their hearts. But it was all temporary. Disposable. Like the plates at our feasts.

CHAPTER 31

DANNY AND THE $500 JACKPOT

One afternoon an envelope came in the mail containing a check for $500. Its rightful recipient was the previous tenant of the apartment, Rubin Shotsky, who had vacated abruptly by dying of a heart attack. Amazingly, the check was accompanied by a check-cashing ID!

This was the third unwitting gift I'd received from Mr. Shotsky, whom I'd never had the pleasure of meeting. When I moved in, I found a bag of bath towels in the closet. I'd felt a bit skeevy about using a dead man's towels, but Mashey had been quick to point out that beggars can't be choosers. The second gift was three cans of Ajax left in the bathroom. I used those to scrub the mold off the tub.

That $500 seemed like five million to me. The problem was, I knew I couldn't pass for someone named Rubin Shotsky at the bank. I needed a man to cash the check. I called Danny, who immediately ran over, snatched the envelope from me, and headed for the nearest teller. An hour later, he returned in his sister's sapphire Chevy with five hundred bucks in his pocket. He shoved three hundred of it into my hand, per our agreement.

I can pay the gas bill, buy groceries, get art supplies! Thank you Rubin Shotsky!

"I'll pick you up at eight!" Danny called out as he drove away, trailing manic, high-pitched giggles.

I put on what I thought was the coolest outfit I owned: purple zebra-print pants, black spandex tank top, leather bomber jacket, and white Capezio shoes. When Danny came back at the appointed hour, I could tell he was already stoned; he giggled all the way over the Manhattan Bridge.

As we crossed lower Manhattan heading for the West Side Highway, he said, "I wanna show you something."

"Are we going back to Christopher Street?"

"*Nah*, something else."

He made his way up to Twenty-Second Street and Tenth Avenue and parked in front of a place called the Empire Diner. It looked like a cross between a 1940s diner and an old train car. Across one side was a big sign that read, "Eat," and the shiny chrome siding gleamed oddly in the midst of the dark and deserted warehouse neighborhood.

"This place is gonna change Chelsea, mark my words."

"I just hope your sister's car is still here when we get back."

The Empire may have called itself a diner, but it turned out to be a high-class restaurant. There was even a guy playing piano in the corner.

"It's open twenty-four hours a day, and at two in the morning, when all the clubs let out, you can't even get in the place," Danny said. "I figured this would be a good time to try it."

There was one empty booth, and as we grabbed it, I looked around and saw that the place was filled with gay men, all dressed in black and looking very chic. *No wonder Danny likes it*, I thought. A slender woman at a table near us had on a cocktail dress and a pink chiffon scarf; the effect was very Audrey Hepburn.

"Celebrities come here sometimes," said Danny, "Gay boys of course, lots of artists . . ."

When the waiter came over to take our order, I opened my mouth to speak, but Danny stopped me.

"We'll both have the steak frites, medium," he said.

"What is a *steak freet?*"

"Steak and french fries, but French style, which basically means expensive. And certainly not kosher." He started giggling and added, "Of course . . . tonight it *is* kosher, because we're Jewish, and we're eating it!"

A drag queen dressed like Marilyn Monroe rolled past our table—literally. She would have been six feet tall in her stocking feet, but on roller skates she was a giant.

The steak was the most delicious I'd ever tasted—nothing like the grayish beef jerky my mother served up, which I'd always had to drown in ketchup just to choke down. This steak was moist and peppery, and when I cut it open, it glistened pink inside. I'd never eaten pink meat.

After dinner, we drove down Tenth Avenue into a warehouse neighborhood filled with wholesale meat businesses closed for the night. The stench of rotting meat was overwhelming.

Two men strolled by us in leather jackets and jeans. One of them wore black leather chaps.

"This is the Meat Market," said my friend and tour guide. "By day, wholesale meat; by night, gay boys, S&M bars, and lots of tranny hookers."

A skinny young woman wearing lots of makeup and a very dirty fur coat stood on the corner with her hands on her hips.

"Chick with a dick," Danny said.

"Really?"

I craned my neck to keep looking at her as we drove past.

Next, we went dancing at a club called the Electric Circus, on Fifteenth Street and Fifth Avenue. A live band stood on stage jamming to some head-banging New Wave, but you could hardly see them through the confetti, disco lights, and fog.

Clad in black jeans, black sneakers, and a black T-shirt, Danny would have disappeared on the dance floor if it weren't for his pink face. We danced like stupid kids who didn't know what rhythm was, jumping up and down and banging into each other like grasshoppers. I closed my eyes and let the music take me on a wild, romping rant of drumbeats. The last time I'd danced to a live band I'd been with Cindy Butler.

At four a.m., exhausted, we made our way back to the Meat Market and bought hot-from-the-oven bagels slathered with cream cheese at a place called Dizzy's. I tore apart the gooey, wonderful mess like it was the last meal on earth, the sweat from the dance floor still drying on my stomach.

"Man, I love it here," I sighed.

"I knew you would. All freaks are welcome in Manhattan."

We sat on a loading dock, smiling at the hookers on their last legs, and the butchers grabbing an early a.m. coffee before starting their eight-hour shifts. As I slurped root beer through a straw, I thought, *This is it. I'm at the center of the place I've always dreamed of. The real New York City!*

•·••·•¸•…•·· ··

One night, over elephant beers, I told Danny about my affair with Cindy. In response, he told me about a place called the Duchess, a lesbian bar on Sheridan Square where no men were allowed.

"You mean . . . every girl in there is gay?"

"Yep. All dykes."

I'd told myself I was bisexual, like a lot of the theater kids I'd hung out with in New Jersey, but inside, I knew the truth. The idea of a bar entirely filled with lesbians sounded like Candyland.

The first chance I got, I caught the 2 train at Kingston and changed to the 1 local to Sheridan Square. There, just across the street from the Village Cigar Store at the corner of Christopher, was the Duchess.

I stood outside the bar summoning up the courage to walk in. It was five-thirty p.m., and I knew I couldn't stay long, since the ride back to Kingston would get dicey after eight. An androgynous-looking woman in a leather jacket, her brown hair slicked back, stepped out to smoke a cigarette. I thought she looked like a female version of the Fonz from *Happy Days*.

Once she'd lit up, inhaled deeply, and let out a cloud of Marlboro smoke, she looked up at me and snickered. "You gonna come in or what?"

"I'm . . . um . . . waiting for someone."

"We all are, honey," she said, and, after a few more deep drags, tossed her half-finished cigarette into the street. Then she leaned in close to me and said, "We don't bite. That is, unless you want us to." Then she chomped her teeth together with a sharp *clack* and let out a wicked chuckle.

I watched her disappear back into the club and just about ran back across the street to the subway station.

Bumping along on the ride home, my heart slowed to normal, and I mentally kicked myself. *Why didn't I just walk in? What stopped me?*

I'd always been so tough. I remembered how happy I'd been, roughhousing with the boys on the school playground in first and second grade. At the grand old age of seven, I'd been completely in my element playing war games in the dirt with my best pal, Ronny.

Mrs. Hendricks, the oldest and meanest teacher in my grammar school, didn't like the fact that I had all male friends and dressed like a boy. After I got into a fight with a boy (and won), Hendricks told my parents I should have a psychological evaluation for "gender confusion."

For eight weeks, every Wednesday after school, I had to go see Miss Ovitz. A tall, pretty woman in her early thirties, she was the first adult I'd ever met who truly seemed to want to know what I was thinking and feeling. She looked into my eyes as we spoke. She asked me about my dreams! Nobody had ever done that.

I told her that I often dreamed I was an Indian warrior on a horse, whooping and shooting and wielding a bow and arrow. "I never dream about being a squaw sitting home in a teepee," I added. "I mean . . . who would want to be *that*!?"

"Not me!" she replied.

I was in love.

I wondered why I hadn't chosen to tell Miss Ovitz about Wonder Woman. I'd tried a few times, but something deep inside me told me that those dreams were too naughty to reveal, even to Miss Ovitz.

When my eight sessions were done, Miss Ovitz wrote up her evaluation. According to my mother, she said, "There is nothing wrong with your daughter. She is just overly creative and a little eccentric. Let her be."

I told everyone in school that I was eccentric; I felt it added to my superpowers. But later that same year was when my parents sent my sister, brother, and me to our version of hell: private yeshiva. By the time the principal took pity on us and pushed us out of there, my superpowers were gone.

After my last day at yeshiva, I ceremoniously removed a serrated steak knife from the meat drawer in our kitchen and slashed to ribbons the maxiskirt I'd had to wear. In Crown Heights, nearly a decade later, I would discard my maxiskirt yet again, this time skipping the knife and instead consigning the thing to a black garbage bag. That bag would then become one in a sea of similar ones arrayed down Kingston Avenue on garbage day. There'd been no ceremony, but as I looked at all those anonymous bags lining the street, I felt a release.

Whoosh!

I smiled so wide it actually made my ears hurt.

My superpowers were starting to come back now that the kryptonite skirt was gone, but apparently, I was still too chickenshit to walk into the Duchess.

CHAPTER 32

THE NEW YORK TIMES

One summer morning, I took a hard look in the bathroom mirror I'd duct-taped to the medicine cabinet. Dark circles hung beneath my eyes. My lips were sunburnt from sitting on the benches of Eastern Parkway. There was a bit of dry blood in the center of my bottom lip where a sun blister had cracked.

I was tired of being hungry, scared, and poor.

I had stopped calling Redbeard, but I remained afraid that he'd send the police after me if I moved out of Crown Heights before I turned eighteen. Anyway, even when I turned that magical age and my prison sentence ended, I wouldn't have many alternatives if I didn't have any money.

I needed to find a job.

I pulled on my cutoff-jean shorts and crossed the street to Uncle Pete's.

"Hola," I said, "got any day-old *New York Times* I could have for free?"

"I got a paper some *pendejo* dropped on the floor," said Uncle Pete. "Half of it is missing." He handed it to me.

"Thanks, *papi.*"

Luckily, what was left of it included the help-wanted ads. I threw myself on the couch with a buttered roll and began to scour the listings. Just about every one of them said, "No experience necessary." Also, unfortunately for me, "Must be a college graduate."

College fucking graduate!?

I thought of some of the rich, preppy kids I'd gone to school with, now in their last year of high school. Soon, they'd be going off to expensive colleges paid for by their parents. I saw them driving off in the Porsches and BMWs they'd been given on their seventeenth birthdays. *Bye-bye, little sweethearts.*

My parents had offered to pay for community college if I were willing to go, but it hadn't exactly jibed with my runaway plan.

I slumped down into the couch.

Fagee shimmied in next to me, took one look at my face, and asked me who died.

"My future," I replied. "I can't afford college . . . so how am I supposed to get a job?"

"Why don't you ask your parents for money?"

"Because I'd rather die."

I kept scanning the ads until I came to one that didn't mention education: "Sell *The New York Times* over the phone," I read aloud. "No experience necessary."

"Well . . ." said Fagee, "You spend all your time talking on the pay phone anyway. You might as well get paid for it."

I knew I didn't look particularly hirable in my torn Levi's and thick black eyeliner, but I'd been blessed with a great phone voice so maybe I had a shot.

Two days later, I took the train to an office on East Thirty-Third Street, where a large middle-aged woman named Dottie said, "Fill out these forms and report for orientation tomorrow." I needn't have worried about an interview.

The phone room had a posh-sounding address—2 Park Avenue—but it was anything but posh. In a large space divided into cubicles, down-and-out drifters of all sorts dialed away. On my first scan, I counted two hippies, one guy who looked like he'd recently been homeless, a few frat-boy college dropouts, an Indian woman in a miniskirt with a white streak in her black hair, a jazz-musician type, an old man who seemed to be sleeping, and a slew of other misfits. It looked like bedlam.

This is my kinda place, I thought.

Most people thought cold-calling was an end-of-the-road job. For me, it was the beginning. I'd soon learn that my shift— the day shift—was the crappy one; all the money was made on the night shift, when people were home from work. But I was glad to work days and avoid having to dodge drug dealers and wild dogs on the way home.

I'd been coached through my script at the orientation: "Hello, Mr. Young. I am calling from *The New York Times* to offer you a wonderful special promotion. We will give you free weekday service for signing up for weekend service . . ."

When I arrived that first morning, most people were already there. Some shook their hands and rolled their necks to loosen up; some drank tea to soothe their voices, but nobody got started until the shift manager arrived—a young woman who looked as if she'd just finished a jog or a workout. She wore sweatpants and a sweatshirt and sported a huge Afro that jetted straight out of the sides of her head, making her look like a Black Flying Nun. She proceeded to take off her sweatshirt, revealing enormous breasts barely covered by a tank top. She shook her sweaty Afro and intoned, "This shift will now begin!"

The chattering commenced immediately and sounded to me like bees swarming.

I sat down and called the first number on the list in front of me. "Hello, Mrs. Wong. I am calling from *The New York Times*—"

She hung up.

Next.

"Hello, Mrs. Johnson. I am calling from *The New York Times*—"

Click.

I made only two sales that day and crawled home dejected. The next day, just as the shift was about to begin, I felt a tap on my shoulder.

I looked up to see Ron, a middle-aged, beatnik-looking jazz musician with a goatee who sat in the adjacent cubicle. He reeked of cigarettes and whiskey.

"It's easier for women to sell to men and men to sell to women," he said. "Just hang up on all the women and keep going. When a man answers, put on your sexiest voice."

"Thanks!"

The next call was a woman, so I hung up.

Another woman.

I hung up.

Finally, a man answered, and I put on what I considered my sexiest voice. "*Hellooo*, Mr. Wilson . . . I am about to bring you excitement every morning."

Mr. Wilson was my first of twenty sales that day, all to men. I high-fived Ron on my way out and floated home without even noticing the catcalls on the 2 train.

Three days later, big-boobed Tilly called me into her office. Her outfit of the day was black karate pants and a matching turtleneck.

"I don't know what you're doing, and I don't want to know, but you're our top salesperson this week."

"Wow, thanks!" I said, unable to keep myself from staring at her mesmerizing breasts.

"I have a face, too," she smirked.

⁕ ⸱⸱⸱⸱⸱⸱

I liked talking on the phone. Maybe it was extra fun because I didn't have my own phone, or maybe I just liked pretending to be someone else. The gig ceased to be primarily about the paycheck. It was the chance to leave Kingston Avenue behind for a few hours every day and check into some other place. I would thrust my head deep inside my cubicle as if it were my own secret tunnel, be whoever I wanted to be, and call dozens and dozens of strangers.

"Hello, Mr. Davis. Are you ready for me? 'Cause I want to give it to you every day . . ."

My first paycheck was $308, and from the way it made me feel, you'd think it had a few additional zeros on the end. This was a fortune to me.

Tilly invited me into the break room for celebratory champagne, which she poured into disposable coffee cups. "Honey, you earned it!" she said as we clinked Styrofoam.

On the way home, two teenage boys in baseball caps took turns swinging on the poles of the 2 train and breakdancing. Then they walked up and down the car with their caps out for money. Feeling rich, I fished out three dimes and dropped them in the taller guy's hat.

"Tzedakah," I said to his bewildered face.

As I was getting out at the Kingston station, two Lubavitch women, young and pretty, rushed out ahead of me. One was unmarried and her long, curly, brown hair cascaded around her shoulders. The other wore a black wig. They looked nervous, probably because it was dark, and the streets were almost empty.

"It's gonna be okay!" I said to them.

The unmarried one smiled. "Yes, *Baruch Hashem*."

I assumed they were on their way to the Machon Chana dorm on President Street. As I passed President, the civilian patrol inched by, a dozen young men crammed into the station wagon, one of them holding a brick. On their own, Chasidic men weren't much to be afraid of . . . but when they banded together, it was a different story. I felt proud that they were taking care of their own and waved as they drove past. Several of them waved back. *Revenge of the nerds*, I thought. Why hadn't we considered that option in grade school?

I cashed my check at Uncle Pete's and bought a nickel bag and a six-pack. The next day, I would go to Pearl Paint on Canal Street and load up on art supplies. I felt the urge to paint returning.

●·····●·····●·····●···●·····

Fagee was at her cousin's in Boro Park that night, so I put one of the four-for-a-dollar mac-and-cheese packets I'd picked up in boiling water, added some canned peas, and sat on my windowsill eating as I looked out at the Kingston night.

I saw two wild dogs come out of the shadows and start sniffing through a garbage bag in front of the closed kosher dairy place.

Where do they go all day? I wondered.

I'd once asked Lifsa why I never saw a Lubavitcher walking a dog. "Because they're dirty and eat dirty things," she'd said. "Definitely not a good addition to a kosher home."

Another few dogs came sniffing around and the first two growled at them until they ran off to find some other treasure. I put my empty bowl aside and lit a cigarette, using the bowl as an ashtray. One of the first dogs, a pit bull mix, must've gotten wind of me; he looked up.

I blew kissy noises at him until he went back to tearing apart the trash. After a few minutes, something startled the animals, and they ran away. The source of their anxiety was a scuffle between a silver-haired Black woman and a young Black man who was trying to take her bag off her arm.

"Give it to me, you fucking bitch, or I'll put a cap in your ass!"

She held on to the bag defiantly.

I saw a light go on in the second-floor apartment next to them, then go off again. I had no phone to call the police, no weapon, no clue what to do . . . but something deep in my soul urged me to action. I stuck my head out the window and let out the longest, loudest, most bloodcurdling scream imaginable. It seemed to come from the loneliest, darkest place inside of me, and once it started, it grew in volume and intensity until it was a granddaddy monster of a scream, too big to ignore.

Lights went on all over the street. The stunned mugger, unable to determine where the scream was coming from, let go of the woman's bag and ran away, nearly tripping over the garbage the dogs had strewn around.

The woman looked around for the source of the siren and found me. She mouthed the words *thank you* and, in the dim light of the streetlamp, tears streamed down her face.

I nodded and watched her hobble home.

The next morning, I found a note pushed through the slot in the door I'd labeled MESSAGES. It read, "Miracles really do happen."

CHAPTER 33

THE KINGSTON CHILL

I looked around my flat. All of the furniture was either liberated street trash or made out of milk crates draped with random bits of fabric. It wasn't much to brag about, but it was all mine; my name was on the lease, and I could do whatever I wanted inside.

I'd never lived anywhere where I didn't have to ask permission before making changes to my surroundings. Outside was a community of people who looked at me like I was an alien, but inside was my very own country.

I set up an easel near the window in my bedroom and loaded up on canvases and acrylic paint. My first creation was a portrait of Grace Jones. I painted her skin sky blue, her pupils purple. She looked like an acid trip. I considered the piece a victory. As I gazed proudly at Grace, I heard knocking.

"Let me in; I got something to tell you!"

Izzy.

"Go away, Izzy."

"You're gonna wanna hear this!"

I opened the door a little but kept the chain on.

"What?"

He pushed against the chain. "You know I could just karate chop this open if I wanted to."

I started to close the door.

"Wait, wait! I really do have something to tell you."

"Spill it."

"Some friends of friends of mine on Flatbush told me that Sherba offered them a few hundred bucks to mug you."

"What!? Why?"

"He wants to scare you out of the neighborhood."

"Izzy, this friends-of-friends stuff is bullshit."

"Yeah, well . . . I'd watch my ass if I were you."

He shuffled away, grinding his jaw. I felt exhausted just watching him. I half-believed him. *It was probably Izzy that fucking Redbeard asked to beat me up*, I thought. But what could I do about it even if it were true?

⁕⸱⸱⸱⸱⸱⸱⸱⸱⸱⸱

That evening, to celebrate having created my first painting in Crown Heights, I stopped in to Uncle Pete's. Hector handed me a Colt 45 and we sat on the milk crates drinking while Uncle Pete worked the counter.

"How you doing, Hector?"

"Not so good, *mami*. I been trying to become a cop, but they won't let me in."

"Why not?"

"Some shit I did when I was a kid."

"Now you're stuck here with me, *papi*!" yelled Uncle Pete. "*Rubia*, let that be a lesson to you. If you get a chance to leave this fucking place, take it. If you wait too long, your ass is stuck here forever."

"Got it."

The next morning, I walked to the kosher-dairy place to pick up a bagel with lox and cream cheese. I waited patiently while the store owner took care of everyone who'd been there when I walked in. Then he skipped over me as if I were invisible and asked the person behind me what she wanted.

"Hey! I'm standing right here!" I yelled.

He ignored me.

I heard a male voice call out from the back of the shop, "*Vas zenen ir tsu rikhter!*" *Yehudah.*

The shopkeeper hung his head and looked at me. "Sorry, I didn't see you there."

I looked at Yehudah and mouthed the words, "Thank you."

"We need a little *meshuga* around here, Famous Rossi," he said, as he did whenever I encountered him. He held the door for me as I exited with my white paper bag.

"What did you say to him?" I asked.

"I said, 'Who are you to judge?' My brethren sometimes forget that they are not *Hashem.*" His kind green eyes seemed to be smiling.

I smiled in return. I hadn't seen very many kind eyes among the bearded. In fact, the last pair had probably belonged to the Rebbe.

"*Zay gazunt,*" I said to Yehudah.

"*Zay gazunt,* Famous Rossi. Some of us are rooting for you."

Had Redbeard really put the word out on me? Danny had warned me that Sherba could make it very chilly for me on Kingston Avenue if he wanted to. I would have felt betrayed, but I'd trusted him about as much as I trusted the Jamaican drug dealers on Eastern Parkway. Actually, *they* had a code, which put them a few notches above Redbeard in my book. My folks had sent this "pious man" money every month to look out for me, and I couldn't think of one thing he'd done to earn it. Now, it seemed, he was actively trying to cause me harm.

●·····●·····●·····●······●·····●··●·····●···●···

The first waves of winter hit, and I moved my easel away from the radiator. I had just finished a portrait of the Rebbe, having spent two weeks trying to capture his haunting, soul-searching eyes.

I came home from work and found Fagee pacing back and forth, wrapped in a blanket.

"This is bullshit!" she hissed. "Your rabbi made them turn the heat off!"

"He's not *my* rabbi! And anyway, he's supposed to help people, not freeze them to death."

"Grow up, little girl!"

I called Danny and he came over with three electric space heaters, one for each room. When I attempted to boil water, I discovered that the gas had been turned off as well—so I used the Mr. Coffee to do the job. "Nobody is gonna force me out again!" I announced. "Not even Redbeard."

"Little girl . . . if Sherba wants you out, you are out." Fagee had a look on her face that seemed as much tired as scared.

"It's gonna be okay, Fagee. We still have electricity."

"For now."

I poured her a cup of tea, and we sat down on the couch. Danny squeezed in next to me. "It's not so bad," he said. "It's almost spring."

Just then we heard a loud crash coming from Fagee's room and jumped up to see what had happened. There was broken glass strewn over her bed. Someone had thrown a brick through the front window.

"That's it!" said Fagee. "I'm going to Boro Park to stay with my cousin."

CHAPTER 34

ELECTRIC WAR

The next day, I came home from work to find all of Fagee's stuff gone. She'd left a pile of dark chocolate bars, a pack of French cigarettes, and a paper bag containing a croissant on the kitchen table. *Slovah, some wars you cannot win,* read a note propped against the bag.

Danny brought me two more electric heaters and covered the broken window with cardboard and gray duct tape. If this was war, I was determined to prevail.

● ·· • ' ·●●···●· · ·

The cough I had got deeper and raspier until I felt too weak to go to work or even down to the pay phone at Hector's to call in. I curled up in a ball and covered myself with blankets— although, thanks to my fever, I didn't feel the cold at all.

The idea of sleeping forever felt oddly comforting. *It would be so easy just to let go . . . go to sleep and never wake up.*

A week into what was probably bronchitis, I heard a knock on the door. I didn't want to pull myself from the black hole I'd crawled into, but, summoning all my strength, I got up and crept down the stairs. I picked up the plank of wood I kept behind the door for protection and rasped, "We don't want any!"

"It's Tilly!"

"Who?"

"Tilly. You know . . . your boss."

I opened the door to find Tilly standing there with a Chinese-food bag. She pushed past me into the hallway. "You haven't been to work in a week," she said. "No call. Nothing. I got your address from payroll."

"Why?"

"Idiot! I was worried about you. You look terrible. And why is it so fucking cold in here!"

"My landlord is trying to freeze me out."

Tilly went to the kitchen and proceeded to pull Chinese-food containers from the bag. "I hope you like sweet-and-sour chicken."

"I do now."

"Good. Make me a cup of that tea," she ordered, pointing to the box of Lipton's near the coffeemaker. "There is a little something called tenants' rights we should talk about."

I filled the machine and turned it on. "I didn't think you cared."

"Don't spread it around."

CHAPTER 35

FOOD

I woke one morning to the sound of rain; at long last the freeze was over. Goodbye, black snow mounds covered in soot. Hello, purifying rain.

I lay listening to the soft vibration of the drops. I looked up at my ceiling. There was a round water spot on the right side, where it tended to leak during heavy storms. The white paint had crumbled around it, so I had moved my mattress to the left, just in case. My ceiling always looked very far away to me, I suppose because I slept so close to the floor.

I rolled myself out of bed, walked to the bedroom window, opened it, and breathed. The air smelled crisp and light, not of car oil and rotting garbage as usual. I hadn't seen green grass in months, but the wind had somehow managed to pick up a hint of its scent—perhaps from as far away as Prospect Park, a mile off. I closed my eyes and inhaled.

I reached my hands and forearms out the window and felt the drops *ping*, *ping*, *ping* against them. I watched the rain collecting in a pool on the faded yellow awning of the fruit market across the way. When the awning got too full and heavy, the overflow poured off its corners onto the sidewalk.

Growing up, we had always lived close enough to the ocean that we smelled the salt water during a rainstorm. Now all I smelled was air, but it was clean air. The only time Crown Heights ever smelled clean was when it rained.

The ocean, the ocean, the ocean. I tried summoning the salt-water smell from my memory of Sandy Hook's Double Vision Beach, where I'd shared a jug of Almaden wine with Sarah as we watched the sun go down.

Men shouting in Yiddish brought me back to reality. Two Chasidic men ran by with their shoulders hunched. For once, their wide-brimmed black hats seemed practical.

Two black umbrellas trotted by.

Umbrellas . . . hmmm . . . I'd lost mine when the billy-club boys had thrown us out of our last place. My landlord sold them for a dollar at his stationery store, but the dollar always seemed better spent on food.

Food . . . The acids in my stomach started churning at the very thought of it. When was the last time I'd eaten? I couldn't remember.

I pulled my arms inside and nearly slipped backward on the wet floor. Reluctantly, I closed the window, then turned my electric heater around, hoping it would dry things up.

I surveyed my kitchen. I had a half loaf of two-day-old Italian bread from Uncle Pete's, a third of a can of Bustelo coffee, and a drawer full of non-dairy creamers I'd swiped from the kosher-dairy place. The last item from Mom's most recent care package, one can of asparagus, sat in the cupboard. I'd only recently found out that asparagus's natural color was green, not the puke-yellow of the canned stuff Mom hoarded. I always saved the canned asparagus for last, when I was desperate.

Even though Uncle Pete and Hector ran a Puerto Rican deli, they always put out a shelf full of freshly-baked Italian bread. In the morning when it arrived, the loaves were perfectly crunchy on the outside and soft like cotton candy on the inside. They went for thirty cents each. You could buy a whole loaf of Wonder Bread for fifty cents, but that stuff paled in comparison to the soft, crusty Italian bread that smelled so inviting as it was being unloaded from the delivery truck. Freshly baked bread—lord, was there anything better than that?

But I never bought the loaves fresh; instead, I'd ask Hector if he had any day-old ones, and he'd usually give me a loaf or two for free. Free overruled fresh.

Making my first cup of coffee always felt like a holy moment. I'd fill the basket of the Mr. Coffee just a little too full so it would be deep and dark, breathing in the smell of the Bustelo or Folger's—whichever had been cheaper. Today, it was the Bustelo.

When it was ready, I poured it to the brim of the "Virginia is for Lovers" coffee mug Mom had wrapped in underwear ten sizes too big and added to a care package months earlier. Then I stirred in a packet of the dry creamer. I didn't care for its cheap chemical taste, but it, too, was free, as I'd swiped two pockets full when the guy at the dairy counter had been ignoring me as usual. (Most of the local merchants did, now that I was wearing Levi's.) Every so often Yehudah would appear, my tiny guardian angel, and scold the offending Chasid in Yiddish for giving me the cold shoulder—but he was only one angel, and there were a lot of shops on Kingston Avenue.

I didn't bother slicing the Italian bread, which was two days old at this point. I tore off a big chunk and soaked it in my coffee. When it was soft and wet, I crammed it into my mouth, dripping coffee down my neck. If I waited too long, the bread would collapse into my cup, and I'd have to eat it with a spoon.

I sat on the itchy plaid couch and turned on the black-and-white television. It got only a few channels, but luckily, a *Love Boat* rerun was on. It was the episode where John Ritter dresses as a woman—a pretty convincing one—to snag a spot on the ship. I laughed at the sight of him.

"Not bad, John!" I said out loud to no one.

I never watched the news, which I knew was filled with

shootings, muggings, fires—things I saw for myself on a stroll down Eastern Parkway.

One can of asparagus and Hector's day-old bread wasn't going to get me far. The kosher markets on Kingston sold canned tuna fish for ninety-nine unaffordable cents. A loaf of sliced bread that I could get at Hector and Pete's for sixty cents was a dollar at the Chasids, and anyway, I was beginning to suspect that I wasn't getting the same price as the regulars. Once, as I watched the red-faced Chasid with the bushy brown beard check out an old lady, I'm almost positive I saw him slide her some change when she paid for a loaf with a dollar bill.

I'd felt powerful when I'd thrown away my maxiskirt, but now all I felt was hungry.

I pulled on my jeans and the black wool pea coat Danny had given me. It was pretty much the worst thing to wear in the rain. It was warm, but when the wool got wet, it felt like an itchy-soggy Brillo pad.

A few roaches scattered as I grabbed a garbage bag from under the sink. I winced. Hector had given me his "secret potion" roach spray, but all it seemed to do was make them mad. What did they want with me, anyway? Surely they knew by now that I didn't have much that was edible.

Using the garbage bag as a kind of awning, I walked to the pay phone in front of Uncle Pete's and called Fagee.

"You still going to Key Food?"

"Did you run out of tampons or something? It's pouring out!"

"I ran out of food!"

"*Sheet!* Stop eating until it stops raining. I'll come by when it calms down."

A Chasidic woman carrying a large umbrella and a bag of groceries walked by. I saw a cardboard carton of eggs on top.

Eggs. I hadn't eaten an egg since I'd left Redbeard's house. Bela had served them on Sundays, baked with tomatoes. The dish was closer to a casserole than the fried eggs I'd loved over well with hash browns at Denny's.

"It's called *shakshuka*," she'd explained.

Whatever it was called, it tasted good.

When the woman noticed me staring at her groceries, she steered a wide berth around me. I was tempted to say "tzedakah!" and put my hand out, but that privilege seemed reserved for Jews who were religious, or at least pretended to be.

I walked into Uncle Pete's. Hector was behind the counter.

"Got any day-olds, *papi*?"

"*M'ita, mami*. Not today, but it's raining. I'm sure to have some tomorrow. I got an old *New York Post* and some platanos."

"I'll take them!"

I'd always been mystified by the large green bananas they sold at the markets on Nostrand Avenue. *Why wouldn't they wait until they turned yellow?* I'd wondered, until Hector had explained the difference between the bananas I'd grown up with and plantains, which had to be cooked before they could be eaten. He and Uncle Pete peeled, sliced, and fried them on a hot plate in the back of the store, then laid them out on paper towels and sprinkled them with salt. One morning Hector gave me a few slices to try, and—holy crap—they tasted better than french fries.

He put a handful into a small brown bag and whirled it through the window in the bulletproof glass as if it were a bag of pot.

Back on the street, a group of children in yellow raincoats followed their mother like four little ducklings. The mother's long black sheitel was drenched and it made me wonder how long sheitel hair took to dry. Longer than mine?

"Hello," I said to her, feeling a sudden sense of camaraderie among the umbrella-less.

She nodded and quickened her pace, hustling her ducklings away from me as they craned their necks to stare.

"It's not contagious," I whispered loud enough to be heard.

Drenched to the bone, I started peeling my clothes off the second I shut the door behind me, laying out my coat, sweat-shirt, sweatpants, even my underwear on my useless radiator. My bag of fried platanos had taken on water as well, but that didn't stop me from inhaling them along with the last of the cold coffee.

Growing up, we'd always eaten until we were full, some-times well beyond that point. Now, feeling full felt like an accomplishment. I'd filled the void in my stomach. For now.

I turned on the shower and waited a few minutes for the hot water to come up. It never got hot and steamy the way I loved it, only just a little warmer than warm. I slathered up the last bar of Ivory soap from one of my Mom's care packages. In New Jersey, we'd always used no-name brands of soap, or tiny bars Mom had stolen from hotels. A class act like Ivory made me feel rich.

When I was done, I pulled on Fagee's old bathrobe, which I'd never bothered to tell her she'd left, and sat on the window-sill. It was really starting to pour.

Where did the wild dogs go when it rained?

I looked at the unfinished painting on my easel. I'd been working on a portrait of a blond female bodybuilder but had run out of pink and orange paint, the two colors I needed for her flesh. All I had left were black and blue—which seemed almost poetic.

I pulled a cigarette out, lit it, and smoked slowly, pondering the bodybuilder. I had particularly enjoyed painting the muscles on her arms and her long, curly, yellow hair. A few days earlier, when I'd stroked midnight-blue into her left quadriceps, I'd felt something stir inside of me. I hadn't even heard Fagee come into the room.

"And who is this creature?" she'd asked.

"I'm calling her Wonder Woman."

"Ah, Wonder Woman. I know this woman, but her hair is black, no?"

"Yeah . . . but—"

"This is a self portrait."

"What!?"

"It is you, silly idiot! It is who you want to be."

That had ruined my mojo.

Now, looking at the canvas, I touched my bicep. Soft. The closest I ever got to exercising was pacing around the living room or walking along Eastern Parkway. But maybe Fagee was right. Who wouldn't want to feel powerful?

It had been easy to impress people with my artistic skills in Rumson. I'd glued pieces of plastic onto the sunglasses of my portrait of Tom Petty, and everyone in my art class had praised it for being "three-dimensional." In Crown Heights, nobody cared that I fancied myself an artist. When I'd asked Bela if she wanted me to teach her children art, she'd replied, "My children study Torah, not art."

I squeezed a smidgen of the navy blue onto the plastic plate I used as a palette, then dipped my brush in and swirled some of it against the lighter blue of the background.

I don't know how long I stood pondering muscle girl, but at some point I heard a car beeping outside and looked out the window. I saw the black town car of Fagee's car service.

Oh, yeah. We'd made a plan a few days earlier to skip the grocery store in our hood in favor of the Key Food on Nostrand Avenue. Any chance I got to hitch a ride out of Chasidland was cause for celebration. I skipped down the stairs and nearly leaped into the back of the town car.

"Ugh, get that itchy wet thing off me!" Fagee cried when my damp peacoat brushed against her.

"I missed you, too!"

We drove past the boys' yeshiva and the last of the Chasidic townhouses. Closer to Nostrand, there was a big empty lot strewn with garbage and old tires. Two ragged alley cats huddled together in one of the tires.

"*Awww*, cute. They're keeping each other warm," I said.

"Those street cats? They would scratch your eyes out if they had a chance."

"At least they have each other."

We passed an abandoned building, the boards over its windows covered in graffiti. Someone had painted "Hello Brooklyn" in red across one of them. A teenage boy in short cornrows walked two large gray pit bulls, one with white spots on its chest like a cow. Cow-spot stopped to sniff the dirt around the fenced-in abandoned building. He lifted his leg. When the boy whistled, both dogs trotted after him.

"Nice to see someone with pets," I said, determined to be cheerful.

"The drug dealers keep those things for protection. Scary *sheet*."

I'd never seen a pit bull before I got to Crown Heights. Fagee had told me she'd heard that the dealers removed their vocal chords and trained them to kill on command; you'd never hear them coming. These were a far cry from the pedigree show dogs of Rumson.

On Nostrand, we passed a West Indian market advertising breadfruit (whatever that was) and a roti joint with a sign outside that said, "Curry goat." Next was a takeout Chinese restaurant, a reggae record store, and then I saw the large Key Food sign.

The driver eased toward the curb. Chasids never shopped at the Key Food. If they'd accidentally wandered near it, the big signs in the window touting oxtails and pork knuckles would have sent them scurrying.

"What the hell is a pork knuckle anyway?" I asked Fagee. She shrugged.

"You haven't lived till you've had pork knuckle stew!" said the driver. "Ain't you never had ham hocks?"

Fagee and I exchanged a look.

"I've tried oxtails!" I said proudly as I stepped out of the car, narrowly averting a pile of dog shit sitting like a welcome mat in front of the entrance.

"Fifteen minutes!" Fagee shouted at the driver as we each grabbed a rusty metal shopping cart.

"Ham hocks and beans!" he shouted back.

The Nostrand Key Food was a major contrast to the markets in Chasidland. Staples such as halvah and challah were nowhere to be found. Instead, there were aisles full of mangoes, plantains, and Spam. And, unlike the markets on Kingston, they would take Mom's coupons. I'd been mortified by her obsessive use of them when I was growing up, but now I couldn't afford to ignore the savings.

Three-for-a-dollar StarKist tuna in oil and four-for-a-dollar Ronzoni macaroni . . . I'd been known to make a month of meals out of these, employing endless variations: macaroni and tuna with mustard, macaroni and tuna with peas, macaroni and tuna with butter . . . Sometimes I'd swipe condiments from the kosher pizza joint and add those to the mix. Macaroni and burnt ketchup sauce with peas was a specialty.

Ronzoni had a product they called "Natural Spaghetti Sauce." I'd seen it advertised on TV as if it were a gourmet thing. Mom's coupons would get it down to two jars for a dollar—cheap, but not as cheap as the tomato paste, so I opted for the paste. What could be more natural than tomato paste and water?

This was not the bright, fluorescent-lit supermarkets of New Jersey, where old women in hairnets offered you free samples of turkey chili or pasta salad in little paper cups. We passed an aisle with a broken bottle of ketchup on the floor, its contents spread out like blood. In Jersey, spills quickly prompted an announcement: "Clean-up in Aisle Three." I'd never heard an intercom at Key Food.

"I'm buying avocados for my face," Fagee said.

I followed her toward the produce section. The floor was scattered with onion skins and rotten fruit that shoppers had tossed out as they picked through for the good pieces. I grabbed a bag of yellow onions and said, "I'll meet you at the checkout."

"Buy something fresh for once in your life besides fucking onions," Fagee snapped. "You only eat pasta and canned *sheet.*"

"Coming from the woman who buys vegetables to put on her face—"

"Avocado is fruit, no? Not vegetable?"

I shrugged and wheeled my squeaky cart toward the frozen section. A large woman with braids that hung to her ass filled her cart with packages of frozen shrimp.

"Big party?" I said.

She looked at me, startled. I don't think anybody had seen a White shopper there since the last time I'd been in.

She smiled. "Just loading up," she said. "They're on special."

One of the last times I'd gone grocery shopping with Mom, she'd wiped out an entire section of Mrs. Paul's fish sticks for the same reason. She'd always seemed to get enormous satisfaction out of grocery shopping. As she prepared for a trip to the store, she'd lay out her many grocery bags on the kitchen table and smile like the Cheshire cat. I never understood why. We had so much food that the garage became a giant pantry and Dad had to park the truck in the driveway.

．‥＊＇‥．．＊＊‥

Fagee dropped me off. I climbed the stairs, dumped my bags out on my rickety kitchen table, and surveyed my haul. Besides the bag of onions and twelve cans of tomato paste, I'd scored a pack of sliced American cheese, eight boxes of pasta, six cans of tuna, a gallon of milk, a pound of whipped butter, four cans of red beans, a bottle of Mazola corn oil, two packages of frozen peas, and a dozen eggs. The receipt read $9.06.

I must have been smiling because I felt the tightness in my face. *No sirree*, I heard my father saying as I stared at the mountain of groceries. *We won't go hungry this month.*

CHAPTER 36

TILLYTOWN

Three months after Tilly called the housing agency, when early spring had begun to warm the air to a pleasant fifty degrees, they came to inspect. Not only did they make my landlord—who liked to pretend he was deaf—turn my gas back on, but they also made him fix my broken window, my wobbly handrail, and the leak in my bedroom ceiling.

I felt downright victorious.

Tilly took me out to celebrate.

We'd planned to meet outside the Seventy-Second Street subway station, and when I emerged, at first I didn't recognize her. She'd pulled her wild Afro into two neat braids behind her head. Her robust figure was hidden under a black trench coat.

"You look like a secret agent!"

"Didn't you know? The phone room is just my cover."

Tilly took me to a nearby movie theater to see *Star Trek: The Wrath of Khan*. William Shatner—Kirk—was now an admiral. Spock was the captain of the *Enterprise*. Ricardo Montalban, whom I had loved on *Fantasy Island*, played the evil Khan. The movie ended with the death of Spock.

When the lights came up, I was crying.

"I love Spock," I said, swiping at my tears. "Can we stay and see it again?"

"You old softie," she giggled. And then she kissed me.

She tasted like popcorn and Dr Pepper-flavored Bonne Bell lip balm.

Everything about Tilly seemed exotic. She bought musk oil from a Muslim man at a folding table near where we stood and wore just enough that it was hard to tell where the musk started, and her sweat left off.

She took me to a basement joint with checkered tablecloths that looked like a cross between a diner and a bar. Men sat at the bar drinking beers across from families shoved into booths. It was called Jackson Hole.

"There are only two things to order here: burgers and breakfast."

When the waiter came to our table, Tilly asked for a cheeseburger.

"Same for you?" the waiter asked me.

"I don't mix my meat and my dairy," I said, to Tilly's obvious amusement. "Can I have a burger with onions?"

"Onions cooked or raw?"

"Cooked?"

"How do you want your burgers?"

"Uh . . . round."

"Shut up, dum-dum," said Tilly. "I'll have mine medium, and she'll have hers well done."

In Jersey, Mom had always cooked our burgers until they lived up to the name we had given them: *hockey pucks*. When we went out to eat, we rarely ordered burgers, and if we did, we didn't specify the temperature. A kosher burger was always well done. It's all I'd ever had.

When the waiter walked away, I said, "I've never been asked so many questions about a burger."

"You'll get used to it."

The burgers were so huge that I couldn't get my mouth open wide enough to take a bite. When I tried, juice and onions ran down my chin and pooled on my plate. I set the thing down and cut it in half.

"Wimp!"

"I can't eat it any other way. This is, like, food for a week!"

"You can always take some of it home. Now, then. How do you feel about Bruce Lee? *Enter the Dragon* is playing uptown."

"Who is Bruce Lee?"

Tilly laughed so hard, she spit out a french fry.

CHAPTER 37

HARRIET AND
THE EGG NOODLES

I wore a pair of my father's old Hanes boxer shorts and one of his worn-out undershirts with the trademark yellow pit stains. I'd swiped them from his dresser drawer before I ran away. I didn't anoint any significance to this action, beyond the fact that I liked the feel of the soft cotton Mom had run through the basement washing machine a hundred times.

I was cooking breakfast for Tilly, who was sitting on the couch wearing nothing but a large Bruce Lee T-shirt. I dumped a packet of egg noodles in boiling water. *What's wrong with egg noodles for breakfast?* Even they looked beautiful this morning.

It was the first time Tilly had spent the night, and I hadn't been sure what to hope for. She had a boyfriend, after all. We'd kissed a few times, but nothing more. In the middle of the night, I heard her rise from the couch and push open my bedroom door. She crawled into bed with me and whispered in my ear, "How long do you want to keep playing this game?"

We kissed for what felt a little bit like forever, then I buried my face between her large, wondrous charcoal breasts, breathing in musk oil and Castile soap: two new scents for my new life. Tilly pushed me back and straddled me. Even in bed she made it clear who was boss.

In the early hours of the morning, she curled up behind me to spoon. I fell asleep trying to remember the last time I'd felt like this: safe.

Breakfast ended up being a concoction of noodles mixed with canned tuna, peas, heavy cream, salt, and pepper. I dumped the concoction into two bowls, and we sat on the couch eating it with spoons.

"White people cook the weirdest shit!"

"Coming from someone who doesn't eat anything that doesn't come with chopsticks or a bun . . ."

We ate in silence for a few minutes, then Tilly changed the subject. "Some of the phone-room gang lives in the George Washington Hotel. It's cheap, clean, private bath—"

"How cheap? Everything I see in the paper is really pricey, plus they require a month's rent and a month's security up front."

"Well, nothing's gonna be as cheap as what you got here, but your neighbors might seem a little happier to see you."

"Maybe. But I'm stuck out here till I turn eighteen."

"It may interest you to know that most parents don't really want to send their *relatively* sane daughters to reform school."

"I don't have *most* parents. Trust me on that."

There was a knock on the door.

"What now!?" I blurted, then got up and stuck my head out the window. My mother and father, always paragons of timing, were standing there with grocery bags.

"Shit, it's my parents!" Visions of Mom chasing Mag down the street with a paring knife flashed across my retinas.

I walked slowly down the stairs, while Tilly ducked into the other room.

"Surprise!"

"Mom, you can't just show up without at least calling the deli and leaving a message for me. It's ten o'clock in the morning!"

"Since when does a mother have to make an appointment—with a deli, no less—to see her own daughter?" She pushed past me and waddled penguin-style up the stairs. By the time she reached the twelfth step, she was completely out of breath, but somehow she completed the trek, hobbled into the kitchen, and dumped the contents of the grocery bags onto the table.

The haul was typical: a bag of bagels marked "day old," an Entenmann's cake marked "on sale," a bag of bruised Macintosh apples, a large kosher salami, three boxes of matzohs, and a plastic grocery bag filled with Burger King mustard packets.

Tilly opened the door of my bedroom and walked into the kitchen. She had pulled on a pair of sweatpants to complement Bruce Lee. "Nice to meet you, Mrs. Ross!" she said brightly. "I've heard a lot about you!" She held out her hand, but my mother just stared at it as if it were a ham-and-cheese sandwich.

Tilly dropped her hand but maintained her brightness. "My name's Tilly!"

My father walked into the kitchen with two more grocery bags, put them on the counter, and turned to Tilly. "And . . . how do you know my daughter?" he queried.

"Actually . . . I'm her boss."

"Do you want a bagel?" my mom said, pushing a bag of semi-frozen Lender's bagels toward Tilly.

"No . . . thank you," Tilly said, reaching for the coat and bag she'd tossed on a chair the night before. "I'm going to leave you to have your family time."

"Be right back," I said without looking either of my parents in the eye and proceeded to walk Tilly down the stairs.

"Don't leave me with them," I whispered when we reached the door, momentarily blocking her way.

"You are on your own, honey. You told me about that kitchen-knife incident and I'm not sticking around to get stabbed like a piece of kosher chicken. You weren't exaggerating—your parents are scary." She kissed me hard on the mouth. "Good luck. Now be a big girl and go deal with your peeps."

And . . . she was gone. I hung my shoulders as I dragged myself back upstairs and into the kitchen.

"I leave you alone for five seconds, and you have a *schvartze* in your house! This is what I send the rabbi checks for? Why not just stab your mother in the heart!?"

"Mom! I told you to stop sending that asshole money. He hasn't done shit for me!"

"Language! You know I don't like those kinds of words."

Schvartze was fine, apparently.

I sat down at the table, tore off a piece of bagel, and shoved it in my mouth. It tasted like freezer burn.

I wanted to tell my mother about the billy-club men, being homeless in Port Authority, what the cop had done, and how both landlords had tried freezing me out. I wanted to tell her that I'd been sick to death for two weeks and it was Tilly who had come over to take care of me. I wanted to explain that the woman she'd just dismissed with one ugly epithet was the first person who'd made me feel safe since I ran away.

But I didn't bother. I knew my rage was bigger than my mother's heart. "You talk about stabbing, Mom? It's a good thing my *friend* left before you could try to stab her, like you did Magnolia!"

"If we get another Hitler, do you really think your *schvartze friend* will protect you?"

"Yes! Actually, I do!"

I looked over at Dad. He was chewing on something. He was always chewing on something.

"You want some Sanka to wash down whatever is in your mouth, Dad?"

He nodded, and I ran some water into a saucepan and set it on the stove to boil.

He came over and sat at the table, tore off a piece of half-frozen bagel and shoved it in his mouth. Choking it down, he said, "Would it kill you . . . would it really *kill you* to have some Jewish friends!?"

After I poured the hot water over the Sanka, I emptied a Sweet'N Low packet into his cup, stirred it a couple of times, and set it on the table next to him. He dunked the rest of his bagel into the coffee and shoved it in his mouth.

"Marty!" Mom barked as if on autopilot. "You have to chew!"

I walked into the living room, grabbed the two bowls of soggy tuna and noodles, and dumped them in the trash.

CHAPTER 38

I AIN'T NO UNCLE TOM

It's odd to say that a drug dealer was a gentleman, but that's exactly what Tom was.

I met Tom early one evening, on the pedestrian island of Eastern Parkway near Franklin. The closest I ever got to enjoying nature in Brooklyn was appreciating the spindly trees along the median. That day, I was trying valiantly to revel in the return of spring while ignoring the broken bottles and the battlefield of dog poop.

I'd been on my way home from work when the conductor had announced that the 2 was making express stops only, and would jump from Franklin Avenue to Utica, skipping Kingston. I weighed my options. Outside the Franklin station, there were always a slew of drug dealers, but it was still a safer bet than Utica at night. The one time I'd exited Utica after sundown, someone had tried to hold me up for my subway token. A friggin' subway token!

It would be dark in half an hour. I chose Franklin.

As I climbed the subway stairs, a group of men wearing their hair in various versions of dreadlocks stood openly sharing a spliff. They looked at me and whistled.

I passed an elderly Black man with a cane. (At the time, anyone over fifty was "elderly" to me; he was probably in his sixties.) He wore his silver hair very short and had on a pair of shiny brown leather shoes, suspenders, and dress slacks, into which he'd tucked a creamy button-down shirt. He reminded me of Fred Astaire. Something about his quiet elegance made me slow my pace.

"Good afternoon to you!" he said in a thick Jamaican accent.

"And to you too, sir!" I replied, a bit confused that I suddenly sounded British.

"Don't worry about them, man. They just young fools!" he said, gesturing toward the half-dozen Rastas who'd whistled. He beckoned me over to where he stood and, despite my desire to get home, I went. "I'm Tom," he said, extending his slender hand, "but I ain't no Uncle Tom." Missing the reference, I could only assume that he wanted me to know he was no one's uncle.

"I'm Rossi, but I'm not Italian," I replied.

He gestured toward a nearby bench, and we sat. I'd like to say I remember most of what Tom and I talked about that afternoon, but what I mostly remember is that he was one of the first adults I'd met who seemed to care about what I was saying.

"And how did a white girl like you end up here?"

"My parents thought if they shipped me off to the rabbis, some of their holiness might rub off."

He shook his head. "That's foolishness, girl!"

While we were speaking, I noticed that the young men who passed us lowered their heads and nodded at Tom.

He answered my question before I asked it.

"I been here a long time—way before they came on the scene. They paying their respect!"

Tom scratched out his phone number on a piece of scrap paper and gave it to me. "If you ever in trouble, girl . . . ya call me!"

I walked away with a new ally.

It never occurred to me that Tom, sitting thirty feet away

from the busiest drug-dealing corner in Brooklyn as if to supervise the activities, was in fact supervising the activities.

Sweet, gentlemanly Tom was the boss.

After my public chat with Tom, the young men who gathered at the corner of Franklin and Eastern Parkway didn't yell vulgar things about my body parts anymore, or hiss, or make kissing noises. They just stood quietly and let me pass. I started not to mind when the train mysteriously went express, and I had to get out at Franklin. Sometimes I got out there whether I had to or not, just so I could stop and chat with Tom.

One sunny afternoon, Tom patted the space next to him on the bench and said, "White woman! Time you know what Black men fear!"

"The men I see around here don't seem afraid of anything," I said, sliding down next to him.

"Oh, no, girl. These men on the corner, they got big fear. That's why they strut around like roosters, man!" He flapped his arms like a chicken. "They afraid of a crazy woman. Not angry, mind you. Gotta be real crazy."

"Why?"

"A crazy woman, she cut a man's balls with a razor blade . . . she scratch his eyes out . . . bite him. A crazy woman is worse than a gun. Worse than a wild dog! Girl, if ya ever get in trouble . . . just make the man think you is fucking cuckoo!"

I considered my outfit of the day: signature zebra-print spandex pants, black Clash T-shirt, and Frye boots. "I can do that," I said, nodding.

•···•·•�····•·· ··

One day on Kingston, a short, pudgy, twenty-something Chasid with a peach-fuzz beard approached me. "Hello!" he said. "I am Hershel, but my friends call me Hershey, like the chocolate bar!"

A Chasid? Talking to me?

"Hi, Hershey, what's up?"

As he shifted from foot to foot, I caught a very potent whiff of sweat and body odor. "I thought maybe you might want to go out sometime," he said.

I thought quickly. "I have a boyfriend," I said.

"That's okay, that's okay," he chattered. "Let's be friends. My father is a pharmacist, and I always have lots of drugs."

I remembered Danny telling me about the source of his free Valium. "The pharmacist's kid is a major-league nerd, even by Lubavitch standards," he'd said. "That's like . . . a nuclear nerd."

As I stood there, Hershel reached into his pocket and pulled out a handful of different-colored pills and held them out to me.

"What are they?" I asked, cupping my hands so he could spill them in.

"I don't know. Valium, uppers . . . I just take one and see what happens."

As I shoved the pills in my coat pocket, I thought about my evening. It happened that I was planning on visiting Tilly in Manhattan, up at 109th and Broadway, where she was staying with her boyfriend Bobby.

I figured 109th and Broadway couldn't be any more dangerous then Franklin Avenue, but it was unfamiliar territory for me and I wanted to get an early start.

"Look, man," I said to my new friend and dealer, "I have to go now. I'm headed to the Upper West Side later, and I have to get ready. For my *date*."

"You can't go up there alone!" he cried. "I'll get my sister's car!"

I couldn't imagine what sort of protection this mousy little guy could be, but riding in a car instead of taking the train—well, that was irresistible. I'd have said yes to a date with Bigfoot if he had a car.

"Pick me up at eight!"

At 10:30, I was pacing around my apartment when he knocked on my door.

"Sorry I'm late," he said. "I had to wait for my parents to fall asleep so I could sneak out."

"Aren't you, like, twenty-four?"

Ignoring my question, he rattled on. "We can take the train right to 110th. It's only a block walk!"

"What happened to your sister's car?"

"It will be okay!"

I followed Hershey to the subway, and we took one he thought stopped at 110th and Broadway. It turned out we were supposed to switch trains at some point; the one we were on wound up depositing us at 110th and Lennox, which was not the same sort of neighborhood at all.

With my mess of blond hair, Frye boots, and a tiny, nervous Chasid next to me, I stood out like a neon sign flashing, "Kill me!"

All we had to do, he told me, was keep walking west until we reached Broadway. "No problem."

It was a dark and spooky walk across 110th Street, along the wall bordering Central Park. A lot of the apartment buildings' lights were out, and a slew of streetlights were, too—their globes broken and the glass littering the street along with other trash. I nearly fell over a stack of old tires and barely avoided piles of dog poop I couldn't see until I was practically on top of them. *Thank God for Frye boots.*

Hershey marched a few steps ahead of me as if he were leading a parade. So much for chivalry.

The glow from one of the only working streetlights kept me from tripping over an overturned trashcan. I'd no sooner recovered from that near-miss when I noticed a half-dozen young Black men sitting on a fence watching us. One of them hissed at me, and I was so startled, I think I screamed.

I blinked and tried to focus. In spite of the sticky summer air, one of the men was wearing a black winter ski cap that must have been sweltering. His arms were scrawled with home-made-looking tattoos. The shirtless guy next to him wore a bicycle chain around his neck. In the center was a wiry-looking guy a bit shorter than the others, wearing a black tank top. He nudged the guy next to him, who had a blue bandanna tied around his head, and they both laughed. I remembered Tom trying to explain gang colors to me and wished I'd paid more attention—not that it would have done much good.

I think they would have let us pass if Hershey had not suddenly thrust his hand into his inside vest pocket and shouted, "You better watch out, I have a gun!"

"*Ooohhh*," came my audible groan. We were toast.

I saw the wiry guy shake his head and didn't want to think what that meant.

I picked up my pace, which forced Hershey to keep up—but very soon I sensed the men following us. *We should run like hell*, I thought, but before I could communicate this to Hershey, I felt a sharp pain, then a stinging in my right calf.

Blood dripped down my leg. I didn't know what it felt like to be shot, but I hoped it was a rock that had hit me and not a bullet.

With no cars, no lights, and no other people on the street, there wasn't much we could do but run. Hershey bolted off the sidewalk into the street, yelling, "Taxi! Taxi!"

I saw the curtains in a few apartment windows flutter, but no lights went on, and I knew nobody was calling 911. Nobody helped a stranger in the night in New York in 1982.

I thought of Tom's advice: *Girl, if ya ever get in trouble . . . just make the man think you is fucking cuckoo!*

I had noticed that the wiry guy seemed to be the ringleader. *What would a crazy person do?* I turned around and ran full force right at him, almost knocking him over, and started jabbering like an idiot. "Did you ever have one of those days where everything is *just a little bit off*?" I screamed, "where all this *shit* is happening, and you don't know *why*?"

My tone was so high-pitched, and I was talking so fast that I sounded like I'd huffed helium. Then I reached into my pocket and pulled out a handful of pills. "*Here!* Take some drugs! I don't know what they are, but they make you high as hell. Anyway, so *my life kind of sucks, ya know*!? I don't even know why I'm here, but things happen and . . ."

On and on I went. Hershey had stopped trying to wave down cars and was staring at me like I had just stepped out of a spaceship.

Wiry Guy grabbed the pills and jammed them into his pocket; then stepped back as I continued to blabber away until, finally, exhausted, I shut up.

"White bitch, you crazy!" he said and smiled wide, showing off a gold front tooth.

"I know, I know! I've always been crazy! I come from a long line of crazy. My mother was crazy as hell. My grandmother too—"

He raised his hand to get me to shut up. "Okay, listen, you're all right, but your friend here disrespected us, so I have to at least hit him. Then we can walk you to where you're going so nobody else messes with you. But he has to walk behind us, cause I ain't protecting his ass."

"Okay," I said, throwing Hershey under the bus without a moment's hesitation. In fact, I wanted to ask if I could be the one to hit Hershey, who was just standing there, goggling at both of us.

Wiry Guy murmured something to his pals, and Blue Bandanna Guy ran over and punched Hershey in the side of the head.

Hershey started screaming, "*HELP! HELP!*"

I saw a venetian blind go up a few inches, but still no lights went on.

Without another word, the young men surrounded me, and we walked down the street with Hershey trailing behind us, all the way to Tilly's boyfriend's building.

"Um . . . this is my . . . stop," I said.

"Let's go on in then," Wiry Guy said, and escorted Hershey and me all the way up to the apartment while his pals waited downstairs.

•···•·•▪....•· ··

When she opened the door, without even asking me who the hell the Black guy and the Chasid were, Tilly hugged me. The now familiar scent of Castile soap and musk oil were like heaven. I drank in her wild Afro jetting out around her pretty face and—as I always did in her presence—felt safe.

"Hey. Nice to meet you," she said to Wiry Guy without missing a beat. She shook his hand, and he nodded. She did the same with Hershey, and I wondered what she must be thinking about the weird little "Mod Squad" I'd assembled. Nothing seemed to faze Tilly.

Wiry Guy scribbled his name—Kurtis—and phone number on a piece of paper and gave it to me. "Let's go out sometime."

"She's got a boyfriend!" yelled Hershey as I walked Wiry Guy to the door.

"Thanks for everything!" I said.

"No worries, but you gotta ditch that little guy, he's a dumbass who's lucky he didn't get his ass kicked down the block."

I looked at Hershey and smiled, then back at Kurtis. "He's gone."

•···•·•▪....•· ··

The next time I saw Tom, I told him what had happened.

"Girl, you graduated from Street University!" he said, clapping.

"What happened to that blood clot?" he asked.

Blood clot?

Hershey walked up to me on Kingston the next day and pulled his jacket open to reveal a knife the size of a small saw. "I'll be ready next time!" he said defiantly.

"Hershey . . . be careful with that thing or it's gonna wind up sticking out of your ass!" As a group of Chasidic men rushed past, I added, "Do me a favor. Next time you see me, do like the rest of your brothers and pretend I'm air!"

With that, I spun around and walked the five blocks to my apartment. To the horror of everyone I passed, I sang Lou Reed's "Walk on the Wild Side," out-of-tune and as loud as I could manage.

CHAPTER 39

WOLF TAKES KINGSTON

Fagee rarely came in from Boro Park anymore. Danny got a new job and was actually working nights when he told his parents he was. Tilly got promoted to the night shift and seemed to spend a lot of her days sleeping. As a consequence of all of this, I was spending far too many nights sitting on the windowsill smoking and watching the dogs.

I called Wolf, my hairdresser pal from Jersey.

"Your hair must be so ugly by now!" he said. "Meet me at Vidal Sassoon!"

The salon was in the General Motors Building on Fifty-Ninth and Fifth Avenue—yet another new and very different neighborhood for me. The smattering of homeless people begging for handouts didn't put a damper on the absolute *poshness* of it all: the Plaza Hotel, with its uniformed doormen opening taxi doors for fur-coated ladies; the horse-drawn carriages lined up to trot tourists around Central Park in old-world style . . . I thought if I breathed in deeply enough, I'd catch the scent of money.

"Never go into Central Park after sundown," Sonya had warned me. But looking at the fancy people lined up to buy hot pretzels from carts or have their portraits done by street artists, it didn't look dangerous at all.

When I reached the GM Building, I walked down a concrete staircase, as Wolf had directed me to do, and found the salon. Four receptionists faced me, frantically answering the phones and jabbering away about appointment times.

I waited for one of them to pause and said, "I'm Wolf's friend."

"Color department is in the back," she responded as I admired her hairstyle, which involved shaved sides and a spiked top.

The salon seemed as vast as a gymnasium and, rather than the bright colors I was used to seeing in Jersey salons, it was completely done up in shades of brown. The effect was otherworldly. I passed a cutting department chock-full of hairdressers fluttering and snipping away at smart women in smocks. Then came a barber's department, full of businessmen and much more old-school. Next was a long row of shampoo bowls—every one occupied by a foamy head—and finally, all the way at the back of the salon, was the L-shaped color department. Four stations lined the short side of the L, and another ten stretched out around the corner. The heads of the women who occupied these chairs bloomed with cascades of folded aluminum foil. One or two sported pink rods that reminded me of Sonya's home perms. I noticed that one of the women, who sipped coffee as she waited for her hair to cook, wore a diamond ring on each finger of her left hand. The effect was blinding.

I spotted Wolf, who was wearing a pair of pointy-toed lizard cowboy boots, tight purple jeans, and a black V-neck sweater. His long, curly blond hair and matching beard and mustache made him look a bit like Buffalo Bill—if Buffalo Bill had worn purple jeans.

"Oh, honey," he moaned as he gave me a quick hug. "You are so ugly. Sit down in this chair and let me fix you right now!"

Over the next two hours, Wolf highlighted my hair, then painted it with sideways stripes. One of his assistants was then pressed into service to wash me out and tuck me under a dryer. Finally, Wolf ushered me back to his chair to finish off my look

with a blow dryer and fancy round brush. When he was satisfied, he whirled me around and handed me a mirror so I could
see the back of my head.

"Well?" he purred.

I looked like a blond zebra.

"Fabulous, isn't it?"

I had to admit, it really was.

"Wait up front, honey—read a magazine or something. I
gotta do up a few more ladies and then I'll take you out."

I did as he suggested, and after an hour or so of catching
up on celebrity gossip, Wolf appeared.

"Let's get our dinner from the salad bar at the deli across
the street, then go out to your place to eat it," he said. "I'm
gonna spend the night, and if you don't like it, too bad."

"I like it, I like it!"

Under a sign that read "Salad bar: $2.25," was the widest
array of ingredients I'd ever seen. I plotted how to cram whatever I could into my plastic container and really get my $2.25
worth. Lettuce, tomatoes, bean salad, three kinds of pasta salad,
artichoke hearts, egg salad, tuna salad, potato salad, carrot
sticks, slices of zucchini . . . Somehow I jammed it all in—and
still managed to shove red Jell-O into the corner.

When we got to the check out, the cashier put my salad on
a scale and announced, "Four dollars and fifty cents, please."

"But I thought it was two twenty-five!?"

"That's per pound, dear," Wolf said, slipping two dollars
into my hand. I fished out the balance from my pocket.

"If I'm going to Brooklyn, I need some vodka," Wolf said,
so we stopped off at a liquor store before descending into the
subway station.

At Kingston Avenue, we got off and weaved our way through
the throngs of bustling Chasidic men and women. It was just
before sundown Friday, so they were in a more than usual frantic
pre-Shabbos rush.

The same group of yeshiva students who'd made a wide arc to avoid me walked too close to Wolf and nearly banged into him.

"Excuse me!" he said. "I'm walking here."

When we'd made our way down Kingston and into my building, I double-locked the door and wedged the metal rod Hector had given me between the door and the base of the stairs.

Wolf took the stairs two steps at a time. "I love what you've done with the place," he said, raising an eyebrow at the milk crates.

"It's bohemian!"

He walked into the kitchen, opened the freezer, and pulled out an ice tray, which he promptly emptied into the sink. Then he filled two coffee mugs with cubes and poured in double shots of vodka. He found a can of Fresca in the fridge and poured that in, too.

"First, we're going to drink," he declared. "Then we're going to eat. Then we're going to drink some more, and then we are going to talk about how to get you out of this depressing neighborhood!"

The bottle of vodka was almost half gone when I heard someone knocking downstairs. I looked out the window, saw Robby, and ran down to let him in. As soon as I opened the door, he shot past me.

"Nice hair!" he shouted as he ran.

"Thanks!"

"Girlfriend! I had a fireman last night. A real fireman! 'Let me see your hose, honey,' I said, and—" When he saw Wolf, he stopped talking.

"Robby, this is Wolf. Wolf, Robby."

For a brief moment, Robby seemed tongue-tied. "Nice to meet you," he simpered. "Are you a friend of Rossi's? Well, I guess you must be or you wouldn't be here . . ."

"We're having vodka and Fresca," Wolf said. "Shall I pour you one?"

"Yes, please."

A few drinks later, I knew I wouldn't have to make up Fagee's old mattress for Wolf.

"I'm gonna check out Robby's renovation," he said to me on his way out the door behind his new friend, my old one. "Don't wait up."

"Not such a depressing neighborhood after all, eh!?" I sneered.

"I wouldn't go that far, dear . . . but even the most depressing neighborhoods have their distractions."

I pushed open the window and sat on the windowsill watching them run down the street. I shook my head, lit up a Marlboro Light, and blew smoke rings into the night.

Hector was pulling the gate down at the store. He looked up and saw me.

"Hola, *mami*."

"Hola, Hector! Do you like my new hairdo?" I twirled my head a few times to show off the stripes.

"You look wild, *mamita*! Like a cat . . . like a wildcat."

"I'm a zebra!"

"No, *mami*. You're what *ate* the zebra!"

CHAPTER 40

NO MORE DANIEL BOONE

They came in waves, the oxidized images that filled the filing cabinet in my head I'd labeled, "The end of my childhood."

One morning Danny came by. I invited him up for a cup of coffee.

"It's 9:45. Don't you have to go to work?" I asked.

"Didn't you hear? I'm independently wealthy."

"More like spoiled. You can't suck off Mommy and Daddy's tit forever."

We sat on the couch, and he put his feet up on the coffee table.

"The patrol beat up a mugger last night," he said. "Some *schvartze* was trying to take a lady's purse. They jumped out and nearly killed him."

"I'm not so sure *schvartze* is a good word, Danny. I don't like hearing it."

"*Schvartze*, matzo. . . . Your friend may be nice, but around here it's the *schvartzes* you have to be worried about."

"Everyone around here is so afraid of Black people. The only bad shit that has happened to me here has been at the hands of the Jews or the cops. *White* people."

As Danny sipped his black coffee with five sugars, I noticed that he seemed more nervous than usual. When he couldn't keep his legs still, he pulled his feet off the coffee table and planted them on the floor.

"There's a party at Izzy's tonight," he said. "Wanna come?"

"I'll pass."

"I'll be there."

"Who else?"

"Izzy's new girlfriend."

"*Nah.*"

"It'll be fun! Come on."

I looked at him and saw some sort of need in his eyes. "Why do you care so much? I never go to Izzy's."

"It's just that I'm going and . . . I miss you."

It was true that I hadn't seen a lot of Danny in recent weeks, but that was mainly because he'd been working in the city. Silly, nervous, giggly, party-hearty Danny had landed himself a real job at a magazine. He even had health insurance.

"Okay. . . I'll come. But only if you never leave me alone with that asshole."

⋅⋅⋅⋅⋅⋅⋅⋅⋅⋅⋅⋅⋅⋅⋅⋅

Danny picked me up that night in his sister's Nova, and we drove to Izzy's place.

"How many cars does your sister have?" I asked as I climbed in.

"She gets tired of stuff quickly."

I'd forgotten how dark Izzy's place was. I had to wait near the door for a minute until my eyes adjusted and I saw what was what.

"Jesus, Izzy, turn on another light."

When he flipped on the lamp near the door, I saw there was nobody else at this "party" but Izzy. And us.

"Where's Izzy's girlfriend?" I whispered to Danny, but before he could respond, Izzy said, "She'll be by later." Then he walked over to his stereo and put on a Rolling Stones album at full volume. When Mick started singing "Satisfaction," Izzy joined in. "He howled, dancing around as he sang."

Danny had taken a seat on Izzy's bed, and I sat down next to him. Even in the dim light, I saw that he was twitchy. I could almost hear his teeth chattering. What was scaring him—Izzy? From what he'd told me, Izzy had been pushing him around since they were kids. I could never figure out why Danny stayed in that friendship.

Izzy pulled a joint out of a pack of Marlboros and shouted, "Let's party!" He lit it up and offered it to me. "Ladies first."

I took a big drag.

"Take another drag, mama, and then pass it to Douchey Dan."

After my second drag, I felt everything in the room, including Mick Jagger, come crashing down around me. It was like a funnel had sucked it all up—the Grateful Dead poster on the wall, the water stains on the ceiling, the gross, soggy mattress under my butt—and slammed it all into my brain. I felt myself falling backward onto the bed.

When I opened my eyes, I was looking at the ceiling. The stains writhed around like something you'd see under a microscope. I heard voices.

Izzy said, "You go first."

I blinked my eyes and tried to focus. When I turned my head, Danny and Izzy stood over me. Neither of them wore pants.

Danny climbed onto the bed and straddled me. He rubbed himself, but his soft penis wouldn't respond. I couldn't move. I felt my body sinking into the mattress as Danny reached down and tried to force-feed his half-flaccid dick into me. I felt the pressure of it, felt it push me open—but it wasn't me anymore. My body wasn't mine. Whatever this was, it was happening to someone else. I tried moving my arms, but they were mush; puddles of pudding.

Everything felt wrong.

I tried to form words, but they wouldn't come. I wanted to focus on Danny's face, but it kept blurring and oozing. I saw four sets of eyes and none of them were looking at me.

"Shit," Danny said, and pulled away. He started massaging himself again, this time more frantically. His dick was so slim and white that it looked like a piece of chalk. For a moment, it seemed to glow in the dark as he frantically tugged at it.

"Just pretend she's a little boy!" Izzy shouted. "You like that, don't you, *faggot*!?"

Something about that word. That horrible-sounding word. In Jersey, I'd heard that word—*faggot*—just before a bunch of dumb jocks jumped on a kid they'd decided was gay and beat the shit out of him.

I forced myself to focus and, with the help of a shocking burst of adrenaline, I snapped out of my stupor. I jumped up like a jackrabbit, startling Danny, and tugged my jeans up from around my ankles. My Frye boots were still on, and I planted my feet wide so I wouldn't fall backward again.

Air. I need air. Got to get out.

I headed for the door but of course it was locked.

I remembered from my last visit: *Izzy has the key.*

"Be quiet! You'll wake my parents up!" Izzy growled, and for one mortifying moment, I obeyed him. *Yes, yes. Wouldn't want to wake the parents up.*

Then the absurdity of that thought kicked in and a scream formed in my chest. Just as I had the night I'd watched the mugging from my window, I wailed like a banshee. I don't know if I formed words or just howled syllables, but it was loud enough to wake the dead—or at least a couple of grownups. I pounded my fists against the door until the flesh on my knuckles tore, and I began to leave smudges of my own blood on the dingy paint.

Finally, the word I had been searching for came: "*HELP! HELP! HELP!*"

Izzy grabbed the rifle mounted on the wall and pointed it at me.

"Sit down and shut up."

I looked at the rifle and envisioned myself surrendering. I saw myself flat on the bed again, with Danny and Izzy taking turns pounding away at me—or trying to. An oddly comforting thought came next: *I'd rather die.*

I kept screaming.

"No one's gonna hear you over Mick Jagger!" Izzy said, attempting a sneer but glancing nervously toward the door.

Where was Danny? I saw him sitting on the bed watching, his eyes as wide as dinner plates.

"Danny," I whimpered, "Help me!"

The sound that came out of him then chilled me to the bone. He giggled. He didn't make a move. His limp white dick hung between his legs like a flag of surrender.

I whirled around looking for a weapon of my own, grabbed the stereo, and threw it to the floor. Mick Jagger wasn't getting any satisfaction now.

"*HELP! HELP!*" I screamed again. "*LET ME OUT!*"

Finally, Danny seemed to come back to life. "Come on, Izzy. This isn't cool," he said, almost in a whisper. He looked terrified.

"It's your fucking fault, faggot!" Izzy screamed. "Do you think nobody knows about your little boys!?"

Still holding the rifle, Izzy turned back toward me, aimed it, and put his finger on the trigger.

"Lay down, bitch, or I'll blow your brains out!"

It didn't matter. He could pull the trigger. Nothing could be worse than giving in to this monster.

"*FUCK YOU, IZZY!!!*" I screamed so loud I thought my throat would rupture. "*HELP! HELP!*"

Izzy dropped the gun and reached out to grab me, but I pulled away and felt his dirty fingernails rake my forearm. My hands felt wet, and I looked down to see blood dripping from my knuckles, leaving a trail on the floor.

I wheeled around and spied some sort of meat stew sitting in a pot on the hot plate. I smacked it so hard my hand stung. The pot clattered to the floor and stew splattered everywhere. The place was starting to look like the crime scene it was.

"Fucking bitch! I'll kill you!" Izzy spat and pressed the rifle to my forehead.

It felt cold.

Nothing to lose, nothing to lose, nothing to lose, I thought . . . but that didn't mean I was giving up. On the contrary, my little mantra was giving me strength. Izzy's arms were both raised to steady the rifle, so I ducked down and slid past him toward the door. I took one last look at Danny, who was still sitting on the edge of the mattress. He'd folded his hands in his lap, covering his pathetic chalk dick.

"Danny?"

His eyes widened but he sat like a statue. Like he was watching a TV show, curious to see how it turned out.

I pounded on the door again.

"HELP! HELP! LET ME OUT!"

After what felt like an eternity, I heard voices on the other side of the door.

"What is going on? Open the door," said a man with a heavy Yiddish accent. Izzy's father, no doubt.

"Be right there," Izzy called out, trying to keep his voice steady. "You better keep your fucking mouth shut!" he hissed at me as he slid the rifle under the mattress and fished the key out of his hip pocket.

When he unlocked the door and opened it, his elderly father and mother were standing there horrified.

"YOUR SON IS A PSYCHOPATH!" I yelled into their stunned faces and raced past them out to the street. I didn't stop running until I'd covered the ten blocks to my apartment.

When I'd steadied my hand enough to get my key into the lock, I pushed the door open then slammed it behind me and wedged the metal bar into place. I mounted the stairs two at a time and finally collapsed at my kitchen table like a sack of wet laundry. Tears of rage streamed down my face and my ravaged hands throbbed like they were on fire as I fumbled for a cigarette and lit it.

* * *

I'm pretty sure I never went to bed that night—just paced and smoked and wept and fumed.

What the fuck had just happened?

I'd slept with Izzy once. Had that given him permission to do *this*?

But it wasn't Izzy who had shoved his half-soft dick inside of me—it was Danny.

Danny.

Sometime in the early morning, I heard Barbra Streisand in my head, singing a familiar song. I raised my own raw voice and joined in.

Tears still dampening my cheeks, I finally dozed off as light leaked in. The last thing I heard as I lost consciousness was the cooing of the pigeons that lived above the fruit stand.

* * *

Sometime later that morning, a knock on the door downstairs woke me.

"Rossi, please let me explain!"

Danny.

I walked down and opened the door a crack, leaving the chain on.

"How could there be any explanation for . . . *that*?"

"It was Izzy's idea! He made me do it! The joint . . . it was laced with something . . . angel dust, I think—"

"Izzy is a psycho! You know that. But you . . . Danny, I trusted you. I only went with you because you begged me. Why the fuck would you do that to me!?"

"I-I don't know," he stammered. "It's Izzy. He gets me to do stupid shit. He always has. I'm so sorry."

"Danny! 'Stupid shit' is putting firecrackers in a beer can. This was way worse than 'stupid shit!'"

A Lubavitch woman pushing a baby stroller slowed down as she passed. She'd clearly heard some or all of what I'd just said and was dying to hear more.

"Shalom, Rivka," Danny said pointedly.

She nodded and kept walking.

"Rossi. I'll make it up to you somehow. Just tell me. What can I do?"

As he talked, I opened the drawer of the filing cabinet in my head. I took the file I'd created titled "Douchey Dan" and placed it in the cabinet behind the ones labeled, "Billy-club Boys," "Redbeard," and "Blow-me Cop." Then I closed the cabinet and locked it.

"Here's what you can do . . . Daniel. You can walk away and leave me alone forever. That's the only thing you can do for me."

"But . . . can't we . . . figure out a way to be friends again?"

"Honestly, Danny? I don't think we ever were friends."

I closed the door in his sorry-ass face and locked it. It would be three decades before I said another word to Douchey Dan.

CHAPTER 41

MAKEUP AND MARIA

I didn't tell anyone what happened in Izzy's basement. Speaking about it would have made it real. It would be two decades before I would tell anyone about that night.

When I finally did open up about "the incident," I couldn't remember what had happened after I made my escape, or what I did the next day or the day after that. I couldn't remember what I saw or who I passed as I ran home—but I remembered every detail of the hours in that dark apartment. It remained perfectly preserved in the filing cabinet in my brain.

In the immediate aftermath, I pulled inward and filled the new space around me with another layer of skin. Tilly was far too busy with her new responsibilities as night shift manager to notice my distance. No one I passed on Kingston Avenue seemed to care about the odd girl with zebra-colored hair and scabs on her knuckles, wearing two layers of skin.

I spent my evenings chain-smoking and painting a female bodybuilder with long black hair. When she was finally done, I scrawled *The Real Wonder Woman* on the back of the canvas with a Magic Marker.

At the phone room, I took my cold-calling job to a higher level of low. I'd found a home in the dark tunnel I created as I talked to strangers. I was the top salesperson for three weeks in a row, and this was notable enough that the *Times* sent a sales manager to plug into my phone from the observation room and see what my secret was. I guess they figured they could add some tips to their sales orientations.

"Mr. Smith, are you ready," I cooed in my sexiest, raspiest voice, "'cause I'm gonna give it to you every day. Oh, yes, honey, get ready for what I'm gonna show you."

"Wh-wh-what are you going to show me?" stammered Mr. Smith.

"Excitement like you never dreamed of, honey. Are you ready for me?"

"Yes . . . yes . . ."

"I need a verifier!" I announced as I aced another sale.

When I stood up to flag down Charlene, the verifier, I saw a woman in a suit on the other side of the glass wall of the observation room. She looked as if she'd seen a ghost.

After Charlene confirmed my sale, I started to make another call, but a hand reached over mine and stopped me from dialing.

"Young woman, you are making a lot of money for this company, and I admire your ingenuity, but Legal would never approve of your . . . techniques."

And just like that, I was out of a job.

I'd managed to sock away a few hundred bucks in my savings account on Utica Avenue, but it was considerably less than I would need to move out of Crown Heights. I needed to find another job.

A few years earlier, I was in my full glory at the Long Branch amusement pier, my summer job for two years, barking into the microphone of the spin-and-win carnival game known as the Cigarette Wheel. "Don't be gay, come on and play," I called out. "There's nothing to it. You can do it!"

I noticed a short, fat, bald man watching me and smiling. When I paused my spiel for a few seconds, he gave me his card.

"You got chutzpah, kid. If you ever need a job, call me."

I'd never thrown the card out. It was in the inside pocket of my bomber jacket.

Nothing to lose . . .

It turned out that the card guy—David—sold designer makeup (minus label) from a concession stand in the arcade: Lancôme, Stagelight . . . all the really good stuff. He and his partner Irwin had recently worked out a deal with two newspaper kiosks in Midtown Manhattan, where they sold makeup from one side of the stands while the candy bars, cigarettes, and newspapers were sold from the other. It was going pretty well for them, and they wanted to branch out to a third kiosk. But David, ever the businessman, wanted to check out the area first.

He rigged up a display table on wheels and hired me to go around with him as he scouted new locations.

"I'll pay you six bucks an hour," he said.

Our first day, I met him Midtown where he unloaded the table from a cargo van he kept in a paid lot. We proceeded to wheel it to West Thirtieth Street, a few blocks from Penn Station, and set up the display, lipstick racks for the Lancôme lipstick and plastic tiers for the Stagelight blush.

"We're gonna make all our money during lunch and after work," he said.

At 11:45 a.m., slews of secretarial-looking women emerged from nearby buildings.

"Watch and learn," David said. He easily charmed them with flattery as he drew pink and red lines on their hands with the lipstick testers. "You see? It's just your color. Brings out your eyes . . ."

I tried emulating him. When a petite, pretty Hispanic woman with bleached blond hair paused in front of the display, I reached for her hand. "Here, let's try a few," I cooed. "This one is definitely *you.*"

"I'll take two," she said, as I gently cleaned her hand with a tissue.

She ran off with her purchase, to lunch, I assumed. A little while later, on her way back past the table, she handed me a folded-up piece of paper.

"This is from a friend of mine," she said, then hurried into an office building across the street.

I opened the piece of paper.

> *Hi,*
> *I've been watching you all day. You look really fun. I love the way you dress, too. I really love your hair. I'd like to get to know you.*
> *Maria*
> *PS that "friend" was me! If you look up, you will see me waving.*

She'd put her phone number on the bottom. I looked up and, sure enough . . . there she was in a fourth-floor window, waving madly.

I waved back.

Having observed the entire thing, David said, "Looks like you've got a not-so-secret admirer!"

Knowing Maria was watching, I spent the rest of the day joking around with David and showing off.

Walking down Kingston Avenue early that evening, I passed Yehudah.

"Hello, Famous Rossi."

I smiled and waved. With his long black Shabbos coat on, he looked even tinier than usual. "Hello, Yehudah."

He gave me the once-over and frowned. "What happened to you?"

I felt a pang of shame and shoved my battered hands in my pockets. "Nothing . . . I'm . . . fine." I tried ducking past his concerned eyes, not wanting to face further questions.

"Famous Rossi?"

"Yeah?"

"Don't ever lose your *meshuga*."

I promised not to.

That night, I went to the pay phone with the little slip of paper. "I got your note," I said when Maria answered on the first ring.

"When can I see you again?" she whispered in a way that gave me a tingling sensation in my chest.

At her suggestion, we made plans to meet at a lesbian bar on the Upper East Side called Peaches and Cream. At long last, I'd see the inside of a real-live lesbian bar! Danny and Izzy suddenly seemed like creatures from another life on another planet.

I hardly slept that night.

CHAPTER 42

PEACHES AND CREAM

Peaches was in a quiet residential neighborhood. As I looked for the address on East Sixty-Fourth Street, I passed two elderly women, one gripping the leash of a well-groomed poodle. A doorman held the door open for her as she said goodbye to her friend and headed inside. I wondered what it was like to be so wealthy you had a doorman.

The first thing I saw when I walked into Peaches was a long bar loaded with mostly older women—older to *me*, anyway. Most were in their thirties and forties and wore office clothes—pantsuits or dresses. A few were more casually dressed in T-shirts and jeans. Some looked a lot like men.

I made a little tour of the place, looking for Maria. There was a dance floor in the back room, surrounded by tables, but it was fairly empty as most of the women were still taking advantage of happy hour at the bar, where a sign advertised well drinks at half-price.

I went back to the bar and ordered one of the only drinks I knew how to order: a Screwdriver.

"The house vodka is half-price," said the bartender, whose hair was short on the sides and long in the back, as if she'd been halfway through a short haircut when she suddenly changed her mind.

"I'll take that, please."

There was still no sign of Maria, so I took my drink to the back room, where I noticed two women kissing at a table in the corner. Coming out of the speakers was the raspy voice of Kim Carnes, singing, "She's got Bette Davis eyes." I sat down at a table, took a sip of my drink, and fell into a daydream that it was I, not Kim, singing. This was one of my favorite fantasies: that I was on stage, a singing superstar.

When I looked up, Maria stood in front of me holding a margarita on the rocks and smiling.

"I love this song, too," she said, pulling a chair close to mine and sitting.

We stayed in the back, talking, laughing, and drinking another couple of rounds. When "Endless Love" came on, Maria stood up and said, "Wanna dance?"

"Sure," I said, wobbling a little as I stood. I was about four inches taller than she was, but somehow, we fit together perfectly as we slow-danced to Diana Ross and Lionel Ritchie.

"So . . . I never asked you . . ." Maria said in that sexy whisper of hers. "Where do you live, anyway?"

"Crown Heights."

"Wow. That's way out there, isn't it? I live with my mom and sister in Queens . . . so . . . I was thinking . . . can we go to your place?"

I just shrugged as if, *no big deal*, and said, "Okay." But actually, my heart was pounding so hard I was sure she felt it.

On the way out with Maria, I noticed a middle-aged, masculine-looking woman standing near the bar. Her short brown hair was slicked back with gel, and she was wearing an orange T-shirt with the number 69 on it.

She looks really familiar.

I stopped and stared at her for a moment and then it hit me. "Ms. Albanoff!?"

She just looked me in the eye and gave a little smile as if to say, *guilty*. Then she put her index finger over her lips.

My first time in a lesbian bar, and I'd bumped into my grammar-school gym teacher.

It was late, and I was dreading the ride home, so when Maria offered to spring for a taxi, I didn't even pretend to think it over. Unaccustomed to traveling above ground, I watched Manhattan speed by along the FDR. When Maria reached out and put her hand over mine, I felt a shot of electricity run through me.

The cab cost eighteen bucks—more than my usual grocery bill for a week—but Maria just pulled out a twenty and said, "Keep the change."

I gave her the two-second tour of the apartment, then said, "Do you want another drink? I've got some vodka in the freezer."

"No," she said, "but I am a little hungry."

I made cheese and mustard sandwiches, and we ate them sitting on the couch. Maria was wearing a soft yellow sweater cut into a low V in front. Around her neck, a gold heart hung from a gold chain.

"I . . . um . . . like your necklace."

"Thank you. My ex gave it to me."

"Your ex?"

"Yeah. Laney. We went out for two years, but I'm single now."

I tried acting savvy as I snuggled up to her and tentatively kissed her neck. "Do you want to . . . fool around?" I asked nervously.

She laughed. "Rossi. Have you ever been with a woman before?"

"Um . . . sure. A few."

"Let me rephrase that. Have you ever been with a *gay* woman before?"

I thought about it for a minute. There'd been Cindy in the Volaré. There was that one night with Mag. There were lots of nights with Tilly, but Tilly had never let me touch her.

Every time I'd tried to put my hand down yonder, she'd pushed it away, saying, "Honey, I got a man with a big dick uptown." The only thing Tilly ever wanted to do was touch me.

The honest answer was, no, I'd never been with a gay woman—though I didn't really understand what the difference was. A woman is a woman, right?

"I guess the answer is no," I replied.

"Well, gay women don't just fool around, honey. We have sex."

Before I could say anything, Maria stood up, took me by the hand and led me to the bedroom.

She took off her clothes slowly, and I did the same, but much more clumsily, tossing them into a pile on the floor.

"Do you know if you're a butch or a femme?" Maria asked.

"I don't think I'm either of those things."

"*Ah*. We call that a switch-hitter."

We didn't fall asleep until the wee hours of the morning, wrapped up in each other and the sweaty sheets. Maria was right. This was neon worlds past *fooling around*.

CHAPTER 43

SIMON SAYS

Robby decided to move to Hoboken.

"Honey, I can't take it anymore. I get hit on more here than on Christopher Street!"

It was chilly the day I helped him carry his boxes down to his friend's van. His coat was already packed, so I lent him my beloved bomber jacket—which he promised to return but never did.

He handed me a leather whip. "Something to hang on your wall."

The last glimpse I ever got of Robby was hanging out of the passenger window of the van yelling, "Cruddy old queers! Come out of the closet!"

•·····•·-•·...•·· ··

One of the catalysts in attracting artists to the hood was a sweet Chasid named Simon, an ex-hippie turned religious. He wore John Lennon glasses and claimed to get flashbacks while praying as a result of his drug-taking days. I don't know if that was true, but he smiled all the time, and his laugh was high and girlish.

Everyone liked Simon, who was petite in stature but didn't seem to be afraid of anyone or anything. Maybe that was because he carried a large lock-jam knife in the pocket of his jeans. He had worn down the spring mechanism so the knife shot out when he flicked it, making it more like a switchblade than a pocketknife.

Simon ran ads that read, "Artists, Renovators, Create Your Own Dream Home." He offered loft-size apartments at a fraction of what they'd go for in Manhattan and threw in free rent plus the cost of materials for tenants willing to renovate.

They came in droves. Well, the "droves" amounted to about a dozen all together, but, added to the handful of artsy outcasts (like me) who had already found their way to the neighborhood, it was the beginning of a scene.

Sarah and John came from Connecticut. They pretended to be poor, but everyone knew they were living on Sarah's trust fund. Rodney, an adorable twenty-four-year-old Black gay boy, moved into a building a block from me, filling the void Robby had left. We became friends in minutes.

Rodney was pursuing a modeling career, to no avail. I was pretty sure he was too short, although, with his cropped Grace Jones haircut and tight jeans, he was pretty damn cute. He liked to draw gorgeous women with Joan Crawford shoulders in whatever outfit he'd just seen in *Vogue*. "Honey," he complained to me one day, "those old rabbis won't leave me alone! They want a piece of this!" He slapped his own ass.

My parents continued to visit every few months, bringing the usual carload of groceries. Perhaps to avoid any more inopportune run-ins, Mom sometimes mailed me a postcard to warn me they were coming—but often they still showed up unannounced. No matter how much fury the sight of them inspired, I was always happy for the (literal) motherlode of provisions. After they left, I would knock on Rodney's door and scream, "Motherlode!" Then he and I would race back to my place and pig out on one of my creations. Stir-fried Hebrew National salami with scrambled eggs and canned peas was his favorite.

Rodney would take photos of the paintings I'd done and turn them into slides. "Girl, you're gonna be a star!" he'd say as he presented them to me.

I toted my slide portfolio into every gallery in Soho. Some of the galleristas would look up briefly and say, "By appointment only." Some would look quickly through my slides, put on a fake smile, and say, "Sorry, but we are booked up for the next two years." One black-turtlenecked young woman sitting behind a counter actually laughed. "Oh, *no, no, no,* thank you," she said, then batted her eyelashes in the direction of the door. The last gallery I walked into agreed to take my slides for review and promptly lost them. I'm pretty sure they just threw them in the trash.

One day, I saw an ad in *The Village Voice* for a loft space on Broome Street that could be rented for private events. A lightbulb went off in my head. When I went to investigate the situation, I met a bearded man named Bugdan with a Salvador Dali mustache. He offered to rent me the 2,500-square-foot, white-walled gallery for a thousand bucks for five days. I haggled him down to five hundred.

When I told Sarah-from-Connecticut about it, she pushed her vintage horn-rim glasses down to the tip of her nose and shouted, "Hell, *yes!*" Evidently her abstract paintings and John's horsey landscapes were getting about as much traction as my creations were. They agreed to put in two hundred dollars toward the rent, plus a hundred toward other expenses.

Roland, a musician who spray-painted scenes of the galaxy, put in two hundred, and Rodney kicked in a hundred to showcase his drawings of nude men. And just like that—without my having to contribute a dime—we had a space for our own Soho show with enough left over for a kick-ass opening party. It was my first experience with "sweat equity."

"Exception" was the name I came up with for the show, under which I wrote, "To every rule there is one." John, whose day job sold insurance for his uncle, printed up flyers, and we each took a pile of one hundred.

I managed to get the *Voice* to cover the show in its "Things to Do" section. The writer called us "nine-to-five artists" and wrote about us as if it were some radical new idea that artists might have day jobs and paint on weekends. (Never mind the fact that the only one of us who actually worked regular hours was John.)

Between our friends and the curious types who read about the show in the *Voice*, our opening night was packed. There must have been two hundred people there. Roland played Santana songs on an electric guitar while the guests drank every drop of the cheap screw-top wine and club soda we provided.

"How old did you say you were?" John asked as he helped me cart more wine from the back room.

"Seventeen—why?"

"You put all this together at your age!? Damn. By the time you're thirty, you're gonna be President."

I looked out at the oh-so-chic Soho types who had wandered in, noting in particular a woman wearing a blue leather dress, high heels, and fishnet stockings. All of this was happening because of me. I felt a wave of pride rush over me.

"It is pretty cool," I admitted.

For the next four days, Sarah and I took turns manning the gallery, but only a few people came in. Sarah's mom bought one of her abstracts, a piece called "Today" that looked like a kite flying over a clothesline. That was the extent of our sales, but honestly, none of us cared. We cut out *The Village Voice* mention and saved it along with the invite, knowing that we'd look back on the experience as a milestone: our very first Soho show.

Simon was so impressed with what we'd put together on Broome Street that he gave us a vacant storefront on Kingston rent-free for a few months to see what we'd do next. "Let's see what percolates," he said, smiling. If only I'd met more Lubavitchers like Simon—or had met Simon sooner—maybe the veil of ice I wore would never have formed. I felt it melting as Simon laughed and told stories about rolling in the mud at Woodstock.

●﹒﹒●﹒●▬●﹒﹒●﹒﹒●﹒﹒

Once the new art space was officially ours, we worked together to clean out the dead cockroaches and prime the walls. We all hung up our work, which sported fancy titles like "Horizon of Solitude" and "Maryanne's Epiphany," and I came up with the name for the gallery: "The Lost and Found." It was the perfect thing to call our showcase for runaways, throwaways, and lost-our-ways. Simon's secretary Carol, a budding portraitist, and I took turns sitting at the front desk.

As a concession to the hood, I hung the portrait I'd painted of the Rebbe. Next to it, I placed my portrait of Grace Jones. "Cool," we all agreed, figuring Grace and the Rebbe had about as much in common as we did with the rest of the neighborhood.

The day before the gallery was to open officially, Yehudah walked in carrying a box and placed it on the desk. It turned out to be a case of decent kosher red wine—not the sweet Passover crap of my childhood.

"For your opening," he said.

"Oh, Yehudah! I can't hug you but know that I am right now."

He smiled and handed me a small plastic bag. "You'll need this," he said. Inside was a shiny new corkscrew. "It's not enough to have kosher wine. The corkscrew must be kosher, too."

"Really? How do you keep up with all these rules?"

"It takes a lifetime. And then some."

Yehudah walked around the gallery looking at all the work. He stopped at the painting of the Rebbe. "Very good. Maybe

Famous Rossi really will be Famous Rossi one day." He bowed his head slightly. "Your guests may or may not drink the kosher wine. More for you if they don't."

With a wave, Yehudah walked back out onto Kingston Avenue.

•··•'·•··•··•··

The Chasids came in, curious at first, then shaking their heads in mild horror. They always stopped to gawk at the Rebbe painting, comforted by the familiar face but shocked to see it in such a context. As they lingered, I would spring out of my chair to greet them, show them around all two hundred square feet of our beloved gallery, and beg them to come again as they backed out the door chanting, "Yes, yes, very nice, yes . . ."

They never came back. No one ever came back. No one bought anything.

I was gallery-sitting one morning when Redbeard walked in. "I came to see this gallery I keep hearing so much about."

I walked toward him and stopped a foot away, knowing better than to close the gap further or try and shake his hand. "Hello, Rabbi," I said, trying for a neutral tone.

"Do you sell these?" he asked, gesturing toward the Rebbe painting.

"Of course. See the price under each one?"

"I see. And how have sales been?"

"Not very good."

"I don't think Lubavitchers appreciate—what would you call it? —*alternative art*."

"I don't think Lubavitchers appreciate alternative anything."

"We don't need it, you see. *We* are the alternative. To the life out there." He gestured vaguely toward the door. By this point, I was used to his refusal to make eye contact with me. There was nothing in the religion that militated against eye contact. In fact, the Rebbe had stared so deeply into my eyes that I'd thought he might see through me to the other side. "There are plenty of other places that appreciate alternative things," Redbeard continued. "One simply needs to seek them out."

As he turned to leave, I had to fight an urge to kick him so hard he'd go flying out onto Kingston Avenue. "Rabbi Sherba!" I called out just as he reached the door. "Is it true you tried to pay someone to mug me?"

He froze for a moment as if considering the question, and I saw his shoulders rise defensively. Then he straightened up and strode out the door without a word. I suppose that was his answer.

When our free-rent period expired, we closed the gallery— but not before an article in *The New York Times* real-estate section called us "pioneers" and declared the artists of Crown Heights a bona-fide movement. The Brooklyn Museum expressed interest in our cause as well. It was all *hurrays* and *hurrahs* and then, suddenly, it was over.

Sarah and John were the first to bail on the hood. They'd decided they wanted to go back to Connecticut, where there was this strange phenomenon called *nature*. They'd been excited to be a part of the movement at first and had enjoyed creating their versions of the same kind of work I was seeing all over Soho. But once they'd achieved their goal of turning a burnt-out dump into a Soho-style loft, the thrill waned. The free-rent ride was over, and they could no longer talk any of their friends into visiting them after dark.

They threw a goodbye party and chattered on about some great pretend "opportunity" they couldn't pass up. I drank their wine and watched them slink off with surrender flags tucked neatly up their asses. Theirs wouldn't be the last "farewell celebration" in Crown Heights, as most of the "pioneers" wimped out and scattered to safer locales.

CHAPTER 44

GROWING UP

The windows in my studio—formerly Fagee's bedroom—let in cascades of sunlight during the day and ghostly amber light at night, thanks to the neon drugstore sign below. I set up my easel in the center of the room and hung my paintings on the walls. In my new temple, clutter would be sacrilege so, other than a stool from which to ponder my work and a salvaged wooden wine crate for storing my paints, I kept the room empty.

I was completely immersed in my work, possessed by it. "Riders on the storm . . ." crooned Jim Morrison from my little stereo speakers as I slashed my brushes across the canvas all night long.

The moment that each of my paintings crossed that intoxicating line between shapeless face or figure and living creation, I felt my solar plexus buzzing. I began to believe I might really be an artist—whatever that was.

One night, three bushy-bearded Russian Chasids knocked on my door.

"What the hell do you want?" I shouted down from the window.

"I come for massage, I come for massage!" the middle one yelled up.

Massage? What the hell?

Then I realized . . . he was referring to the sign I'd painted over my mail slot when I'd attempted to go into business as an art teacher. "That's *messages*, you idiot! Not *massages!*"

•·····•·········•···

Talent or no, my fantasy of becoming the next Andy Warhol was dying on the vine. Without much money coming in, I could buy only a few colors of acrylic. My work became mainly black, white, and red. I painted faces with red eyes and purple skin. I thought they were beautiful.

Fagee made the trek from Boro Park one night.

"These faces," she exclaimed, "they look like demons! Would it kill you to paint a flower? Everything looks like it is bleeding!"

"That's me on the inside, honey!"

But the truth was, the rebellious fury that had fueled my teenage self, driven me to leave home and never look back, had begun fizzling out. I could no longer hide from the shocking truth that I had no idea what I actually wanted to do with my life.

Late one night, I sat on the windowsill smoking and watching the dogs while the last layer of paint dried on three red, black, and purple strippers dancing across a sixteen-by-twenty-inch canvas. My back teeth ached from grinding them in my sleep. My body ached from some strange ailment I could never identify. Questions that had spun around in my head since Fagee's "paint a flower" comment came to the front of my mind.

Was it my anger that was hurting me physically? What might it feel like to just stop being angry? Was that even possible?

I picked up the plastic plate I used as a palette and mixed white and red acrylic until I got something close to bubble-gum pink. *Bubble Yum*, I thought, snickering. That's what the pretty, popular girls in Rumson had chewed by the mouthful as they traveled in packs like pretty little wolves looking for the weaker, less popular girls to judge, insult, and ignore. I'd never been a Bubble Yum girl. I was old-school: Bazooka—the small pink squares that came wrapped in tiny comics and left your hands smelling sickly sweet for hours. I was a Bazooka girl with a brandy chaser.

Just the thought of the Bubble Yum girls seemed foreign to this place. Then I thought about the clusters of bewigged young women who huddled whispering about me and gig-gling as I passed them on the street. I thought about the tall, pretty girl in the beige silk head *schmata* sneering at me at the kosher bakery. Were these people really so different from the Rumson girls?

I painted the Bazooka pink I'd created onto the skin of one of my strippers and retreated to the windowsill to smoke and let her dry. As I admired my smoke rings drifting off into the amber light, I noticed a lone figure walking down the street. It was half-past midnight. No one except cops and criminals walked around at that hour. As the figure emerged into the neon glow, I saw who it was: Danny. He would know that there was a good chance I was up, probably smoking out the window.

Sure enough, he looked up and saw me. He seemed wide-eyed and bewildered, like a baby who had just awakened from a nap. Was that what Danny was? A six-foot-two baby with a budding beer belly?

He raised his right hand slowly and rocked it back and forth in a tentative wave.

I stared at him.

He kept the gesture going, a big baby rocking his hand. He looked so pathetic I had an urge to wave back—but then I thought about my hands. The scabs had healed months earlier, and Fagee had given me a bottle of liquid vitamin E to help with the scars. Mercifully, she hadn't asked what had caused my injuries, but were there really so many explanations for bloodied knuckles? Most of the wounds had faded, but the scar from the deepest cut, on the large middle knuckle of my right hand, remained even after I drowned it in vitamin E. That white crescent wasn't going anywhere. Eventually, I'd found the poetry in having a battle scar on my Fuck You finger.

Could I simply decide to not be angry anymore?

I glanced back at the Bazooka–Bubble Yum dancer poised in front of her red-and-purple sisters. She looked fake.

I flicked my cigarette out onto the street and slammed the window shut. When the paint dried, I'd cover that pink back up with blue and purple. I wasn't yet ready for pink.

· ··· ·· ·· ·· ·· ··

Rodney came by one Sunday morning dressed in the shortest shorts I had ever seen on a man. He'd completed the look with a pair of red cowboy boots and a pink tank top.

"Girl! It's gay Pride. You are coming with me to the parade."

I rubbed my eyes and looked at the clock. 9:00 a.m.— entirely too early to be going anywhere with anyone. I'd been on a roll with my dancers and hadn't stopped painting until sometime after four. "Rodney, come back later, okay? When I'm awake?"

"Girl, no way! This is only the most important day of the year! Get your ass in gear, I mean it! Get down here and let this fabulous creature in!"

What choice did I have?

The minute he got upstairs, Rodney started rooting around in my closet and bins for something acceptable. While I bustled around making double-strength Bustelo, he cut three inches off a pair of my Levi's shorts. By the time we left my place, we were wired to the gills, and I was dressed in short shorts, my Frye boots, and a black tank top. We looked like twins . . . well, sort of.

"Girl, you look fierce!" he announced as we ran down Kingston Avenue toward the subway holding hands. The Chasids clucked away as we passed, but we couldn't have cared less.

As we sat on the 2 train, I leaned in and whispered, "Do you think it's okay that I'm going to the parade?"

"Why wouldn't it be?"

"Because . . . I'm not gay. I'm bisexual."

Rodney leaned back and started to laugh. "*Uh-huh*," he said, then laughed harder. When he finally came up for air, he said, "Let me ask you something, Ms. Rossi. When you think of dick what comes to mind? Give me one word."

The filing cabinet in my brain pushed open a crack and a quick flash of Danny's luminescent rod leaked out. I winced and slammed the file shut.

"Chalk."

"*Hmm*. Not sure I even want to know where that came from. Now think about pussy and give me one word."

I skimmed over Tilly, Mag, and Maria and went straight to the back seat of the Volaré.

"Warm," I said with a soft smile on my face.

"Girl, first of all, everyone but haters is welcome at the gay Pride parade. Second of all, you're about as bisexual as I am!"

We switched trains for the local at Chambers Street and emerged at Sheridan Square, into the most breathtaking scene I'd ever witnessed. Thousands of beautiful people marched along the street, danced on floats, and cheered from the sidelines. There were lavender balloons everywhere, people hanging from windows shouting. Someone threw rainbow-colored beads at me, and I put them on. A float on a flatbed truck rolled by filled with dancing muscle boys and drag queens. A man wearing nothing but a jock strap and high heels swanned down the middle of the street grinning at the crowd. A woman in a studded choker was being led along on a leash by her leather-clad partner. An elderly woman walked by holding a young man's hand and a sign that read, "I love my gay son." The crowd went wild for her.

I thought about my parents shipping me off to the rabbi so I'd be somebody else's problem. Was this what they'd been afraid of? Not my smoking or drinking or general rebelliousness, but the fact that I might be a lesbian?

I tapped Rodney on the shoulder and whispered in his ear, "Rodney! I think I'm gay!"

"Girlfriend, get over yourself. You're the biggest dyke I know, and you might as well shout it out loud and proud, honey!"

"I'm gay!" I tried to proclaim, but it came out muffled and halfhearted.

"Girl! Is that all you got? You're a big ol' dyke. You were born a dyke, you'll die a dyke, and you better start letting the world know about it!"

"*I'M GAY!*" I shouted. And it felt damn good.

Long after the parade was over, Rodney and I lingered on Christopher Street. The pavement was littered with confetti, trash, and a lot of drunk, passed-out, or just tired-ass people like us. A bearded, muscle-bound guy, shirtless in a pair of leather chaps, spotted Rodney. I watched as they exchanged looks. Rodney had explained to me earlier in the day that when men stared at each other and neither looked away, they were cruising.

"Girl, can you make it home without me?" he whispered.

I nodded, and he followed his new friend toward the piers without a word.

On the 2 train back to Kingston, I picked the confetti out of my hair and thought about all that I'd seen and felt. The train was packed with my new compatriots, men and women who'd clearly been part of the festivities. We shared smiles all around as the crowd gradually dissipated. By the time the train reached Grand Army Plaza, the only parade-goer left was me.

When I closed my eyes, I could still see thousands of gay people cheering with joy, out and proud. The image would remain etched in my brain forever. There was no question about it anymore: I was as gay as anyone could be and I wouldn't have changed that fact for the world.

●····●'·●●····●····

The next day, I called up Sonya and Sarah. "I'm gay!" I announced when Sonya picked up.

"Doy!" she said, laughing. "Tell me something I don't know. Let me put Sarah on."

"What's up sister?" Sarah said.

"I'm gay!"

"What a surprise," she said, the sarcasm dripping. "We were wondering how long it was gonna take you to figure that out. Even my mother said she thought you were a lesbian."

"I hate that word. It sounds like a disease."

"What do you prefer, then?"

"How about just *gay*?"

"Okay then. Happy gay-day, Rossi!"

●····●'·●●····●····

Sarah couldn't come to her dad's place because her mother was making her study for the SATs, but Sonya invited me for the weekend anyway.

When we went out for a walk, she said, "I want to show you the shortcut to the East Side—through Central Park."

I thought about Union Square Park. "Is it safe?"

"It's okay in the daytime. You just have to careful under the bridges."

There was an island of floating garbage in the pond. I saw an old tire washed up on the bank.

"They keep saying they're gonna clean it up," she said.

We entered an area with newly planted trees and lots of flowers. An old man sat on a bench feeding the pigeons. Kids played in the grass.

Seeing all that nature reminded me of *The Wizard of Oz*, when it went from black-and-white to full color right before your eyes.

When we got back to her dad's place. Sonya took his vodka out of the freezer and mixed it with apple juice. It tasted so good, we each had three. Then she ran a bubble bath for me.

I closed my eyes and submerged in the bubbles. *Peace. Bliss.* Something jolted me out of nirvana.

"Make room, bitch," Sonya said, sliding in behind me and straddling me with her legs.

"Now that you're gay, we might as well save some water."

She soaped up my back and then my breasts. It was sexy for a moment. I turned and kissed her, but when we opened our eyes, we both laughed.

"Well . . . we can cross that off the list," she said, cracking up all over again.

Sunday rolled around fast. As I prepared myself to catch the 2 train for Chasidland, I felt like a coal miner getting ready to go back underground.

"I don't know how you do it," Sonya said, her eyes tearing up.

"It's still better than going home," I said.

·····•····•···•···

The *Voice* came out on Wednesdays, and everyone looking for a job or an apartment grabbed the first one they could find. Some people even went to the newsstand near the *Voice* offices on Tuesday night, where the first batch was delivered around midnight.

One Wednesday, I saw an ad for an apartment in Chelsea

with a "shared bath" for only seventy dollars a week. When I got there, I realized the place was some sort of flophouse filled with transients. There was a front desk behind bulletproof glass and a communal "living room" with a big TV and a dozen men and a few women watching it. The whole scene reminded me of *One Flew Over the Cuckoo's Nest*.

A scruffy-faced man with a cigarette hanging out of his mouth came out from the bulletproof booth to show me the available room. It was about a hundred square feet and came with a single bed with a mildew-stained mattress on it (at least I hoped that's what the stain was). A wire rack of rusted metal shelves stood against one wall.

"You have to pick all your personal stuff up off the floor before you leave in the morning," the scruffy man said. "We hose the place down every day at one o'clock."

My grand tour complete, we retreated to the hall, and he closed the door behind us. I noticed there was a six-inch gap between the bottom of the door and the floor.

I went to see an apartment on East Third Street and First Avenue. As I pushed the front door open and stepped into the vestibule, I felt something crunchy underfoot. It was a pile of hypodermic needles. Empty beer cans were strewn around as well, so it must have been quite a party.

I buzzed the apartment, and a Puerto Rican man came down the stairs to let me through the inside door. "Junkies," he said shaking his head. "They're like cockroaches. No . . . I like cockroaches better because I'm allowed to kill them."

The apartment was an L-shaped studio. When I opened the cabinet under the sink, the brownish floor came alive. In the battle of man versus cockroach, the bugs were clearly winning.

"You want it? It's $300 a month."

"I'll think about it."

The long-awaited freedom bell of my eighteenth birthday came, and naturally, I threw a party. The centerpiece of the buffet was stir-fried sliced Hebrew National hot dogs and macaroni. Fagee brought French apple tarts and Tilly brought a small birthday cake into which she'd stuck a candle in the shape of a number *one*.

"It's your first birthday as a legal adult," she explained.

Hector and Uncle Pete brought a malt beverage called Champale, which was supposed to be a cheapo substitute for champagne. It tasted like sweet beer.

When I blew out my candle, I made a silent wish: *Please, Lord, get me to Manhattan!*

CHAPTER 45

LEAVING KINGSTON

I spent a weekend at Sonya's and came home with two birthday gifts: a bottle of jasmine bubble bath, and a Talking Heads album. It was late in the afternoon on a Sunday, and the Chasids were buzzing about, enjoying their favorite day to socialize. I waved at Hector, who sat on a milk crate in front of the bodega, then pushed my key into the lock on my front door. Before I'd even turned the key, the door swung open. I saw bits of broken wood on the floor.

I looked for the metal rod and found it in its place, leaning against the wall behind the door. Rod in hand, I carefully climbed the stairs. My heart pounded. I had no idea what I would do if I met whoever had broken in.

I owned so few things that it wasn't hard to take inventory. My little black-and-white TV set and beloved Radio Shack stereo were gone. I moved on to the bedroom and opened the closet. Nothing seemed amiss there. I looked into my art studio, and all seemed in order. Finally, I entered the kitchen. The Hebrew National salami from my last motherlode was suspended from the string that turned on the kitchen light, swaying in the faint breeze.

Clearly, the thieves hadn't been in any rush. They'd made a meal out of the few groceries I had and left their dirty plates on the kitchen table. A half-eaten bagel sat hardening on one, leftover potato salad curdling on the other.

The bathroom door was open, but the shower curtain closed. Gingerly, I reached in with the rod and poked open the curtain.

Empty. Just as I was about to leave the bathroom, I looked down and saw a large turd floating in the toilet.

"Hector!" I called out the window. "Can you come up here!? I need . . . help!"

After he'd looked around a little, he said, "They knew you were away. That's how it is around here. They know everything."

He flushed the toilet, then went and got his toolbox and fixed the door as best he could.

"*Mami*, wedge the pole behind the door tonight. Tomorrow I'll call my cousin Ramon, the locksmith. He'll hook you up."

"Should I call the cops?"

"Nobody bothers to call the cops around here."

I threw out the food they'd eaten, and the plates and forks, for good measure. I poured bleach into the toilet.

When I was satisfied that I'd removed all traces of my intruders, I put the bag containing my now-useless album and bubble bath on the stand where the TV had been. Then I walked over to the couch and sunk into it, exhausted. From somewhere that felt ancient, a wail rose up out of the pit of my stomach. Tears sprung from my eyes and streamed down my face endlessly.

"Why!?" I asked the ceiling.

"Why?" I whispered.

When was it going to stop?

Two months later, I had my answer when an envelope arrived from my mother with a check inside. I had inherited $5000 from my aunt Roslyn, who had left instructions that I get it when I turned eighteen.

Along with the check was an index card covered in my mother's unmistakable scrawl:

> *Slovah, you're eighteen now, a legal adult. I hope you will use your gift from your aunt wisely. Know that we did the best we could.*

I shook the envelope one last time and out fell a few coupons for a free salad bar at Wendy's.

I hadn't known Roslyn particularly well. I was eight when she died and remembered that she'd played the violin beautifully and had varicose veins in her legs. But for me, the most notable thing about her was something I heard at her funeral. One of the old ladies whispered to another, "She was a lesbian, you know." She said it as if she were saying, "She was a murderer, you know." It was the first time I'd ever heard the *L* word.

Roslyn had never had kids, so she left what little she had to her baby sister's children. In the end, it wasn't hard work or bravery that delivered me from Crown Heights; it was lesbian Aunt Roslyn.

I woke up on the breezy fall Monday that would be my last day in the hood rubbing the scar on my Fuck You finger. There were days when everything felt like poetry.

I'd told Hector he could have the couch and mattresses. My parents had agreed to store most of my stuff in their basement in Rumson, so my father drove in in the Datsun truck to pick it all up. As I watched him carefully wrap blankets around my paintings before loading them into the back with my clothes and other stuff, I had a flashback to one of my earliest memories.

I'd just gotten my first bed, and lying in it, I felt lost. My crib had felt so safe, but this was like floating in a big, wide ocean. I must have started crying, because my father came in and tucked my soft cotton baby blanket all around me. Then he made a little wall of pillows to protect me.

Dad tied a cord around the blanketed paintings. "That oughta be safe enough," he rasped. I had an urge to hug him, but I just couldn't bring myself to do it. I put my hand on his shoulder and said, "Thanks, Dad."

Just before he left, I handed him a coffee in a Styrofoam cup, "for the trip back."

He kissed me on the forehead. "Your mother would never admit it, but she hated you living here."

"That makes two of us."

"Three."

As I watched him drive off, I rubbed the place on my forehead he'd kissed. The last time my father had kissed me that way, I'd been six years old.

I double-locked the door and gave Hector the keys.

"*Mami*, you go and keep on going. Don't ever come back to this shithole."

⁕·····•·ª•····ª· ··

I moved into an apartment on Twenty-Third and Lexington, in what used to be the George Washington Hotel. It had been declared "apartments" without any apparent change to the space. Each unit looked exactly like what it was: a hotel room with a microscopic bathroom and nothing resembling a kitchen.

I checked in with two suitcases of New-Wave clothing, a shopping bag of art supplies, and Sonya's jasmine bubble bath. The building didn't ask for a security deposit or insist on doing a credit check—which was good, because I'd yet to get my first credit card.

For $400 a month, I had my own phone, a bed, a dresser, and twenty-four-hour-a-day room service from a diner downstairs that had once employed Rita Hayworth.

The first night, I stood under the hot shower as my little bathroom filled with jasmine-scented steam. I wanted to wash it all away—the feral dogs, the yarmulkes, the cop, the billy clubs, Danny and Izzy, my violated apartments, and my violated self. I felt it all swirl off me and down the drain with the soapy water.

By morning, I had all but forgotten Kingston Avenue.

Or so I told myself.

CHAPTER 46

HARRIET

I lived at GW for a year. Every time I was late on my rent—by even one day—they locked me out. On top of that, the absence of a kitchen drove me crazy. I was blowing my rent money in the goddamn diner!

As much as I loved solitary living, I left GW and moved in with Wolf—an arrangement that lasted just a year as well. I would have stayed longer, but Wolf's crazy tabby cat, Eric, tried killing me every time I got my period. No matter how much Wolf loved me, he loved that satanic beast more, so that was that.

Somehow, I lucked into a large two-bedroom on Bank Street in the West Village—considered dirt cheap at eight hundred bucks a month. The reason for the bargain price was that it was on the top floor of a six-story walk-up, but that was a compromise I was happy to make. Pieces of the ceiling would fall once or twice a year, and the claw-foot tub was in the kitchen—but it was in Greenwich Village, it was mine, and it was big enough to share with Alison—the beautiful Grenadian waitress I'd met at my first cooking job.

When Alison left me for a six-foot-tall Amazon from Copenhagen, I was devastated. I still loved the apartment, but now everything in it reminded me of her. One morning, as I lay on the couch picturing Alison with her Danish model and trying to summon up the energy to go to work, the phone rang.

"Yes," I said, barely able to force the word out of my mouth.

"Slovah. It's your mother!"

"Mom."

"Why do you sound so down?"

I made it a habit never tell my mother when anything was wrong. Two years earlier, I'd admitted to her that I had a cold, and she was still mailing me coupons for half-price cough syrup.

That day, I was too sad to pretend.

"I'm depressed, Mom. I broke up with someone."

"Oh. Was it that guy in Newark?"

"What guy in Newark?"

"David something . . ."

"Mom, I never dated anyone from Newark. I don't know who David Something is."

"So . . . who?"

"It was Alison. You know, the woman I've been living with for the past three years?"

"Oh, her. You know, she sounded so nice over the phone, I never dreamed she was Black."

"Mom! What does that have to do with anything!? She was my girlfriend!"

I expected her to scream.

"Oh . . ." She paused. "I knew that."

"You did?"

"A mother always knows."

Wow.

"We all have female and male genes, Slovah. It's just as natural to go one way as the other, I understand this. But your life will be a lot harder this way."

I just about passed out. Was this the same woman who had once threatened to stab Magnolia with a dull paring knife?

"Did you ever . . . ?" I stammered, completely shocked at myself for asking.

"Well . . . When I was a college professor, I had a student who was very sad, and I would sometimes hold her hand. She looked at me in a certain way. I knew what she wanted. And . . . it was hard not to give it to her. Very hard!"

"Mom! Really?"

"I have to go now, Slovah. Bertha Immerman is here with the Archway cookies for the sisterhood. Now, don't talk about any of this . . . stuff with your father. He wouldn't understand!"

My mother, who had shipped me off to Redbeard for not being a 1950s-style "nice Jewish (heterosexual) girl," was coming around. Just as I was marveling at the new and improved Harriet, she added, "I've looked into this, Slovah. For your sake. If you want to change, we can send you somewhere. I'll pay for it."

"What do you mean?"

"There are places that can cure you of . . . what you are."

"No, Mom. I like myself the way I am."

"You could fight it, Slovah. Try. Your life will be so much easier if you can."

Years later, I'd remind her of that conversation, depicting it as a warm and fuzzy bonding moment between us. But in reality, she'd implied that what I had was a sickness that could be cured. She'd offered to send me to conversion therapy to make my life "easier."

•·····•·•·•·····•·····

I caught the Academy Bus for Red Bank and stared out the window for the entire hour-and-fifteen-minute ride. For years, I'd been riding this bus, grinding my teeth the whole way until my jaw hurt. But this time, the outrage I usually experienced had given way to something else: fear.

Please, please, don't let it end like this.

As I approached the door to my mother's room at Riverview Hospital, I heard her voice but her words sounded broken. *"Aterrr. Aterrr!"*

"Here's your water," the nurse said gently. I watched her help Mom drink from a plastic cup. When Mom looked up and saw me standing there, she tried to smile but only the right side of her mouth arced upward. The left side of her face hung down like a puppet with its strings cut.

I moved in past the IV drip and heart monitor machine and kissed her on the broken side of her face.

"Avaaa. Avaaa."

"That's right, Mom. Your Slovah is here."

I'd spent most of the bus ride in a panic that I wouldn't have a chance to say goodbye—that I'd never have a chance to make things right. "I love you, Mom."

"Av uuu. Av uuu."

· ··· ·· ·· ·...·· · ·

A year after I left Crown Heights, Yaya married an Irish Catholic line cook named Dirk. When I came home for a visit a few weeks later, I found all the mirrors covered in towels and my mother rocking back and forth on the couch crying inconsolably. "My *shana madelah* is dead," she wailed.

It was an odd feeling, not being the black sheep of the family.

"She's not dead, Mom. She just fell in love."

That brought about another fit of hysterical sobbing.

She sat shiva for my sister for a month.

I wondered how Mom would have felt if I'd married a woman. Would it have been okay if the woman was Jewish? It didn't matter anyway; the only place I could have done it at the time was in Denmark.

Mendel traded in one mother for another and moved in with our aunt in Los Angeles. Dad started staying out late after racquetball to "go drinking with the buddies."

Mom's stroke sucked everyone back in. I began to visit every other month.

I wasn't a four-star chef, or anything close, but I'd learned a few tricks during a brutal year of interning at an all-boys misogynist colosseum of a kitchen. I'd parlayed that into a succession of cooking jobs, culminating in a gig as sous chef for a boutique catering company. I was a food professional—though not exactly eons past my days of stir-frying Hebrew National hot dogs.

A year after Mom's stroke, I decided to go home to Rumson every other weekend and cook for my parents.

Mom was undergoing physical therapy to try to regain the use of her left side and terrorizing the nurses Dad hired until they quit. Her hoarding had gotten so bad that the dining room now housed a mountain of flashlights with bank logos, mismatched plastic place mats, coffee mugs with real estate agency logos, hundreds of bags of stale pretzels, packs of granola bars so old they were covered in dust, old magazines, newspapers, and Sabbath candlesticks. A narrow pathway through it all provided access to the kitchen.

Nobody was ever as happy to see me as my mother. "My *shana madelah*! Come give your mother a hug!"

When she noticed the bags I carried, she said, "Since when do you bring groceries to your mother?"

"I'm a chef now, Mom. I'm going to cook for you."

"I've got Empire kosher fried chicken. It was on special."

"We're gonna have chicken in orange mustard glaze, haricot verts, and basmati rice!" I announced, showing off.

"You know your father can't have salt. No sugar for me—my diabetes. And we only eat kosher chicken. No dairy."

"Mom, I have met you before."

She shrugged. "Marty, I have to go to the bathroom!"

I watched as he trudged into the kitchen and helped her stand up. She grabbed the walker and as she shuffled past me she said, "Remember, no salt."

CHAPTER 47

THE RIOTS

In August of 1991, I took a job cooking at a supper club in Tribeca. Most of the line cooks were either from Jamaica or Africa and they chatted away on their breaks in a language I couldn't understand. One day, in the lull between lunch and dinner, I heard the Senegalese grill man talking with the dishwasher and swore I kept hearing the word *Jew* popping out from their French patois.

"What are you talking about?" I asked.

"The Jews that killed those kids," he said in his French African accent.

"What kids?"

"A Jew mowed down two little kids. The little boy is dead. They are rioting in Crown Heights!"

"Was it an accident?"

"Who the fuck knows, man? But they ain't arresting the guy who did it, that I do know. Ain't gonna arrest no Jews in Crown Heights, only the Black man."

"You know I'm Jewish, right?"

"Yes, man, but you're a different kind of Jew."

"What kind is that?"

"A cool one, man."

On my way home from work, I stopped at a newsstand. All the papers had headlines about Crown Heights, and I bought a copy of each one. As soon as I got into my apartment, I turned on the news.

The first thing I saw was a photograph of the Rebbe. Seeing his face in that context felt strange. What did the Rebbe have to do with some poor dead kids? Next came footage of a crowd of people running for cover as rocks and bottles were hurled. The news anchor explained that a driver in the Rebbe's motorcade had struck two seven-year-old Black children on President Street near Utica Avenue. One little boy, Gavin Cato, was dead. His cousin, Angela Cato, was in critical condition.

The crowd had beaten up the driver. The private Jewish ambulance Hatzalah had then arrived and picked up the Jewish driver while leaving the children on the ground. That's when the crowd erupted.

The tension I'd always felt simmering just under the surface had exploded in wild fury. There was looting, breaking windows, smashing cars, and chanting: "No justice. No peace!"

In apparent retaliation for the car accident, Yankel Rosenbaum, a twenty-nine-year-old student, was stabbed four times and died at the hospital.

Crown Heights was on fire. Screaming protesters swarmed in front of 770, throwing rocks and bottles. When Mayor Dinkins showed up to quell the outrage, they threw bottles at him.

Police in riot gear were called in to keep the peace.

I slumped down on the couch as I watched the recap. How had I missed all of this? I'd been so buried in my intimidating new job supervising the cranking out of a thousand supremely mediocre meals a day that I hadn't turned on the television once since I was hired.

Anya, Lifsa, and finally Fagee had gotten out of Crown Heights. The last time I'd seen Fagee, we'd shared a bagel and cream cheese at a diner on Twenty-Third Street. "I will miss these bagels," she'd said sadly. She was moving back to France.

The last time I'd seen Anya, we'd shared a cigarette on a bench on Eastern Parkway. I remembered the sad look on her face that day. I should have known what was brewing.

"I miss the cows," she'd said.

"The what!?"

"The cows on the kibbutz. I used to tend to them. They're dumb as shit, but they look at you so sweetly with their big, dumb eyes. I've never had anyone look at me as sweetly as those cows."

"That's really sad, Anya," I said laughing, "What about me? I look at you sweetly all the time!"

"Yeah, but you've got smart eyes. To really feel unconditional love, you need a baby or an idiot. Or a cow."

When Anya moved back to Israel, I flashed on an image of her tending her cows with a big joint in her mouth.

One by one, the Crown Heights angels who had made the worst time in my life a little easier had spread out across the globe and fallen out of touch. They were still beacons of warmth for me, though, and always would be.

•·····•·····•·····•·· ··

I looked at the phone sitting on my desk. I longed to call them all and commiserate about the riots. But—it occurred to me in horror—not only did I not have any of their phone numbers, I didn't even know their last names. My lifeline, my sisters-in-arms, my kosher-pizza-and-cheap-wine buddies . . . they were all just first names to me.

The only person I'd hung out with in Crown Heights whose last name I knew was *Danny Cohen*, and I wasn't about to call him.

I thought of Yehudah, the lifer, and Simon who had followed the hippie trail from Woodstock to Haight Ashbury and finally to the Lubavitchers at age twenty-five. I thought of Tom standing guard on Franklin Avenue—sweet, gentlemanly Tom. I thought of Hector and Uncle Pete salsa dancing in the deli. These five very different men had one thing in common: they'd all been kind to me. I hoped they were all right.

I didn't give a rat's ass what happened to Danny Cohen.

Sitting in my air-conditioned apartment with my feet up on the coffee table, I felt a pang of guilt. I'd been so engrossed in my life that I'd been oblivious to a nightmare unfolding in the hood. A little boy and a student were dead. Cops had been shot; even a TV news anchorman, Tim Dolan, had been beaten nearly to death.

The Jews were calling it a pogrom.

I remembered my mother talking about pogroms when I was eight years old.

"What's a pogrom?" I'd asked her.

"That's when the crowds come to kill the Jews, Slovah. If you ever hear that word, run."

Now I felt helpless and guilty. Surely there was something I could do? Something I should do? Why did I care so much about the place I'd once considered to be my prison? Why did I care so much about the people who had shunned me?

"You can leave Kingston Avenue," the kosher-dairy shop-keeper had once said to me, "but it's always on you. The road sticks under your feet."

•···•·•..••...•· ··

One day, Yaya went over to Mom and Dad's in search of free groceries. The lights were all off and Dad's truck was gone, so she assumed no one was home and let herself in. She walked into the living room and turned on the light to find Mom sitting on the living room couch she used as a bed, staring at the wall.

"What are you doing, Mom?" Yaya said, startled.

"Waiting to die."

Back then, nobody knew much about things like OCD or depression. Certainly, my family didn't. We only knew that Mom had "lost her drive." I started calling her once a week to give her pep talks, as if *drive* were something you could force-feed a person.

I'd started writing a cooking column for *Provincetown Magazine,* and when my first piece was published, I clipped it out and mailed it to my mother. In it, I poked a little fun at the way she'd stopped cooking once she got her first microwave, and I was a little nervous about how she'd take it, but I hoped she'd be proud of my accomplishment.

She called a week later. "Slovah, you've immortalized me!"

"So . . . you don't mind that I made a little joke about you?"

"I love it! I sent Marty to make a hundred Xeroxes at the drugstore. I'm going to mail it to everyone! My famous daughter!"

I hadn't heard my mother sound that happy in years. Was her drive coming back?

"Slovah, you're a writer like your mother. Promise you'll keep writing about me."

"How could I not, Mom? There's so much material!"

The last time I'd heard a cackling laugh like the one that came out of her at that moment, I was still living at home. I'd been sitting by her side helping her clip the expiration dates off coupons. In the middle of a stack of special offers for Ragu tomato sauce, she found a ten-dollar bill she had hidden "for a rainy day."

"Slovah!!! It's raining!" she exclaimed. "Time to go to Dairy Queen!"

· · · · · · · · · · · · ·

My parents were on a highway in North Carolina, driving back from Florida for a family Rosh Hashanah reunion at the Rumson house, when Mom went into cardiac arrest. She never made it home.

While she drew her final breaths, I was on my way to the gathering with a wonderful surprise for her. After a decade of listening to her go on and on about how I should go to college, I'd finally signed up for the fall semester at a city school called Empire State College. I'd promised myself—and her—that the moment I had a reason to go to college, I would, and now I had one. That article in *Provincetown Magazine* had made me want to be a better writer.

"I'll never get to tell her now," I cried to Tilly.

"She knows, honey. A mother knows."

CHAPTER 48

1994

The morning of June 12, 1994, I was sitting on the windowsill of my West Village apartment sipping Bustelo. I flipped open *The New York Times* and scanned the headlines.

Rebbe Schneerson was dead.

I felt as if I'd gone into a *Star Trek*–style transporter back to 1981. In an instant, I felt it all: the fear, the loneliness, the hunger—and the moment that the Rebbe had stared into my soul with his deep-set, kind, sad eyes.

Now he was gone, and I was overcome with a feeling of loss for both him and my mother. Grief for the two of them merged into one black hole of pain.

I heard Fagee's voice in my head: *The Rebbe blessed you. That is forever!*

On a quiet afternoon, in the lull between Rosh Hashanah and Yom Kippur, I returned to Kingston Avenue. Notebook, pens, chewing gum, and subway tokens in hand, I made my pilgrimage, intent on saying goodbye to the Rebbe in person—or at least on his home turf—and perhaps burying the last bits of rage that still sparked up whenever I heard mention of Crown Heights.

I was voluntarily going back to my former prison. On the 2 train to New Lots, I still stood out among the crowd of staring

West Indian passengers. It was midafternoon. The businessmen were already at work and the kids were not yet out of school. This had always been my time to ride the trains.

Two Lubavitch men diagonally across from me seemed to sense I was headed for Crown Heights, but when I attempted to make eye contact, they quickly returned to their prayer books. How familiar it felt as I sat there trying to decide who I had more in common with, the Lubavitchers or the Jamaicans.

When I climbed out of the subway, 770 shot up before me. I squinted at it as my eyes adjusted to the sunlight. The old shrine to the Rebbe was getting a facelift, complete with new iron fencing and real stone steps. Work crews scurried around the aged façade like flies around roadkill, attacking the brown structure mercilessly with their tools.

Modern alterations to this dinosaur seemed almost blasphemous.

Pushing past a stream of Chasidic men working hard not to let their bodies touch mine as I passed, I took the side steps up into the women's tower. Nothing had changed. Prayer books were scattered across the pain-inducing wooden benches thick with layers of dull brown paint. A sign posted on the wall read "Please don't talk in shul."

Who was there to talk to, anyway?

Peering down at the main floor, I saw a hundred or so men in prayer shawls and tefillin. Most seemed in a state of despair or frenzy, chanting to themselves in near delirium as they mourned their leader. The smell of sweat and dust and candle wax wafted through the air with the help of a row of ceiling fans.

I sat down on one of the benches. Two old women a few feet away looked me over and whispered.

I began reciting one of the few prayers I knew by heart: "*Yis gadal ve yis Kadash she mei raba . . .*"

When the women realized I was reciting the Mourner's kaddish, they nodded their approval and turned away. Evidently, it was okay for a woman to wear pants if she was mourning the dead.

The last time I'd been inside 770 was to celebrate the Rebbe's eightieth birthday, along with thousands of Lubavitchers— more than I'd ever seen in one place. The Rebbe had sat on his red chair and spoken in Yiddish for hours. There had been so many women crammed into the tower that I'd narrowly escaped a full-blown anxiety attack. When someone stepped on my foot, I couldn't even look down to see who'd done it. Just as I was sure I was going to pass out, the strangest thing happened. Out of the avalanche of Yiddish pouring from the Rebbe's mouth came something I understood.

"*Nashama.*"

Soul.

He said it several times. He was speaking about the soul.

It felt like a doorway had opened to let in a radiant light.

"*Nashama.*"

His was a simple message, really. He wanted his followers to fill their souls with godliness, not gold.

I stood tippy-toed to peek out over the crush of women and caught a glimpse of the fragile-looking old man with the strength to speak for hours without notes.

"*Nashama.* I hear you," I said just above a whisper. And at that precise moment, with ten thousand Chasids between the Rebbe and me, I saw him glance up.

Did I imagine it?

"*Shhh!*" the irritated woman wedged next to me said as she jabbed me with her elbow. "Be quiet."

"*Nashama!*" I said back to the startled woman.

Nashama, I said to myself.

I was absolutely convinced that he had heard me.

•···•·•\••···•·· ··

Now he was gone.

I walked to the locker section of the women's tower and sifted through the tattered Hebrew books, searching for something to shake away the cold settling inside me. The bulletin board on the wall was covered with notices: "Moshiach Car Service," "Wigs by Deborah," "Babysitter available . . ."

Modern facelift aside, 770 was almost as I remembered it—but it seemed subdued, especially for the High Holidays. Missing were the thousands of visitors who'd poured onto the streets during the lull in the "Days of Awe." They'd come by the busload and fill the takeaway meat store with cries of "Me next! . . . Kishka, one pound!" Huddling together in the dairy eatery, they'd sip their strong, bitter coffee, then tear off bits of sweet, fruity strudel as a chaser.

To a tourist, Kingston Avenue probably looked much as it had a decade ago. Ess & Bentch luncheonette was still there; so were the mom-and-pop grocery stores and Raskin's Fish Market. I passed the Mitzvah Tank and Weinstein's Hardware, then entered the Judaic gift shop, which reminded me of a souvenir stand my family had visited in Memphis the year Elvis died. Prints, paintings, key chains, postcards, biographies, letters, and posters of the Rebbe filled the store. I didn't know whether to laugh or be offended. Commercializing the Rebbe!? What next—Rebbe T-shirts? Then I saw those, too.

The merchant seemed amused by my purchase of a set of Rebbe postcards I simply couldn't resist. I smiled as he counted out my change, and asked, "Was it crowded here for Rosh Hashanah?"

He looked up.

"No, not at all. Not like it used to be." He reflected for a moment, then sighed. "People used to come from all over the world to see the Rebbe, but now . . ."

"Now?"

"Now, we are just a small community in a high-crime neighborhood in New York City. Why should they come?"

"I used to live here."

"Everyone seems to have a connection to this place, even Barbra Streisand. I bet you don't miss it, though. Maybe the memories, but not living here."

The customer behind me was getting restless, and I sensed that old disapproval: *Don't talk to the outsiders.*

My conversation with the shopkeeper ended politely, and I exited onto Kingston. The Lubavitchers seemed to move more slowly than I remembered, as if they were just going through the motions. Sleepwalking. The community did not have that buzz of life and nervous energy that used to fuel the air like electricity before a storm. I suddenly felt like I was watching a crowd of background extras in a big-budget movie.

A brightly colored banner bearing the Rebbe's image stretched across Kingston Avenue announcing, "Welcome, Moshiach!" A flag proclaimed, "Moshiach is on the way. Be a part of it."

The movie continued.

I made my way a little farther down Kingston Avenue and walked into Uncle Pete's bodega. The bulletproof glass was gone, and the counter was painted canary yellow. Behind it, a Puerto Rican woman sold cigarettes.

"Is Uncle Pete or Hector here?"

"Pete!? He gone long ago . . . back to Puerto Rico. I bought the bodega from him in '92."

"What about Hector?"

"I think he move to Jersey City."

I nodded and looked around. The place was cleaner than I remembered it, with a wider assortment of canned goods: Goya beans, Campbell's soups . . . I guessed the new owner wasn't in the weed business.

"If you ever see Hector again, tell him La Rubia stopped by."

"Okay, *Mamita*."

I walked over to the kosher pizza joint, my old hangout. It, too, looked like it had undergone a facelift, and sported a bright neon sign that read "Kingston Pizza." Inside, it felt more like a Wendy's than a Jewish pizza joint. Full-color fluorescent signboards advertised tahini, babaganoush, falafel, baked white-fish, kugel, and pizza. I stuck with what I hoped was a safe bet: falafel and an iced tea.

A few non-Chasidic locals—pioneer artists, I gathered—stood in front of me at the counter, pooling their small change to make a purchase. Their kind had been sprouting up in patches along the outskirts of the community, drawn by the relatively large spaces and low rent. After piling up all of their collective pennies and nickels on the counter, they received one slice and a side-order of stuffed grape leaves. The gray-haired Israeli behind the counter mumbled, "Why not throw in a few quarters for once. Make my day!"

I approached him. "Is Uzzi still here?"

"Uzzi? No. It's my place now. Why? Does he owe you money?"

"No."

"Good for you. He owes everyone else."

Pushing my luck just a tad, I said, "I haven't been here for a while. It feels different but I can't quite figure out what's changed . . ."

"Everything is the same!" he barked.

"But aren't there fewer people now that the Rebbe is gone?"

As if intoning a prophecy, he replied, "Four hundred people are coming in four days!"

As I sat down at a table with my food, a Lubavitch girl sharing a pizza with her parents shot me a startled glance, then turned her back. What was she scared of? An unfamiliar white lady in jeans, I guessed.

Lucky for her, I was just passing through.

Back on the Avenue, I closed my eyes to try to feel the old hum of life, but everything felt still. Crown Heights had deflated.

A group of moms in matching wigs trotted past, pushing their babies in strollers, dragging toddlers by the hand. They stared through me and continued on. One thing hadn't changed: I would always be an outsider here.

I walked by my last apartment in Crown Heights, the only one for which I had an actual lease. The bachelorette pad over the pharmacy had been my fortress—until it was broken into, that is. The large two-bedroom for which I'd paid $250 a month was now a podiatrist's office.

I remembered the parties I'd had there, among the milk-crate chairs and laundry-basket coffee table. I'd created feasts of spaghetti in tomato sauce out of a jar chased by countless beers and joints rolled with the good stuff from the Rastas across the Parkway.

I remembered Danny. I heard his high-pitched giggle. How many nights had he giggled away on my couch. Until . . .

Until.

"You can always trust a boy with a yarmulke," Mom used to say.

You were wrong, Mom.

I kept walking.

A stocky man who was all but obscured by a wondrous, bushy red beard displayed his wares on the sidewalk: children's books and toys. To my surprise, he smiled at me. I stopped to talk.

Searching through the Jewish storybooks, I tried to find the least threatening voice in which to inquire, "How has it changed here since the Rebbe died?"

"Who are you?" he asked in a heavy Russian accent. "Do you write for a newspaper?"

"Well, no. But I am a writer."

He froze.

"I used to live here . . . ten years or so ago. I remember the Rebbe and all the people."

He shrugged.

I sighed and murmured the password he'd been waiting for: "I am Jewish."

He looked into my eyes as if searching for something.

"We are waiting for Moshiach."

The movie inside my head resumed.

"How long will you wait?"

"I am not a rabbi. I can only say that we are just waiting."

Suddenly, the question I'd been carrying around all day was answered. I felt ridiculous for not understanding the situation from the start. The inhabitants of Kingston Avenue were not sleepwalking. They were waiting. This was a community caught between departure and arrival, between sorrow and rejoicing, frozen in time, waiting for the resurrection of the Rebbe.

The man continued, "The people here are closed. In Russia, it was not so closed. The children are open, though. My son turned five years old just a few days ago. I gave him a stuffed animal and a book. He opened the window and threw them out. 'I want Moshiach!' he yelled." The man looked up at me. "Children say more than adults sometimes."

There were police on almost every corner. They seemed to be waiting as well, or just going through the motions, making a show of beefed-up protection. As always, crimes could be committed on the other side of the tracks in Bedford Stuyvesant, but not here.

A television news crew pulled up to 770 and jumped out like a SWAT team. The Lubavitchers scattered like rabbits as a female reporter approached me. "Do you think they'll let us film in the synagogue?" she asked.

I shrugged, feigning ignorance, and strolled away, suddenly protective of the community. Maybe I was more of an "insider" than I'd realized.

As the reporters wandered around looking for someone who'd provide a sound bite, I felt myself going back in time as the bitter taste of how it had all ended filled my throat and clouded my senses. I needed to pace to clear my head.

I needed to escape again.

Making my way back to the subway as day ebbed into evening, I felt the urge to run—to run as fast as I could until the road ended and then find another one and keep running. Instead, I breathed in and out, calming myself as I plodded down Kingston Avenue. *Plip, plop, plip, plop.* I felt bits of who I had been dropping to the ground behind me—emotional garbage now, crumbs of the girl who had lived for a while among the believers.

On the platform waiting for the 2 train, two Lubavitch schoolgirls huddled against the wall. One read aloud from her prayer book.

"Excuse me," I interrupted. "Would you mind if I just asked you a question?"

"*Shhh!*"

I waited as she finished her prayer, then spoke again. "With the Rebbe gone, do you think the crowds will return?"

She looked into my eyes as she thought about it. "Some will come. Some will not. My friends ask me, 'Why do you still go to the Rebbe's synagogue without him?' I answer, 'Because his essence is still there.' I believe some will come for his essence."

Her friend jumped in. "We go on as usual, but we are a little sad."

It was the first time that day that anyone had admitted his or her feelings to me. *We are a little sad.* I thought of the Russian man's words, "Children say more sometimes."

"I'm a little sad, too," I replied as I headed toward the door of the incoming train. "Thanks for reminding me."

CHAPTER 49

FINDING MY JEWISH

By the time I left Crown Heights, I felt about as Jewish as Jesus. (Well, maybe not quite *that* Jewish.) I didn't want anything to do with yarmulkes or shul. I felt practically anti-Semitic.

Anti–Chasi-mitic, I corrected myself.

When I was a kid—long before my Crown Heights adventure—I accompanied my parents to the Orthodox shul they went to in New Jersey for the High Holidays. My mother would forgo services, instead sitting perched in a large armchair in the lobby with a white lace doily bobby-pinned to her head. I guess she felt that just being in the building was enough. I tried sitting through the services, but the separation of men and women, and the "only the men are allowed at the pulpit" thing, filled me with fury.

I would storm into the lobby and fall into the chair next to my mother. "Women should be up there too!" I'd rage. "We're just as smart!"

"We're smarter!" she'd reply.

Mom used her lobby time to impart her special brand of wisdom to her children. "Slovah, as you go through life, you may have a nice meal, a warm bed, a good experience, but no one ever got anything from paying a compliment. Instead, you must find some little thing to kvetch about; maybe the food isn't hot enough or the carpet isn't clean. If you can find some little thing to complain about, they'll give you something: a free meal, a discount, a cup of coffee. This wisdom I impart to you, my Slovah."

* ··· * · ·•....•· · ·

The only person who could have enticed me back to an Orthodox shul at this point was my father, but that wasn't going to happen. Three months after Mom died, Dad had met a woman named Natalie at a Jewish senior center. Natalie liked to be the center of attention; she objected to all talk about my mother. My father, who had been *yes*-ing Harriet for thirty-nine years, began *yes*-ing Natalie instead. The photos of Mom were put away, the Xeroxes of newspaper clippings about her triumphs in local poetry contests hidden. It was as if my mother had never existed. Soon, Dad moved to San Diego with Natalie, and none of his children were allowed in their home.

What was the point of my father keeping kosher and going to shul on Shabbos if he was walking out on his own children? So much for Orthodox Jewry.

I heard from a pal about a gay synagogue in the city, Congregation Beit Simchat Torah. Evidently, it got so jammed during the Jewish holidays that they had to rent out part of the mammoth Javits convention center. I decided to visit the place.

When I walked in and saw men with men, women with women, black, white, Asian, Hispanic, Israeli, Indian people, lesbians with babies, adoring grandparents, and a female rabbi standing at the podium, I knew I'd found a home.

Thousands of people attended my first Rosh Hashanah at CBST—as Congregation Beit Simchat Torah was known—and the choir raised the roof with song. "*Oseh shalom bimromav,*" I joined in at maximum volume. As I sang, I felt my heart lifting. It was the first time I had fully opened myself to Judaism since I'd caught the eye of the Rebbe. "*Hu ya'aseh shalom aleynu!*"

"*Nashama*," I whispered. "I hear you."

I'd been looking for a place to go for Yizkor, the break during the Yom Kippur service when the spouses and immediate family of those who have recently died stay to pray for them.

In my childhood, all the kids would leave during Yizkor while all the grownups stayed—and of course I'd relished escaping the boredom of the service to run around in the grass out front or, as a teenager, sneak cigarettes. I'd called Yizkor the "us and them" service. We were the "us," chasing each other through the poorly tended grass. The sad, old adults were the "them," bent, teary-eyed and serious, chanting in Hebrew and whispering silent messages to their lost loved ones.

But in September of 1992, as I'd stood to leave with the other young people, the rabbi had looked over and motioned for me to sit. My mother had passed away a few days before Rosh Hashanah and I had become an official member of "them."

At CBST, I felt I'd found a place to say the prayers for Yizkor.

"*Nashama*."

I'd found a home.

●·····●·´·˜●···●··· · ·

I would never have predicted that my hippie-dippie friend Sarah would go from peace, love, and Todd Rundgren to the life of a corporate banker, but that is exactly what happened, right after she graduated from Sarah Lawrence College. The bigger shock came eight years after that, when she quit banking to become a Jewish charity fundraiser and something of a Jewish scholar. By the time the Rebbe died, Sarah had become a full-blown expert in the faith.

Over a "kosher-style" dinner one night, Sarah said, "You know, Rossi, I've been thinking. Maybe all those years ago, when the Rebbe gave you the blessed wine and gave cake to the rest of the seven hundred women, he was protecting you."

"From who?"

"The Rebbe was so pious. He knew everything. He knew how judgmental his community could be of outsiders. He wanted to show them that he considered you worthy of respect."

"I never thought of it that way."

"Did you know that the *ba'al teshuvas* are considered one step holier than those born into the Lubavitchers?"

"Really? Is that because we've been put through the mill?"

"Exactly. You've gone through the trials of the outside world. The Rebbe didn't just want to single you out. He wanted to honor you."

⁕⸳⸳⸳⸳

On September 11, 2001, I ran up to the roof deck of the East Village building I'd lived in since 1999 and watched in horror as the towers of the World Trade Center burned.

"How do you think they'll put the fires out?" I asked my neighbor, Nick.

"Helicopters," he replied.

This was Manhattan, the city of my dreams, the place I'd longed for during the two years I'd been exiled in Crown Heights. Now its tallest skyscrapers—symbols of its centrality in the world—were on fire.

And then just like that, I saw a flurry of what looked like silver cards in the air as the first tower fell. I'd never heard a sound like the one that followed, and hope never to again: screaming from all sides—from rooftops, fire escapes, streets— as we simultaneously witnessed the unthinkable.

•·····•·•~•...•~··

On September 16, I hopped a pickup truck and grabbed a hard hat. With my volunteer ID hanging from my neck and a ventilator mask clutched in my hand, I headed to St. Paul's Church at Ground Zero to feed the first responders.

"She's a chef!" the security guard announced, and everyone clapped.

I flipped burgers on three small backyard barbecues for firefighters, cops, Con Ed workers, and volunteers. According to reports I read later, I helped feed a thousand people my first day. I would take breaks from grilling to push a wheelbarrow filled with Gatorade to what they called the "pile," then hand cold drinks to firefighters crawling around on the smoldering remains of the towers.

I'd gotten my friend Brian a job organizing the socks, Band-Aids, eye drops, and other supplies that had been donated by the boxload. As we worked side by side, we looked out at the ruins of the towers. We were both covered in dust, and when we blew our noses, black soot came out.

"Hell of a place to spend Rosh Hashanah," Brian said.

"Yeah, but I wouldn't want to be anywhere else in the world. Would you?"

"Nope."

An army chaplain set up an impromptu Rosh Hashanah service. Along with a hasty assembly of other Jewish workers, I watched a rabbi in camouflage and yarmulke, his beard long and white, offer prayers and blow the shofar. The mournful sound of the ram's horn resonated off the remnants of broken buildings and broken hearts. At that moment, I felt as close to *Hashem* as I supposed I would ever get.

"Everything in my life brought me right here," I said to Brian.

"I know what you mean."

As I did every year since I'd found them, I attended Yom Kippur services at Congregation Beit Simchat Torah. They rented their usual space in the Javits Center, but that year the synagogue was sharing the mammoth venue with the command center for "the disaster."

As we made our way to services, we encountered ranks of state troopers and police on their way to the convention center for their own purposes. Most of the side streets leading in were blocked by police barricades, and helicopters buzzed overhead. It felt like entering a war zone.

CBST was known for its diversity, but that year every imaginable kind of person was in attendance: black men in yarmulkes, white lesbian mothers of Asian babies, elderly men escorting elderly wives, young Jewish men with their boyfriends and mothers, hipsters with shaved heads and facial piercings, devout Jews wearing *tallis* and their own embroidered yarmulkes . . . and me.

It wasn't until near the end of the service, during the sermon, that the real magnitude of what we were all feeling hit me.

Rabbi Sharon Kleinbaum spoke. "When services began, I told you that this was our largest Yom Kippur attendance ever, at least four thousand people, but since then, we have added chairs. There are now six thousand people here tonight!"

She asked the front row to stand and look back, the people in side rows to stand and look toward the center. And when all of us were facing one another, fully aware of the size and power of our numbers, she gave voice to what we were all thinking.

"This is something close to the number of people missing at the World Trade Center."

Many started to cry. I was one of them.

The rabbi tried to find the words to help us all make sense of this unfathomable tragedy. "Our broken hearts are part of who we are now," she said.

Mine felt as if it were held together with duct tape and bubblegum. I thought back to the day my parents dropped me onto the couch of Redbeard. I thought back to the day I heard about my mother's death on her way to our family reunion. I thought back to the day the Rebbe died. I had been sure I had no room in my heart for more pain . . . but now thousands more lost souls resided there.

I'd traipsed through the dust of Ground Zero, so thick it felt like fresh snow. What was in that dust? *Who* was in that dust? I'd fed firefighters digging through rubble with badly burned hands, looking for their friends and colleagues. One day, as I made my way through the pile, I saw that someone had scrawled a message into the dust on an abandoned car windshield: *They may take our bodies, but they'll never take our souls.*

It was time to say Kaddish for them all. "*Yis'gadal v'yis'ka-dash sh'mei raba.*"

Our broken hearts are part of who we are now.

CHAPTER 50

LA FAMILIA

I spent a year and a half with a six-foot-two blonde German runway model named Heidi. It was a relationship built on sex and free dinners at the club where I was chef. Most people we knew considered us to be a glamorous couple: the chef and the model. But every time a holiday rolled around, Heidi was conveniently unavailable.

"Aren't we going to spend Thanksgiving together?"

"Have to take care of my mom—her back is out."

When Heidi bailed on Valentine's Day because of a toothache, I called bullshit.

"What the fuck, Heidi? Why do you blow me off every single holiday!?"

She hesitated, then said, "Because if we spend a holiday together, then it's like we're really a couple."

"And that's bad because . . . ?"

"Because if we were really a couple that would mean I'm gay and . . . I don't want to be gay."

Before the next holiday rolled around, Heidi left me for a man she met at a Club Med.

Tilly had long since married a cartoonist and moved to Chelsea, but we'd meet one Monday a month for drinks.

"Tilly, why did she leave me?"

"Honey, anyone could tell from a mile away that that girl wasn't available. A better question is, are *you* available?"

"What do you mean? Of course I am!"

Waving her finger in the air, Tilly explained myself to me as only Tilly could do. "Rossi. You spent three years with that Grenadian chick who only cared about herself, two years with that Dominican chick who only cared about herself, a year and half with this German giant who really, *really*, only cared about herself. I don't know what or who fucked you up so badly, but you've got one whopper of an intimacy issue!"

"I dated you for a minute, didn't I?"

"I rest my case. I am not gay. You need to get over yourself and find a woman who can love you as much as she loves herself. Someone who feels like *family*."

"Well, not like *my* family."

"Good point."

I thought about the morning decades earlier when I'd scraped together enough change to buy a buttered roll at Uncle Pete's. When I'd pushed my pile of mostly pennies into the bulletproof glass turnaround, Hector had laughed. "*M'ita, mami*, don't your *papi* ever give you *dinero*?"

"My parents suck! The only thing they give me is shit!"

"No brothers, sisters?"

"They're useless!"

"*Mami*! *La familia* is everything! Do you know how lucky you are? All these gringos come and go, but *la familia* is forever, man!"

⁕⸱⸱⸱⁕⸱⸱⸱⸱⸱⸱⁕

My family did rally together after Mom had the stroke, but once she died, we went our separate ways.

My mother had never forgiven Yaya for marrying a non-Jew. It was only when she left her husband and showed up with an adorable two-month-old baby boy named Drew that Mom agreed to start talking to her again. Even then, it was never the same. She started calling Yaya *Pat*.

"Why do you keep calling her *Pat*, Mom?" I asked.

"Because my beautiful daughter Yaya is dead. This is my friend Pat. She is a loose woman. Pat her on the head, her legs fly open."

But Mom was so smitten with baby Drew that she agreed to let "Pat" move into the top floor of the two-family house in Carteret that her sister Roslyn had left her.

Yaya and Mom had been fighting when Mom died, and the news of her demise seemed to push the already fragile Yaya off the deep end. She rarely left North Jersey after that.

Mendel moved out of our aunt's house eventually, but never left Los Angeles. Dad remained shacked up with his mean-spirited girlfriend in San Diego. I stayed in Manhattan and kept as far away from all of them as I could.

Mendel met Delia, an Israeli, at a Jewish singles dance, and they were married a few months later. A month after my Mom died, they had a baby girl and named her Hannah after Mom's Hebrew name. Then they had another baby girl and named her Tovah.

No one in the family expected what happened next.

Mendel began wearing a yarmulke and let his beard grow. His wife covered her head in a scarf and dressed their daughters in maxi skirts and shirts with long sleeves, just like the girls at Machon Chana.

"Are you Chasidic now?" I asked when I saw him, thoroughly horrified at the thought. I didn't know if it was because of the private Hebrew school Mendel had put the girls in to honor our mother, or just because he yearned for a sense of community, but he had become über-religious.

"We're not Chasidic," he replied. "We're ultra-Orthodox."

I still couldn't tell you the difference.

One Saturday night, an hour after Shabbos ended, I got a call.

"Sis, we're coming to town and want to visit 770!"

"Not Times Square, Broadway, the Statue of Liberty . . . ?"

When we met in front of his hotel, I almost didn't recognize my brother. He'd gained thirty pounds and, between that and his thick beard and black fedora, he looked like a middle-aged rabbi. He would have fit right in at Redbeard's.

Mendel pushed right past his wife and daughters and came running toward me. "Doo!" he crooned my childhood nickname. He hugged me so hard I started to cough. "I can't wait to see your old haunt!"

"You know I didn't exactly want to go there, right?"

Mendel looked down at his shoes and cleared his throat, just as he had when we were kids. "Mom and Dad never told me what happened. Only that you were going to stay at a rabbi's house. To tell you the truth, I was kind of jealous."

"You thought it would be fun to go live with a rabbi?"

"I was dying to get out of Rumson, but I was too scared."

"I never thought I'd hear you admit that."

"Doo. It's like there was a big bowl of bravery, just enough for each of us to get a third, but you took all of it."

"You and Yaya had kids. I am definitely not brave enough to do that!"

•····•'·•◦···•··· ··

We drove over the Manhattan Bridge, down Flatbush, past Grand Army Plaza, and parked on Eastern Parkway. Twenty-one years had passed since I had been abandoned by our parents in this place, and now I was being dragged down Eastern Parkway by Mendel's two joyful daughters.

At ages eight and ten, the girls were beyond excited to see the great Rebbe's shul.

"Let's go, Aunt Rossi! I want to see the Rebbe!" said the older one, Hannah.

"You know he's dead, right?"

"Yes, but his essence lives on!" said Tovah.

Funny, I thought, *that's just what the young girl in the subway station had said.*

"And his chair!" added Hannah.

"Now, girls," I said. "Remember what I taught you! Never walk when you can sashay!"

I started strutting down the street like a supermodel, and the girls giddily followed.

"Sashay! Sashay!" they screamed in delight.

As we approached the old synagogue, Delia got out her video camera. She taped Mendel touching the brick wall outside, then her daughters doing the same. She taped me rolling my eyes.

Inside 770, the girls ran up the stairs to the women's section while Mendel stayed downstairs to pray with the men. As I lingered at the base of the stairs, I saw a young Chasidic man staring at my shoulder, where my tank top left part of my winged-lion tattoo exposed.

I waved at him. "It's very holy!" I said. "The Lion of Judah!"

I let the girls drag me upstairs, leaving Delia behind. Within seconds, I was covered in a film of sweat. "Some things never change," I said under my breath—but loud enough to draw a hissing "*Shhh!*" from one of the older women.

Like I said.

An hour later, we three emerged drenched onto Kingston Avenue to rejoin Delia. A half hour after that, Mendel bounded out, gleeful.

"I feel so holy!" he proclaimed.

"Oh, you're holy, all right."

The banner with the Rebbe's picture still stretched across Kingston Avenue, welcoming Moshiach.

"They are still waiting for him to come back," Delia said.

"It's gonna be a long wait," I said.

A tour bus disgorged loads of bewigged women wearing long skirts over leggings. "And this was the Rebbe's shul!" announced the tour guide through a scratchy microphone.

Walking down Kingston Avenue, we passed the kosher-dairy luncheonette, Weinstein's Hardware, and the Judaic gift shop. The shop windows were filled with Rebbe keepsakes: T-shirts, key chains, postcards, photo albums. The girls dragged their parents inside while I stayed on the sidewalk enjoying a moment of sunshine.

I looked up and saw Simon, my old ex-hippie pal. His dark beard had turned white, and he walked with a bit of a limp, but he still smiled with his whole face.

"Simon!" I shouted, momentarily forgetting the rules, and going in for a hug. He stepped back before I touched him.

"Virtual hug then!"

"You look wonderful!" he said.

"You look old!" I said, and we both laughed. "Do you still have that big knife?"

"Yep. And I gave one to each of my six daughters, too."

"Simon. I'm so happy to see your *punim*! How is Yehudah?"

"Yehudah? Which Yehudah?"

"I never knew anyone's last name. I don't even know yours."

"Silber. Simon Silber at your service."

"Well, Simon Silber, I want to thank you. You were nice to me when I needed it the most."

"Who on earth wasn't nice to you?"

"Once I started wearing jeans, most people."

"I hate to hear that." He looked as if he might cry. "You were so easy to be nice to."

As I pondered that unlikely fact, the girls emerged from the shop with their Rebbe keychains and postcards.

"Come on, Aunt Rossi!" they shouted, grabbing my hands, and starting to drag me down the block.

I looked back at Simon. "Meet my nieces, Simon. Want to tag along on our tour of the neighborhood?"

"I'm sorry, Slovah, I have to work. But call me." He closed the space between us and gave me his card. "I'll tell all the Yehudahs I know you said hello."

I shepherded my brother's family down Kingston and pointed out where I used to live—the bachelorette pad–turned– podiatrist's shop.

I could almost see the teenage me looking out the front window blowing smoke rings.

"Hey, girls, what do you think of the place? I only paid 250 bucks a month!"

"Did the Rebbe ever come over?" Tovah asked.

"No. We . . . weren't that close."

Mendel looked up and then back at me and said, "I wish I'd visited you then."

I patted him on the back. "Somehow I don't think you would have dug the fact that I was gay and had a Black girlfriend."

"*Shhh*," Delia said. "We haven't told the children about any of that."

I rolled my eyes and remembered quite clearly why I'd remained distant from my brother and his posse.

•···•·••••···•·

I met Lyla—a pretty Italian girl with rich black hair—in Provincetown through mutual friends. We spent the week laughing and exploring the many wonders of the seaside town, then stayed in touch after we got back, but never became more than friends.

"You know she likes you, right?" my pal Charlotte observed.

"It would never work. She's not my type."

"And what's your type?"

"Androgynous, kinda butchy-futchy."

"Alcoholic, conceited, dishonest, self-absorbed . . . am I missing anything?"

I decided to give Lyla a chance.

One night after we'd met for dinner, I took her hand and said, "Let's try a little experiment." We stood close together and began kissing . . . and it was sweet. Uncomfortably sweet.

I stepped back and looked at Lyla looking at me with dreamy eyes. We'd been laughing all evening. Now we were kissing.

You need to find a woman who feels like family.

Within a week of that kiss, it became hard to imagine life without her. It still is.

• ⋯ • ˙ ▪▖⋯ ▪ ⋅ ⋅

In 2010, I started something I'd never had: a friendship with my father. He had been unhappy with his mean girlfriend for years and wanted desperately to leave her. With no one else he could trust, he decided to rely on me, the black sheep of the family. I would fly out to San Diego, he'd pick me up, and we would go straight to Anthony's on the Bay for fish.

On a visit in 2011, Dad dropped a pile of unpaid bills on the table and started to cry. I'd only ever seen him cry twice: once when his sister died, and once when my mother did.

"Can you help me, please, Slovah? It's all getting to be a bit too much for me."

My tough World War II–vet dad, who'd never needed anything from anybody, needed me.

"Of course, Daddio. I'm here for you. I'll always be here for you."

From that moment on, we switched roles. I became the parent and Dad became my large, white-haired child.

• ⋯ • ˙ ▪▖⋯ ▪ ⋅ ⋅

Just back from a trip to California, I was grilled by my friend Wolf. "Your dad abandoned you in Crown Heights, hooked up with that witch right after your mom died, and walked out on his kids. How can you be doting on him now?"

"It's kind of like going back and doing for him what I wished he'd done for me. All those years of being poor and alone in New York City . . . I could have used a father."

* * *

When Dad fell in the shower in 2012, I moved him into a quiet apartment in an assisted living center on Pico Boulevard in Los Angeles. His apartment had a sliding glass door that opened to a patio in the back, where a single beam of sunshine broke over the concrete structure in the late afternoon.

I took it upon myself to provide as much love as I could slather on him and enlisted my girlfriend Lyla's help as surrogate daughter when work kept me away. I pampered him with his favorite treats: kosher hot dogs with sauerkraut and mustard (cut into four portions to keep him from choking), Chinese vegetable rolls with the red sauce he loved, dairy-free apple pie, bananas. The man loved bananas.

For four years, I flew out to spend a week with him every other month. Visiting Dad was like calculating a tree's age by counting its rings. At every visit, I noted a steady, slow decline. His attempts at walking disappeared; his ability to converse dwindled to the point where he could get out just a sentence or two.

One afternoon, while Lyla was fetching Dad coffee from Starbucks, I asked, "Dad, do you like Lyla?"

He nodded his head.

"You know we're together, right?"

He nodded his head again and said in a scratchy voice, "'At's okay!"

"Dad. . . how would you feel if we got married?"

His eyes grew wide. "Abomination!"

Some things even senility can't soften.

By the stricken look on my face, Marty sensed something was suddenly wrong. "Lyla! Where's Lyla? Lyla!"

"She'll be back soon, dad. She went to get your coffee."

"Lyla," he said again as he slipped into a doze in his chair.

•····•·•◦····•·· ··

In his last year, I put Dad into hospice care. He loved the extra attention and flirted shamelessly with the new nurses.

"Tell him you're sorry for whatever!" a pal advised me, knowing my father's time was growing short.

"*I'm* sorry!? He was never there for me!"

Then again . . . what could it hurt?

"Dad . . . we fought a lot when I was a kid. I was very wild. You were so strict . . . but I want you to know . . . I forgive you."

He looked at me with murky eyes and smiled. "I forgive you, too."

You forgive me!? I wanted to scream. *You abandoned me when I was sixteen and didn't give a fuck about me till I was forty-six!* But instead, I said, "Dad . . . I'm sorry I gave you such a hard time."

"Yes," he smiled and nodded in approval.

Winning Dad's approval had never been at the top of my list of priorities, at least not consciously. I guess it had been easier to embrace rebellion than try and fail to live up to his standards. Throughout my childhood, his smiles and nods had been visible as rarely as double rainbows. But in his last years, I won a nod every time I walked in the door. *There's my beautiful daughter who never forgets me!* he'd say—if not in words, then in gestures.

On one of my last visits, I helped the nurse position him in bed so she could change him into his pajamas. As she pulled off his shirt, I looked at his torso: not bad for eighty-nine. With his little pooch of a belly and soft white chest hair, he looked like a teddy bear. I reached over, petting his belly for a moment and thought about our vacations at the Jersey Shore. When I was six, Dad had held me up over the crashing waves to keep them from sucking me away. He'd seemed like a giant to me then. Now, my GI Joe giant of a dad was a childlike teddy bear.

"I love you," I said.

"I love you, too," he said, almost singing it.

Would this day be our last together?

"Dad . . . has Mommy been coming to see you?"

"She's gone."

"Yes, I know, Dad, but in your dreams?"

"Yes," he said as he started to blink the sleep away.

"Tell her I miss her."

"Okay," he said, closing his eyes.

I left two bananas by his bed.

CHAPTER 51

BREADCRUMBS
ON THE PATH

"**I**'ll be right over," Ted called out.

As the Q&A continued at the Jewish Book Festival in Naples, poor Ted was getting quite a workout. Audience members waved their hands in the air furiously as he dashed madly over to one after another with the microphone.

I'd been told that the more questions you get at one of these events, the better you've done. If they want to get rid of you . . . it's just crickets when the MC asks, "Are there any questions?"

As Ted scurried over to somebody at the far left of the stage, I glanced up at Danny.

He caught me looking and waved.

I felt a headache forming.

Danny was dressed in yellow golf shorts and a white button-down shirt that hung untucked over his protruding belly. His curly gray hair was unkempt. To a stranger, Danny probably looked like somebody's father: approachable, kind. Safe.

He'd always looked safe.

The mic squealed as a woman grabbed it and asked, "What's your favorite thing to cook?"

"Oh . . . that changes every week. Right now, it's Korean barbecue beef. Last week it was jerk chicken."

An elderly lady asked, "Is your mother alive?"

"No. She's gone to an all-you-can-eat salad bar in heaven."

"Good, 'cause this would kill her," the woman managed to squeeze in before Ted coaxed the mic back. "You telling everything, I mean!"

"Actually . . . I think she would have loved it. She was always after me to make more Jewish friends, and here I am with two hundred friendly Jews in one room!"

The crowd erupted.

A short, plump woman with blond hair that was white at the roots stood up. "I have three granddaughters and I'm buying each of them your book, so they know what chutzpah looks like."

"*Aw.* Thank you so much, sweetie. What's your name?"

"Esther!" the woman belted out proudly.

"Esther!" I said. "Queen of the Jews."

"Honey, today I think you're the Queen of the Jews!"

There was a smattering of applause.

After what seemed like hours of banter, Ted came up to the stage and announced, "Chef Rossi will now be signing books at a table in the lobby."

The crowd clapped as I gave a little nod and a wave, then carefully made my way down the stage steps. The last thing I wanted to do was top off a great afternoon by free-falling into smoked salmon.

Danny had crept into my thoughts in the few days before the appearance. Could it be that I had caused him to material-ize? And if I had conjured him up, could I unconjure him now?

No such luck. He was the first person in line at the signing table.

"Ruthie! Ruthie!" he called to a Rubenesque brunette stand-ing behind him. "This is Rossi! Rossi, this is my wife, Ruthie!"

Ruthie grabbed my hands in delight. "Oh, Rossi, I've been hearing about you for years! I am thrilled to finally meet you!"

"Th-thanks?" I stammered. The dusty old filing cabinet in my head shuddered. Over the years, I'd purged most of the files from it: the billy-club boys, and the cop at Port Authority . . . but there was one file left in there and it was labeled *Douchey Dan*.

"So . . . how did you two meet?"

"The old-fashioned way," said Ruthie. "We were fixed up by Danny's sister."

"Right," I said, shaking my head to clear it. "The one who bought a new used car every five minutes."

Ruthie looked puzzled. "Bertie doesn't drive," she said.

"Rossi, didn't you ever figure it out?" Danny said, giggling like a maniac. "Those were all stolen cars!"

"All that time, I was riding around in cars you stole!?"

"Come on . . . I didn't steal them. Izzy bought them from some guy in Bed-Stuy for twenty bucks. We'd just drive them around for a few days and dump them."

"Weren't you afraid of getting caught—going to jail?"

"*Nah.* Nobody gave a shit back then. The cops had way worse problems to deal with out there than a couple of white boys joyriding around in a stolen car."

"Izzy did go to jail," Ruthie chimed in.

"Years later," added Danny as if that made it better. "For illegal gun possession."

As a line formed behind him, Danny came around the table and threw his freckled arms around me, then squeezed tightly. "We couldn't believe it when we saw your name and picture in the brochure!" he said.

I didn't squeeze back.

Even after all these years had passed, I recognized the smell of sweat mixed with Johnson's baby powder. There had been a time when I'd loved his smell. It had been the smell of friendship and fun and adventure. The smell of laughter.

Then it became something else.

If betrayal had a smell, for me it would be sweat mixed with Johnson's baby powder.

No mystery how I'd recognized Danny in the crowd, in spite of the fifty pounds he'd put on. It was those squinty eyes. He'd always looked like he was staring into the sun.

"So . . . what are you two doing in Naples?" I asked, having no clue why I was making small talk when all I wanted was for them to leave.

"We spend a lot of time down here with Ruthie's mom," Danny replied.

"She's eighty-five," Ruthie added.

When I inquired as to whether they had children, Ruthie pulled out her phone and flashed a shot of two teenagers, a girl and a boy.

"My son Aaron just turned nineteen. He's in college. My daughter Sophia is seventeen, just about to graduate from high school."

"Wow . . . she's the same age I was when I met Danny."

"You were that young? He always makes it sound like you were some worldly creature!"

Danny started shifting from foot to foot as he watched us talk. Three decades had passed, and he still did his nervous foot dance. Or maybe he was thinking back, too.

"I'm wondering why you and Danny didn't stay in touch," she added. "He speaks about you so fondly."

"Does he?" I'd made a point never to talk about him. That would have made him real. "We . . . had a . . . falling out way back when. It's . . . kind of a long story, maybe best left in the cobwebs."

"Those cobwebs can be a bitch," she persisted. "Maybe it's time to clear them away?"

I opened my mouth but nothing came out.

"I don't know how long you're in town, but . . . would you consider coming to my mother's house for lunch or dinner tomorrow? She took the kids and went on a cruise, so we've got the whole place to ourselves."

"Cruising at eighty-five? Good for her."

"Rossi, I am a believer that things happen for a reason. You two crossing paths thirty years after you met feels like *beshert* to me."

Fate? I sighed.

After extracting the name of my hotel from me, Ruthie and Danny grudgingly stepped away from the table to let the grumbling people behind them have their shot at me. "Don't ignore the signals," Ruthie said as she pulled Danny after her into the departing crowd. "I'm going to call you later!"

I tried to keep smiling as I chatted and signed, but I felt the filing cabinet in my head spring open and the dusty old file marked *Douchey Dan* push itself up to be read.

Was it time to forgive?

•··•᾽·•᷈•·•᷈· ··

That night I lay in bed next to Lyla, staring at the ceiling.

"Are you going to sleep at all tonight, honey?" she said softly. "Do you want to take half a Xanax?"

"I don't know." I turned to look into Lyla's eyes.

"Look . . . he did a terrible thing to you all those years ago, unforgivable things. But you've been hanging on to the pain of it—the shame—for a long time. Danny is like this big black hole in your childhood. Wouldn't it feel great to deal with it and . . . close the hole?"

"I guess so . . . unless I'd be closing it on my foot or something," I said. "Just . . . make sure I don't kill him, will you?"

Lyla kissed me softly and smiled. "Please make sure *I* don't."

CHAPTER 52

BEEF STEW

We were sitting in the back seat of Danny and Ruthie's silver minivan, but I wasn't sure how I'd ended up here. True to her word, Ruthie had called our hotel room repeatedly the night after my book talk, pleading with me to come over for a meal before we left Naples. After the sixth call, Lyla had talked me into accepting the invitation. "Remember what Rabbi Sharon said on Yom Kippur about forgiveness?" she'd said. "You have to forgive to let go of that stone you're carrying."

"I've got quite a few of them."

"And acid reflux and headaches and trouble sleeping."

I looked down at an old Almond Joy wrapper on the floor by my feet, a half-eaten bag of Doritos curled up next to it for company. Lyla hitched herself up to brush bits of popcorn off the seat beneath her.

Danny sat in the front passenger seat, and I examined his short, kinky hair, gray flecked with brown. I remembered how hard and coarse it had felt the first time I'd affectionately petted the back of his head, a million years ago, when we were friends. His hair reminded me of a terrier's fur, but curlier, like a poodle's. I'd loved watching him charging toward me on the street, my big, puppy-dog friend with the flame-red hair. He'd seemed so full of life that walking wasn't enough for him; he'd bounced.

For a moment, I felt a smile form. Then I remembered that same coarse red hair soaked in sweat, sharp, like a pine-tree in my hand, as I pushed him away, hard. My puppy dog had gone rabid.

"Don't mind the mess," Ruthie said. I noted that she was a cautious driver, always coming to a slow stop, always signaling a turn well ahead of time. "We made the mistake of leaving the minivan with our daughter for a few days when we flew up north on business, and I think she used it for a rolling party."

"It's nice," Lyla said, attempting to be polite. "What is it? A Chrysler?"

Danny turned around and smiled at her. "Only the best for my Ruthie."

"It was my birthday gift a few years ago. Well, I thought it was a gift, and then I realized I'd be doing all the driving. Mr. Macho here hates to drive."

"Miss Rossi here only drives about once a year." Lyla said, and they shared a laugh.

Danny changed the subject. "You still like music?" he asked, turning to look back at me. "You used to like New Wave, I remember."

Thank God Lyla was doing most of the talking. "Rossi here is more into Barbra Streisand these days," she said. "She's not that wild little girl you once knew."

"God, I love Barbra!" squealed Ruthie. "Danny, put on the Barbra!"

He nodded and slid a CD into the player and out came the unmistakably lush, powerful voice. Barbra sang right into my ear from the speaker behind my seat.

"Great sound in here, right?" Danny boasted. "Like surround sound. But don't be too impressed with us. We still use a CD player."

"No bluetooth?" Lyla asked.

Danny turned in his seat again and smiled widely. "These are the only teeth I have."

"Not blue," I managed, trying to join in. "Maybe a little gray."

•····•· ·•₂···•· · ·

In high school, Barbra had been my dirty little secret. I'd stuck safety pins in my T-shirts and hopped around with my friends to the Sex Pistols and Ramones, but when I was in my small bedroom with the door shut, it was Barbra I listened to over and over again.

"On A Clear Day," had been my favorite. I sang it over and over again.

I didn't know why the lyrics in that song resonated, but I remembered humming them as I walked around Port Authority with nowhere to go, afraid to stand still too long in any one place.

The morning after "the incident" with Danny, I'd paced around my apartment belting them out as loudly as I could.

•····•· ·•₂···•· · ·

Ruthie pulled into the driveway of a yellow two-story home with a terracotta tile roof. Two wooden doors covered two garages. I could just make out a swimming pool in the backyard, the water twinkling in the late-day sun.

"Pretty," Lyla said.

"Pretty awesome. My folks bought this house years ago," said Ruthie.

Danny hopped out of the car and opened the door for me, bowing his head. "My lady," he said, holding out his hand for me to take as I climbed out of the minivan. I ignored it.

Ruthie elbowed him in the ribs. "Honey, Rossi's not the 'my lady' type."

"Oh, please. What isn't ladylike about Rossi?" Lyla said, laughing. "She puts on a good show, but she doesn't have a masculine bone in her body."

I glared at her, then watched Danny and Ruthie walk up the driveway to the house. Danny had a grass stain on the back of his shorts. He shuffled along cautiously, as if he were afraid of falling, the way old people do.

I wondered when he'd lost his bounce.

Lyla put her hand on my shoulder. "Are you sure you want to go through with this?" she whispered.

"No."

"We can just stay for a little while and leave before dinner, if you're not comfortable. You never have to say a word."

"Let's just see how it goes."

Ruthie's mother's house felt warm and friendly. In the living room sat a plush beige cotton couch covered in throw pillows, an old quilt tossed over its side. Two leather recliners completed the seating arrangement.

In the kitchen sat an old wooden table with six mismatched painted wooden chairs. A bowl of oranges was surrounded by magazines and newspapers.

This was not a house for show; it was a house for living in.

Ruthie directed us to the glass table on the back deck overlooking the pool, and when we were seated around it, she brought out four glasses and a pitcher of iced tea with floating lemon slices, along with a bowl of red-pepper hummus and a basket of sliced pita. "Have a little nosh while I get the rest of the food ready," she said, disappearing back through the sliding door.

In a minute, she was back with a bowl of sliced cucumbers. "Almost forgot . . ." she said. "This is for Miss No-Gluten Rossi."

Danny dipped a piece of pita into the hummus, then folded it into his mouth. "I'm starving!" he said.

As Lyla poured the tea, she inquired, "So, Danny, what do you do for a living?"

"I'm a real-estate broker."

"You're not doing commercial art anymore?" I asked.

"*Nah*. Too many newfangled things to stay on top of. It stopped being fun when the computers took over."

I watched him chug down his iced tea, then refill his glass.

We sat enjoying the sunny day in silence until Ruthie reappeared with a large wooden bowl of tomato-and-onion salad. The minute she put it on the table, Danny reached for it, but she slapped his hand.

"So, Rossi," she said, using a large wooden spoon to dollop tomato salad onto my plate, "how did you and Lyla meet?"

"Through a friend in Provincetown. It's a six-hour drive from New York, but we love it there. The funny thing is, when we got back to the city, we realized we only lived six blocks apart."

"We go to all the same places. We probably passed each other on the street a hundred times." Lyla laughed.

"It was kismet." Ruthie smiled. "And you make such a cute couple."

Danny stood up from the table. "Nature calls, ladies."

Lyla stared at him as he walked away, her eyes narrowing. She hadn't liked him from the moment she'd met him. She had her reasons, of course.

It was a different story with Ruthie. We had both warmed to her instantly. She was kind, friendly, and genuine, with no pretense—the kind of woman you wished were your sister or your mother. I bet her children adored her.

Ruthie put a bowl of gluten-free pasta salad on the table, followed by a platter of roast chicken and finally, a large plate of grilled asparagus.

"I don't know if we're calling this late lunch or early dinner, but enjoy!"

I looked at the asparagus.

"Do you know I was sixteen before I learned that asparagus didn't grow in a can, and that its natural color was, in fact, green?"

"That's right!" Danny said, returning from the bathroom. "I forgot about your mother's canned asparagus and all those weird things you made with it! Canned asparagus stew, canned asparagus stir-fry, canned asparagus and pasta, canned asparagus and scrambled eggs . . ."

"You can get pretty inventive when you're poor," I said, and for a few seconds, I flashed back to Danny feasting at my beaten-up table, laughing at all of my jokes.

"How is Harriet these days?" he asked, breaking the spell.

"She passed away in '92, sadly. But I've got a feeling she's still here."

Somehow, Ruthie found room for a tray of strawberries on the overflowing table. She sighed as she finally shimmied onto her own seat and scooped some salad onto her plate. "Rossi. You and Danny have so much history together. What on earth happened between you?"

I had almost forgotten why I'd come. The late-day sun was starting to fade, and a warm breeze had picked up. How could I tell this cheerful woman with kind eyes what her husband had done to me a lifetime ago?

I sat for a few seconds quietly. "What do you think happened, Ruthie?"

"Well, I think you were very young, and maybe you got close with Danny and had certain feelings for him, and maybe it was unrequited, and—"

I started to laugh. "No, Ruthie. I was never interested in Danny that way." I let myself steal a look at Danny, who had begun to giggle nervously—his trademark.

"Do you want to tell her, Danny?"

He squinted and shrugged. "Rossi . . . I really don't know why we stopped being friends."

"You don't know!?"

"That was such a foggy, hazy time for me, those Crown Heights years. All I remember is . . . there was this time at Izzy's and . . . I had to get out of there."

"But you came to my house after!"

"After what?" Ruthie jumped in.

I took a deep breath.

Lyla put her hand on my arm and petted me softly. She leaned in. "It's up to you," she whispered.

Just as I was thinking, *Maybe we should just say goodbye and get out of here*, I heard Danny mutter, "It was nothing, really. We were just kids . . ."

Nothing!? I felt the acid from the tomato salad rise into my throat.

"Danny, for fuck's sake! I was seventeen. *I* was a kid. But you were twenty-three!"

"What happened?" Ruthie asked softly.

"What happened was, I was a teenager alone in Crown Heights—a little rocker chick in a sea of Chasids. Then Danny came along, and he became my guardian angel. At least I thought that's what he was. He had this crazy, scary friend—Izzy—who I hated. One night, Danny pleaded with me to go with him to Izzy's apartment. For a party, he said."

Danny started to say something, but Ruthie elbowed him into silence.

"When we got there, it was just us. And Izzy."

"It was always a party if you were there!" Danny chimed in, trying to lighten the mood.

I couldn't even look in his direction as Ruthie smacked him hard on the shoulder. "Shut up, Daniel. Let her talk."

"Izzy gave me a joint to smoke, and . . . there was something in it besides pot. I started . . . seeing things, got weak, passed out. He'd planned it all. *They'd* planned it all. Drugged me."

Ruthie tore at the paper napkin in front of her.

"When I came to—sort of—Izzy and Danny weren't wearing pants. My jeans were pulled down. I heard Izzy say, 'You go first.'"

Ruthie put her hand over her mouth, her eyes filling. "Oh, God." She turned and looked at Danny, then back at me. "Did he? Did they?"

The scene I'd filed away for so long unspooled in my mind—Danny stuffing his semi-hard dick inside of me—but I couldn't bring myself to say the words.

"Danny . . . started, but I guess his heart wasn't in it. His . . . penis wasn't cooperating." Feeling a wave of compassion for Ruthie, I continued to soften the edges of the story. "I think Danny was afraid of Izzy. He'd gone along with the whole thing because he was too scared to stand up to him."

"That's no excuse!" Ruthie said.

Of course, she was right.

"I managed to get up off the bed and try to get out of there, but Izzy had locked the door with a key. He had a gun and started chasing me around with it."

Ruthie started to cry. When Danny reached out to comfort her, she shrugged him off. I still couldn't look at him.

The scar on my Fuck You finger started itching like crazy, and I rubbed it. When I caught Ruthie looking, I put my hands in my lap.

"At one point, Izzy put the rifle to my head and told me to lie back down, but—I guess I figured I had nothing to lose—I screamed so loud that I finally woke up Izzy's parents, who lived upstairs. When they banged on the door and forced Izzy to open it, I got the hell out of there."

Tears streamed down Ruthie's face. "Our Sophia is seventeen," she said. "If someone did something like that to her, or even tried it, I swear to God I'd kill them!"

"I don't remember any of that," Danny said nervously. "I was always so stoned back then, I . . . Rossi. I'm so sorry that happened."

Ruthie smacked him hard on the arm and said, "Shut up! You're just making it worse!"

I don't know what I'd hoped would come of it all. Maybe I'd wanted Danny to take some sort of ownership of what he'd done. I felt a wave of anger rise up inside of me and Lyla must have seen it on my face. She reached out and squeezed my shoulder. "Breathe, honey."

I took a deep breath, then looked Danny straight in the eye for the first time since I'd begun talking. "How can you say you don't remember? You came to my house the next day completely sober and tried to apologize. You said Izzy had planned the whole thing. That he had laced my joint with angel dust."

He sat there, shaking his head. "I'm just . . . so sorry. I don't remember any of that."

Ruthie rose and put her arms around me. "You were such a brave girl," she said. "You deserved better." She straightened up and glared at her husband.

"I'm . . . sorry it happened," he said again, louder this time, but it still came out sounding like a question.

Ruthie walked into the kitchen, and I heard her blowing her nose.

I felt nauseous as I watched Danny pick the top off a macaroon that sat on a plate meant to be shared by all of us. Then, my revulsion gave way to a kind of calm.

"I don't remember what I had for lunch the day after Izzy's," I said. "I don't remember if I went to work that week or even if I had a job. But I remember every insanely tiny detail of what happened in that basement. I remember the dust and the smell of mold and body odor. I remember the water stains on the ceiling, the fan that screeched like a dying bird. I remember the sound of the pot of beef stew clanging to the floor and splattering everywhere when I smacked it off the stove. I remember the feeling of Izzy's rifle pressed against my head and the frozen look on your face when I begged you for help."

I looked back toward the sliding door, then back at Danny. "I remember you entering me when I was barely conscious," I growled. "It was a lot worse than what I described to Ruthie, and you know it. There are a lot of things you may have forgotten, Danny, but there's no way you've forgotten tricking your best friend into smoking angel dust and then raping her."

Raping. Rape.

I'd never used that word for what happened, not even in my own head, until I told Lyla about it. It was about two years into our relationship. We were sitting in front of the fireplace sipping peppermint tea, and, for whatever reason, I told her about the night at Izzy's.

As soon as I stopped talking, she said, "Baby, that's rape."

"It is?"

"It's a drug-facilitated sexual assault. Rape in the second degree, if you want to get technical. What that guy Izzy did with the rifle? That's aggravated assault with a deadly weapon."

My soft, kind girlfriend who liked to sip peppermint tea before bedtime was also a savvy, street-smart lawyer. I forgot that sometimes.

As the light began to leave the patio, Danny stared at me with vacant eyes, clearly in a daze. He picked the coconut off another macaroon.

When he opened his mouth to repeat how sorry he was "that happened," I fought an urge to leap across the table and slap the coconut out of his mouth.

"I . . . I'm going to go help my wife," he said in a low voice, backing toward the sliding door.

When he'd closed it behind him, Lyla leaned toward me and, through gritted teeth, imitated Danny's lame excuse for an apology. "'I'm *sooo* sorry that happened to you.' He couldn't even say, *I'm so sorry I did that to you!* He doesn't fucking get it!"

"Ruthie does, though," I pointed out. "He was a coward back then, and I guess he still is."

"Well . . . you did it. Confronted him with the truth. How do you feel?"

"Disappointed . . . but not really surprised. At least it's out of me and onto him."

"I hope she gives him hell."

⁕ ⸳⸳⸳⸳⸳ ⸳ ⸳⸳⸳⸳⸳ ⸳ ⸳

When I'd pictured the scene in my mind, I hadn't thought about what would come after everything was out on the table. I felt terrible for Ruthie, and so did Lyla. We made an awkward attempt at complimenting her on the food and the house . . . but when she offered to call us a taxi, we both exhaled with relief. The second it arrived, she walked us down the driveway. Danny stayed at the front door.

Ruthie kissed Lyla. "You have a very brave girlfriend."

"Yes, I do."

Then she wrapped her arms around me.

"I'm so sorry," I said.

"*You're* sorry!? No, honey. You have nothing to be sorry about. But my husband up there, oh, he's going to be very, very sorry."

In the taxi on the way back to our hotel, I turned to Lyla.

"It's like everything I hoped I might get from Danny, I got from Ruthie."

"Some people are just weak, honey. That's his burden to bear. It's not yours anymore. Let it go."

I stared out the window as we drove past the palm trees and pastel houses. I opened the window.

"Air conditioner is on," barked the driver.

I ignored him and let my hand lace through the warm air as we drove. The basement, Izzy, Danny—I shook it all off my fingertips like grains of sand and let it blow away in the warm Florida wind.

The filing cabinet in my head was now empty, except for a little splattered beef stew.

"Let's go swimming in the hotel pool," I said to Lyla. "I hear there's a waterfall."

CHAPTER 53

PASSING THE TORCH

In 2012, Lyla and I took my nieces, Hannah (who now called herself Ruby) and Tovah, to see *Wicked* on Broadway. They both wore the ultra-Orthodox uniform—maxiskirt falling below the knees, long-sleeve shirt to cover the elbows and collarbone—but Ruby's sleeves were rolled up.

"It's so hot out tonight. Would God really mind if you wore shorts?" Lyla asked.

"No, but it's what I want," said Tovah.

Ruby just smiled.

During intermission, we wandered out into the lobby.

"Do you girls want anything?"

"I'm okay, Aunt Rossi. I have water in my bag."

"What are you having?" Ruby asked Lyla.

"I'm gonna have a cocktail!" she replied.

"Can I come stand in line with you?"

"That's my sister," said Tovah, shaking her head as she watched her sister wade toward the bar.

I looked at Tovah's pretty face. After she graduated from high school, she was going to move to Manhattan to attend Stern College, a Jewish school for women. She planned to be an accountant.

"I'm glad you want to have a career and not just get married and have kids," I said to her.

"I want that, too, but I can have both."

"Yes, you can, sweetie. You can have everything."

After the show, we streamed through the exit with the crowd, then stepped off to the side. I looked at Ruby's long black hair reflecting the lights of Broadway. At nineteen, she was entering what I hoped would be the happiest time in her life. Shapely, with almond chocolate eyes and long lashes, she had clearly taken after her Persian mother. She reminded me of Anya.

"Your father says you're going to go to some singles mixer tonight that Chabad is throwing?"

She turned to me, dark eyes twinkling, "Get real, Aunt Rossi!"

And there, in front of the escaping theater crowd, Ruby pulled off the maxiskirt to reveal a black miniskirt underneath. Then she pulled off her sweater to unveil a low-cut silver halter top. She slid her sneakers into her bag and pulled out a pair of pink pumps.

"Holy cow!" said Lyla.

"Hot mama!"

"That's my sister," laughed Tovah.

"I'm going to a party in Brooklyn. You ladies wanna come?"

"Oh, Ruby, we're old. Your aunt wants to go home and drink a tall glass of water with a spoonful of Metamucil," Lyla said. We all laughed.

I put my arms around Ruby and breathed in the sweet smell of mango body lotion mixed with perfume. In an instant, I had a flash of the dark-haired baby I'd held in my arms only a few months after my mother had passed away.

I thought of Mom and smiled. *I'll always see two of you. One as you are now, and one as my darling baby.*

"Ruby, you are clearly the Rossi of your family."

"I'll take that as a compliment from my cool New York aunt."

"You go on, Ruby Tuesday. Have fun. I am officially passing the torch to you!"

She winked and kissed me on both cheeks—"the Persian way," she'd explained years ago.

She skipped toward the subway station, then paused and looked back. "Aunt Rossi, I do just what you taught me when I was little. I never walk—I sashay!"

"Sashay away!" I called out as I watched her disappear into the crowd.

Lyla and I walked Tovah to her dorm, then headed east—to where the tourists don't steal all the cabs—and caught a Yellow straight down Second Avenue.

CHAPTER 54

OLD NEW YORK

My mother once told me that no matter how old I got, she would always see two images when she looked at me: me in the present day, and me as a baby. At the time, I was a teenager with pink highlights wearing a Sex Pistols T-shirt.

"I still see you as my little baby girl."

I don't have children, but I like to think of New York City as my child, and I understand what my mother meant. When I walk through Tompkins Square Park, past the baby strollers and the dog run, I also see "Tent City," where the homeless lived for so long that they actually collected mail at their tents. I see the gangs of punk-rock kids in Mohawks and spiked leather jackets.

"When did Alphabet City get so family-friendly?" I asked a pal one day.

"Nobody calls it Alphabet City anymore."

I long for the old Second Avenue Deli, where an eighty-year-old waitress in a bouffant would serve up pastrami and a joke. "You know what they say: Where there's a will, there are relatives," she'd crack as she set down the overflowing oval platters of half-sour pickles and cabbage salad. I took my parents there once. Dad flirted with the waitress while Mom pushed all the pickles into a plastic bag and stuffed it in her purse. It's a Chase Bank now, but I swear I smell pastrami near the teller windows.

Scary and smelly old Union Square Park is now pristine, packed with locals reading books they bought at the nearby Barnes & Noble, and tourists munching on artisanal bread, cheese, and fruit from the farmers' market. I remember the first time I walked through it en route to my "job interview" for selling metal etchings. I can still see the man sitting on the bench shooting up heroin at eleven a.m.

The Apple Store in the fancy "meatpacking district" used to be Western Beef, a fantastic low-budget grocery where you could buy huge slabs of meat along with cartons of premade coleslaw and potato salad. It was my go-to store for the two summers I spent working as a chef on a yacht.

Danny and I sat on the hood of what I'd thought was his sister's car, eating bagels from Dizzy's while hookers sashayed by. That stretch of the far west side is all designer boutiques and expensive eateries now. People have brunch on the corner that used to house The Vault.

The part of Franklin Avenue in Brooklyn that used to be Tom's domain and a haven for Jamaican drug dealers is now one of the hottest blocks in the borough. I recently had to wait an hour for a table for brunch at a Mexican restaurant there.

When I hop the train to Forty-Second Street, I find myself on a relatively clean, air-cooled number 2 filled with people who look like they're late for the office. But I can still see the red-bereted Guardian Angels patrolling hot, graffiti-encrusted cars. I can still hear the sharp whine of the worn-out brakes as the train lurched into each station as if it might be the last stop ever.

Forty-Second Street is Disneyland now, complete with humans dressed up like Mickey and Minnie and Elmo, clowning around and posing for selfies. Video ads thirty feet tall play on the sides of skyscrapers. But I can blink and see the

XXX theaters, peep shows, dive bars, and yet more hookers. I still picture the marquees that read "GO-GO," "ALL NUDE REVIEW," and "LIVE GIRLS!"

I look at all the taxicabs and Ubers racing by and remember the bulbous Checker Cabs, so roomy in the back that they had "jump seats." Even back then, only one of every four cabs was a Checker, but those were the ones you wanted. I think the last time I saw one was in the late eighties.

On the top floor of my doctor's office overlooking Time Square, I take in the view. My old friend the Empire State Building is there to greet me, but she stands shoulder-to-shoulder with dozens of new neighbors, all windows and glinting steel.

"What is that tall, skinny building over there with all the glass?" I ask.

"Which one? That sounds like all of them."

My mother and father are together somewhere else now; there is no one left to see me as a baby girl. But those of us who arrived in New York decades ago and stayed will always see her in her gritty glory, even as we wait in line for an overpriced brunch.

I meet fewer and fewer people who remember when Manhattan was wild. You had to watch your ass, for sure, but it was also a haven for dreamers, outsiders, and artists. There were real neighborhoods filled with mom-and-pop stores. Old women sat on folding chairs in front of tenements and kept track of who came and who went. The Bowery had flophouses and homeless drunks, but it also had CBGB, Allen Ginsberg, Blondie, and the Ramones.

When I get back to my neighborhood, I cross through Tompkins Square Park. On a bench is a man in a motorcycle jacket with the sleeves cut off, eating a Snickers bar. His hair is sculpted into a pink Mohawk, and he has about a dozen piercings in his right ear.

I swear I want to kiss him.

A THOUSAND THANK YOUS.

Looking back, I sometimes wonder how I survived those dark early years. Many times, when all seemed bleak, a simple act of kindness sustained me, and I was able to keep moving forward.

Thank you, Trey Moynihan, for your unbreakable friendship of forty-plus years.

Thank you, Jeni Weber, for introducing me to theater, cappuccino, and hope.

I hold a special place in my heart for my Crown Heights sisters, Fagee, Anya, and Lifsa. Ladies, I don't know where you are, or even your last names, but I know that you saved me.

To Hector and Uncle Pete, if you are alive, I know my book will find its way to you. You gave me *comidas*, *cervezas*, and a safe place to ride out the storm. *Muchas gracias, papis*.

I was blessed with an unlikely angel who remained my champion until he left this earthly plane. Thank you, Mr. T., a.k.a. Charlie Thompson.

For Mike Simon, my big-hearted Chasid friend. I give my heartfelt thanks for choosing kindness instead of judgment.

For Rebbe Menachem Schneerson, I give my love and gratitude. Rebbe, I didn't join the Chasidic fold, but you touched my heart and caused me to slow down and listen when all I wanted to do was run.

Thank you, Rabbi Sharon Kleinbaum, for helping me find my way to my very own Judaism, one that understands and accepts that love is love.

I have been blessed with the guidance of several brilliant, cuttingly honest women who steered my book along its journey. Thank you, Nancy Murrell, my first and constant editor and dear friend. Thank you to the wondrous Jeananne Pannasch who believed in me when few others did. Thank you, Helen Eisenbach, for lovingly guiding me in the right direction. Thank you to the awe-inspiring Laura Ross for being the guardian angel/midwife who helped bring this baby into the world. Laura, you will always be my liger, half lion and half tiger.

All that I am is because of my larger-than-life mother, Harriet, who taught me that food equals love. Mom, I will always be your Slovah.

For my father, Marty, caring for you was the greatest honor of my life. Thank you for letting me in before the finish line.

My heartfelt gratitude goes to my partner, Lydia DeLisi, for teaching me that forgiveness is more powerful than revenge. Honey, I love you and always will.

For my beautiful nieces, Hannah and Tovah, who have shown me that you really can have it all: Orthodox Judaism, education, career fulfillment, family, love, and joy. Ladies, I am so proud of you.

Lastly, this book is dedicated to women of any religion who feel trapped, who go to sleep at night dreaming of the life they wish to have. It may feel as unreachable as pedaling to Mars. It is to you, my silenced sisters, that I say, rise. Your destiny is calling. Come out, come out and live.

MENDEL'S SONG

My baby brother, Mendel, passed away weeks before this book was going to print. He had a wild, zany, fun-loving spirit.

When we were kids, he loved terrorizing his older sisters. I often thought if you looked in the dictionary under "annoying baby brother" you would see a picture of Mendel.

I figured he would grow out of it, but like Peter Pan, he never grew up.

He loved amusement parks, candy, pizza, popcorn, french fries, and video games.

He adored being a father. Having children was a perfect excuse to be one himself. I can't imagine anyone with a more fun dad. At one point he even purchased a "Partridge Family" style bus to cart his kids around the country on family vacations.

Mendel planted potent seeds of love in his children that grew and blossomed.

I close my eyes and see him in heaven, terrorizing our sister, Yaya, who always gave it back to him threefold. I know they're having a blast.

ABOUT THE AUTHOR

ossi has been published in outlets including *The Daily News*, *The New York Post*, *Time Out New York*, and *Mcsweeney's*, to name a few. She has been the food writer of the "Eat Me" column for *Bust* magazine since 1998, hosts her own hit radio show on WOMR and WFMR in Cape Cod called *Bite This*, now in its nineteenth season, has been featured on The Food Network and NPR and has been a popular blogger for *The Huffington Post*. Her first memoir, *The Raging Skillet: The True Life Story of Chef Rossi* was published by The Feminist Press to rave reviews. In addition to memoir, Rossi has written two full-length plays, a number of one-act comedies, a one-woman stage adaptation of *Queen of the Jews*, and launched the *Raging and Eating* podcast.

Author photo © Quyn Duong

SELECTED TITLES FROM SHE WRITES PRESS

She Writes Press is an independent publishing company founded to serve women writers everywhere. Visit us at www.shewritespress.com.

Uncovered: How I Left Hassidic Life and Finally Came Home by Leah Lax. $16.95, 978-1-63152-995-5. Drawn in their offers of refuge from her troubled family and promises of eternal love, Leah Lax becomes a Hassidic Jew—but ultimately, as a forty-something woman, comes to reject everything she has lived for three decades in order to be who she truly is.

Joyful, Delicious, Vegan: Life Without Heart Disease by Sherra Aguirre. $16.95, 978-1-64742-063-5. Augmented with personal anecdotes from the author, guidelines from two leading cardiologists, and information about the unexpected joys of a vegan life, this recipe book empowers women to protect themselves from the number one killer in America—heart disease—by learning to prepare delicious, healing, plant-based foods in their own kitchens.

Away from the Kitchen: Untold Stories, Private Menus, Guarded Recipes, and Insider Tips by Dawn Blume Hawkes. $24.95, 978-1-93831-436-0. A food book for those who want it all: the menus, the recipes, *and* the behind-the-scenes scoop on some of America's favorite chefs.

The Skeptic and the Rabbi: Falling in Love with Faith by Judy Gruen. $16.95, 978-1-63152-302-1. When Judy Gruen marries the man she loves—who happens to be an Orthodox Jew—she embarks upon a serious spiritual quest that is by turns poignant, deep, and hilarious.